Sylvia Porter's Planning YOUR Retirement

Sylvia Porter's Planning YOUR Retirement

New York   London   Toronto   Sydney   Tokyo   Singapore

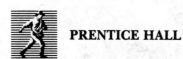 **PRENTICE HALL**

Simon & Schuster, Inc.
15 Columbus Circle
New York, NY 10023

A J. K. Lasser Book
Published by Prentice Hall

J. K. Lasser, Prentice Hall and colophons are
registered trademarks of Simon & Schuster, Inc.

Manufactured in the United States of America

1 2 3 4 5 6 7 8 9 10

Librai y of Congress Cataloging–in–Publication Data

Porter, Sylvia
    [Active retirement companion]
    Sylvia Porter's active retirement companion.
        p.   cm.
    ISBN 0–13–877812–4
    1. Retirement income–United States—Planning.   2. Retirees—
—United States—Finance, Personal.   I. Title.
HG179.B5695   1991   91-6061
332.024'01—dc20   CIP

Contents

DISCLAIMER

This information is intended to provide general information and background and is distributed on the basis that the publisher and copyright owner are not engaged in rendering legal, accounting or other professional services.

Should legal, accounting or other professional assistance be required, the services of a competent professional should be sought.

The publisher, copyright owner and authors disclaim any personal liability for advice or information presented herein.

Part I

Financial Planning for Retirement

1

Financial Planning

What is your greatest worry as you approach retirement? For many of us, it's the fear that we will run out of money, that we will end up becoming a financial burden to our families or to society, or both. But if you carefully plan for your retirement, and keep your financial house in order, your worst fears about money need never come to pass. You should be able to remain financially self-sufficient for the rest of your life.

To begin with, if you have any options, you should not retire until you feel financially able to do so. That's when most of us elect to retire anyway. Unless you can prove to your own satisfaction that you can afford to stop working, and if you have a choice, don't give it up. That's the best common sense advice anyone can offer you. Some companies encourage employees to continue working beyond retirement age, if only part time. Take advantage of that policy, if you need to. If that's not possible, look for part-time work with another firm or consider starting your own part-time business. Entrepreneuring on a modest scale can be both financially rewarding and fun. Chart 1 enables you to see the alterations that will take place in your lifestyle, both of income and outlay, upon full-time retirement.

Your financial planning for retirement hopefully began many years ago when you started a program of saving and investing for the day you would quit your job and begin living a life of leisure. As you approach the actual moment, little should be left for you to do but add the finishing touches to a financial plan that will assure you of an adequate income for the rest of your life. If you have saved enough, and made your investments work hard enough, you will have retirement income equal to about two-thirds of your working income, for that's what experts say most of us need to maintain the standard of living we enjoyed during our working years. You will also have investments that will grow along with the cost of living (inflation beaters) so that you won't outlast your money.

CHART 1 Your Check List of Changed Retirement Expenses	Less		More	
Expenses	*Expenses Eliminated*	*Expenses Reduced*	*Expenses Added*	*Expenses Increased*
Debts				
Principal and interest on:				
Residential mortgages	☐	☐	☐	☐
Investment mortgages	☐	☐	☐	☐
Loans, notes, margin accounts	☐	☐	☐	☐
Balances due on installment payments	☐	☐	☐	☐
Payments on borrowings from your employer or benefit plans	☐	☐	☐	☐
Other	☐	☐	☐	☐
Taxes				
Federal income taxes	☐	☐	☐	☐
State and local income taxes	☐	☐	☐	☐
Social Security contributions	☐	☐	☐	☐
Residential real estate	☐	☐	☐	☐
Investment real estate	☐	☐	☐	☐
Other	☐	☐	☐	☐
Living Expenses				
Food and beverages at home	☐	☐	☐	☐
Food and beverages away from home.....	☐	☐	☐	☐
Household supplies	☐	☐	☐	☐
Housing, maintenance, utilities	☐	☐	☐	☐
Clothing (purchases and care)	☐	☐	☐	☐
Transportation (including autos, gas)	☐	☐	☐	☐
Insurance premiums	☐	☐	☐	☐
Entertainment, recreation, vacations	☐	☐	☐	☐
Medical and other health expenses (unreimbursed)............................	☐	☐	☐	☐
Contributions, donations, gifts.............	☐	☐	☐	☐
Education and day care	☐	☐	☐	☐
Child support and alimony paid...........	☐	☐	☐	☐
Grooming and other personal care........	☐	☐	☐	☐
Other (pets, legal, accounting, etc.)........	☐	☐	☐	☐

Source: *Sylvia Porter's Active Retirement Newsletter* (SPARN) 11/88.

YOUR FINANCIAL PROFILE

As you approach retirement, sit down and figure out your financial profile. Write down the sources and amounts of your income, including your Social Security income, pension benefits and the return on your accumulated savings and investments. Then make a list of your expenses. See how much more you have coming in than going out (or vice versa). That's called your *cash flow*. Now, make another list of your financial assets, including your home and other real estate, your collectibles, antiques, jewelry and other valuables, the cash value of life insurance policies—anything you own that you could sell or otherwise convert to cash. Chart 2 is a worksheet to help you define your current statement of income and expenses.

If you find that you can live on your retirement income without changing your lifestyle and without dipping into your pool of capital from time to time, you are fortunate indeed. Financially speaking, life has been exceedingly good to you, or you have been a very wise financial manager. If you find, however, as most people will, that somewhere down the road you could run out of money, particularly if you live twenty, thirty or even forty years longer, then you must do some hardheaded financial planning.

The solution to your immediate problem might be simple. If you are short of monthly income, for example, you might find that selling a piece of raw land you own and investing the money in an income-oriented mutual fund will not only make up your income shortfall, but allow your investment to grow along with inflation. An alternative approach to an income shortfall might be selling your house, investing the profit, and moving into a modest apartment. This step could allow you to lower your monthly housing expense while substantially increasing your monthly income. On the other hand, you may feel that such a move would reduce your standard of living to a point you find unacceptable. Then you must look for another solution. Perhaps you won't take that long-coveted trip around the world this year. Perhaps you will sell a piece of expensive family jewelry, or a painting, or a vintage car you've owned forever—or all of them and more. Perhaps you'll break the "plastic addiction" and stop using most of your credit cards, reducing your consumer interest expenses. Perhaps you'll go back to work part time. Whatever your answer, the point is you must find an answer. You can't ignore the problem. It won't go away and it won't solve itself. The most fundamental principle of financial planning is taking charge—taking charge of your money and your life. As you confront retirement, it is more important than ever that you remain in control. If you make a mistake when you

CHART 2

Your Current Statement of Income and Expenses

INCOME   Year: _____

Total employment income .... $ _____

Self-employment income ....   _____

Profits from business/partnership ....   _____

Interest, dividends, rents, royalties, fees ......   _____

Child support and alimony received ....   _____

Social Security, pensions, annuities ....   _____

Other ....   _____

TOTAL INCOME .... $ _____

EXPENSES $ _____

Debts

Principal and interest on:

Residential mortgages ....   _____

Investment mortgages ....   _____

Loans, notes, margin accounts ....   _____

Balances due on installment payments ....   _____

Payments on borrowings from your employer or benefit plans ...   _____

Other ....   _____

TOTAL PAYMENTS ON DEBTS ....   _____

Taxes

Federal Income taxes ....   _____

State and local income taxes ....   _____

Social Security contributions ....   _____

Residential real estate ....   _____

Investment real estate ....   _____

Other ....   _____

TOTAL TAXES ....   _____

Living Expenses

Food and beverages at home.. $ ____

Food and beverages away from home.............................. ____

Household supplies... ____

Housing, maintenance, utilities...................................... ____

Clothing (purchases and care).. ____

Transportation (including autos, gas)............................. ____

Insurance premiums.. ____

Entertainment, recreation, vacations.............................. ____

Medical and other health expenses (unreimbursed)....... ____

Contributions, donations, gifts....................................... ____

Education and day care.. ____

Child support and alimony paid...................................... ____

Grooming and other personal care.................................. ____

Other (pets, legal, accounting, etc.)............................... ____

TOTAL LIVING EXPENSES....................................... ____

TOTAL EXPENSES... $ ____

POSITIVE (NET) CASH FLOW

TOTAL INCOME LESS TOTAL EXPENSES.............. $ ____

INTO SAVINGS.. ____

INTO INVESTMENTS.. ____

are younger, you may be able to earn your way out of it. In retirement, that becomes much more problematic.

PREPARE FOR THE UNEXPECTED

You must also be prepared to face unexpected drains on your financial resources in retirement. Because of increasing life spans, one or both of your parents may still be living when you retire. If they run out of money to pay their own way, you may have to chip in hundreds of dollars a month toward their living expenses, including food, rent, transportation and some medical costs. You yourself may be seriously injured or suffer a costly, long-term illness. Some retirees even have to take in grandchildren for a time, either because their sons and daughters get divorced or fall victim to a catastrophe such as a fatal or disabling automobile accident. All these possibilities should be acknowledged and taken into account in your retirement planning.

BALANCE YOUR BUDGET

But your first obligation as the chief financial planner for your own retirement is to bring your expenses in line with your income. You should also leave room for your investments to grow in value to counter the slow erosion of the value of money. Historically, the dollar has lost about half its buying power every seven to ten years, depending on the rate of inflation during the given period. Perhaps down the road, when you are seventy or older, you may feel comfortable dipping into your capital occasionally. But you should not begin retirement by spending more than you have coming in each month. To do so is to court disaster at a time in your life when you are least able to cope with it. Follow the instructions in Chart 3 and you can estimate how close your planning is coming to your financial aims.

If a balanced budget is the first law of economic survival in retirement, the second law is preservation of capital. You'll be bombarded by well-wishers with hot tips on stocks, bonds, real estate, gold mines, oil wells and myriad other "investment opportunities." Many of them will be legitimate. You may lose money by turning some of them down. But better to lose a little money "on paper"—by not investing—than to risk your life savings.

The safest of all investments are treasury securities, backed by the full faith and credit of the U.S. government and its authority to levy taxes. Next safest may be mutual funds that invest in treasury securities. Certificates of deposit and money market mutual funds also are considered safe investments, and there are other safe ways to make your money work for you. We will discuss most of them in later chapters. Real investing takes hard work and careful thought. The point here is that no investment objective is more important during your retirement than holding on to what you have. Once lost, you may never be able to get it back. And remember, almost without exception, when a deal sounds too good to be true, it probably is. Somebody who doesn't care about your future is trying to take your money away.

The third law of economic survival and prosperity in retirement is this: When you need financial or other advice, rely on professionals only. If you require the services of an accountant, call one you know you can trust. When you need legal assistance, call a lawyer who specializes in the field, whether it's wills, trusts, probate, divorce or real estate. When you need a financial planner, seek out a professional with top-flight credentials. You can begin by asking relatives, friends, colleagues, bankers, accountants or other business people for recommendations. If that doesn't work, ask the Institute of Certified Financial Planners, based in Denver, Colorado; the International Association of Financial Planning, based in Atlanta, Georgia, or the National Association of Personal Financial Advisers, based in Buffalo Grove, Illinois, for the names of several of their members in your area. Financial planning is not regulated by federal or state agencies, and membership in professional planner associations is voluntary. The bottom line is that anybody can hang out a financial planner shingle and go into the business. That is why it's vitally important that you thoroughly check out any planner you may consider hiring and paying a fee for financial advice. Generally, it's wise to interview several planners and make other inquiries before coming to a final decision. Use the selection criteria below as a guide.

SELECTING A FINANCIAL PLANNER

- Question each prospect about their formal education as well as their specialized training and experience in the field.

- Ask about memberships in professional organizations that have qualifying standards for planners.

CHART 3
Will Your Retirement Income be Enough?

(1) Annual retirement income you will need (expenses) or desire (expenses plus)— *in today's dollars* .... $ _____

(2) Adjustment for inflation:

  (A) About when will your retirement start? (Enter 5, 10, 15, or 20 years.) .... _____ years

  (B) Your estimate of average annual rate of inflation between now and your retirement (enter 4%, 6%, 8%, or 10%) .... _____ %

  (C) Refer to "Calculating" table below. Enter number from table where years (from #2A above) and inflation % (#2B) intersect .... _____

  (D) Multiply projected retirement income (#1 above) by number in #2C. This is your retirement income adjusted for inflation .... (#1 × #2C =) $ _____

(3) Your estimated retirement income from current sources:

  (A) Annual income you now project from Social Security, retirement plans, savings, investments, etc.—*in today's dollars* .... $ _____

  (B) Your estimate of average annual rate of growth or cost-of-living adjustment (COLA) for amount in #3A (enter 4%, 6%, 8%, or 10%) .... _____ %

  (C) Refer to "Calculating" table below. Enter number from table where years (#2A) and % of growth/COLA (#3B) intersect .... _____

  (D) To calculate the increased value of your projected annual income when you will need it for retirement, multiply #3A by number in #3C ...... (#3A × #3C =) $ _____

(4) Will your retirement income be enough?

  (A) Which is larger: the amount on line #2D or on #3D? .... $ _____

  (B) How much larger is it? ....

  (C) *If the amount on line #2D is larger, you will need more retirement income. If the amount on line #3D is larger, you will have enough retirement income.*

Table: Calculating Annual Rates of Inflation and of Growth/COLA

Years	4%	6%	8%	10%
5	1.22	1.34	1.47	1.61
10	1.48	1.79	2.16	2.59
15	1.80	2.40	3.17	4.18
20	2.19	3.21	4.67	6.73

Source: *Sylvia Porter's Your Finances in the 1990s* (SPYF 1990s) pp. 294–5.

- Ask each prospect whether they are registered with the Securities and Exchange Commission.

- Ask for the names and phone numbers of current clients. Find out whether these clients are satisfied, and how they rate the service they receive.

- Make sure any planner you consider is willing to sign a financial planner disclosure form like the one on page 000. This form will tell you whether or not the planner is selling financial products, such as annuities, insurance policies, mutual funds, limited partnerships or other types of investments that may compromise his or her objectivity as your personal financial advisor.

- Make sure you understand how each prospect is compensated for his or her work. Some planners are paid only on the basis of flat or hourly fees. If a flat fee, what is it based on? Others are paid only through commissions on investment products which they sell to you. Still others are paid on a combination of fees and commissions.

- As a general rule, we would hire only a Certified Financial Advisor (CFA) who works in the profession full time. We would not want a part-timer with dubious credentials within a country mile of our retirement nest egg. We would also prefer a planner who works on a fee-only basis, because that should guarantee greater objectivity in selection of investment vehicles. The National Association of Personal Financial Advisors (NAPFA) offers a booklet entitled "Why Fee-Only Planning," and explains how fee-only planners work on a fee-for-service basis. They do not receive sales commissions, referral fees or reimbursed costs from the implementation of recommendations made to clients. The booklet also explains how planners work with attorneys, actuaries or other professionals; how they charge for their services; how investment recommendations get implemented and many other questions a potential client might have. Copies of the booklet may be obtained by writing to NAPFA's executive director, Margery Wasserman, at 1130 Lake Cook Road, Suite 105, Buffalo Grove, IL 60089.

- A final word of advice: Never give any financial advisor discretionary authority to make investment decisions for you. It is your hard-earned money. You must be responsible for it. Your planner is there to advise and instruct, but the decisions must be yours.

A good planner can help you in a great many ways. Initially, your planner should provide you with a written analysis of your financial situation, including a balance sheet showing your assets versus your liabilities (your net worth) and a minimum one-year cash flow statement. After taking into account your tax bracket, your financial objectives, your risk tolerance and other factors, your planner or adviser will probably suggest ways of improving your money management to help you achieve your goals. (Stay away from any planner who glosses over your finances and feelings and launches immediately into a sales pitch for an annuity, mutual fund or some other financial product. "Reposition your assets" is a code phrase for commission salespersons, meaning sell one thing and buy another.) Any planner who has not done a thorough analysis of your finances and feelings is certainly not to be trusted to recommend products to you.

When the proper time comes to recommend products, your planner should spell out the assumptions on which the recommendations are made and offer several alternatives, with arguments for and against each, so that you have choices. When your financial plan has been completed to your satisfaction, set up a schedule with your planner for regular reviews and for monitoring changes that have to be made from time to time.

Among the things a planner or advisor cannot do for you is assemble your financial data and set your goals. Unless you are willing to speak up, neither can your planner know for sure that you understand the terms being used, the risks of various investment decisions, or the possible alternatives. Don't be afraid to ask questions, no matter how dumb they may seem to you at the time. Forget about dumb, and forget about not questioning your planner's judgment. To the planner you may be a valued client, but you are only one of many. Your financial plan, on the other hand, is your lifeblood.

When the plan is complete, you must be prepared to stick with it. This is the key to the success of both your choice of a financial planner and of the plan you work out together. Otherwise, you have wasted your money and, just possibly, jeopardized your financial future. In the final analysis, it's all up to you and your will to make it work.

The level of your financial and emotional comfort with your planner may be tested as soon as you begin calculating the adequacy of your financial resources for retirement, many planners say. You may not like the idea of drawing on your principal when you retire, but some people find they have little choice. Their resources simply are not adequate to throw off the income they need, or feel they must have, to meet living costs or maintain a desired standard of living. If you find yourself in a situation where you must dip into your principal, the trick is to conserve capital for as long as possible.

MANAGING EXPENSES

As a first step, divide your living expenses into two categories: monthly and periodic. Monthly expenses will include food, housing, utilities, local transportation and entertainment costs, among others. Periodic expenses might include travel, club dues, tax payments and quarterly insurance premiums.

Try to meet your monthly expenses from current Social Security, pension or investment income. Avoid digging into your principal to meet monthly bills. Once you have identified your periodic expenses, set up an automatic capital withdrawal plan under which the funds you need are transferred into your bank account at the appropriate times. Mutual funds are especially useful tools for this purpose because you can withdraw fractional shares. Selling odd lots of individual stocks is considerably more costly. Chart 4 is the layout for that most essential factor of all financial planning, the budget.

Retirement portfolios should be structured first to meet income needs, then to yield a growing stream of income over the years, since inflation causes money to lose some of its value year after year. Here is a relatively simple three-step strategy for achieving income growth during retirement:

- Delay the availability of some of your assets, unless you need the yield from your entire portfolio for living expenses. Zero-coupon treasury bonds, which you purchase at a steep discount, are a safe vehicle for building future reserves during your preretirement or early retirement years.

- Tax-deferred annuities are another method of achieving income growth both before and during retirement. At age 59½, you can withdraw any part of the annuity without incurring an added tax penalty. Interest on any part of the annuity you don't withdraw accumulates tax-deferred. You may also elect to take a guaranteed lifetime income based on the size of the annuity.

- You should also consider putting some of your surplus cash into conservative total-return stock mutual funds, letting your dividends accumulate and the value of your shares appreciate, providing protection against inflation. Income from these funds tends to cushion the downside in a down market, and your dividend should rise as the blue chip, high-capitalization companies the funds own increase their dividend payouts.

	CHART 4 Your Budget. Period: _____		
	Expected This Period	Actual	Actual vs. Expected (plus or minus)
Income items	$ _____	$ _____	$ _____
Expense items: Fixed expense items	$ _____	$ _____	$ _____
Variable expense items	$ _____	$ _____	$ _____
Net (income less expenses)	$ _____	$ _____	$ _____
Net application (into savings, investments, specific goals)	$ _____	$ _____	$ _____

Source: SPYF 1990s p. 21.

Ideally, you would begin retirement by plowing all your dividends back into your stock funds. Later, if the need arises, you could begin drawing the dividends for living expenses. Eventually, you might take dividends and a portion of your equity through an automatic withdrawal program. As noted earlier, this is a particular convenience of mutual funds.

SHEPHERDING YOUR ASSETS

A surprisingly large number of people who are otherwise well organized neglect to keep accurate records or to monitor their assets. They risk becoming victims of fraud or neglect, or of needlessly losing opportunities for gain. Some even forget what they own. On Wall Street, the stories of these people are legion.

Jim M. moved all his securities to a new broker, warning the broker that he did not want to trade. Three months later he checked his statements for the first time to discover his account was being churned. Some of his favorite stocks had been sold out to buy "dogs."

For the most part, New York's social life occupied Mary S. One day she called the trust officer of her bank in high dudgeon. "I just checked my statement. When I was twenty-one my father gave me 1,000 shares of this small company's stock. Your statement says I own 10,000 shares. How could you make this mistake?" The banker explained: "It's no mistake. You haven't been monitoring your assets. The modest company in which your father invested is now an industrial giant. It's been thirty years, and the stock has been split numerous times."

In contrast to these two examples, Gene B. monitors his assets almost too closely. Acting against all conservative advice, he made small fortunes for himself and others by following some of his own basic precepts. "I never lost so much," he says, "that I couldn't reenter the market. Most of my assets are always in a safe harbor. I buy modest amounts of many new, selected issues and watch these stocks by the hour. I'm my own analyst. I call the CEOs and the treasurers frequently. If they won't see me or if I get wrong answers, I sell within the hour. It takes time, knowledge and vigilance, but an aggressive investor can win. I owe it all to having lived with a chronic disease most of my life. Diabetes taught me to keep everything in balance."

You don't need to work as intensively as Gene B., but you do need to: (1) Review your entire holdings at least twice a year; (2) monitor your stocks monthly or weekly, according to their vulnerability; and (3) watch the economic news daily. You also should schedule a general checkup of your investments around the time you go for your annual physical examination. Here are ten basic questions you should ask yourself:

1. Have my long-term goals changed in the past twelve months?
2. Are my short-term objectives being met?
3. Should I exchange stocks or bonds that are generating taxable income for securities that yield a tax-free or tax-deferred return?
4. Are the holdings in my portfolio overweighted in a single company or industry?
5. Have securities acquired through programs offered by my employer or former employer altered the makeup of my portfolio?

6. Have I investigated whether my company has such programs, and if so, how would my participation affect my portfolio?
7. Is this the year I retire? Change jobs? Change residence? What effect will this have on my holdings?
8. Is a major variation likely in my earnings over the next twelve months (a wedding, graduation, birth of a grandchild) that will require me to sell securities?
9. Do I have sufficient cash and liquid assets to meet emergencies?
10. Is my net worth increasing at a rate compatible with my risk tolerance and comfort level?

Ask yourself also whether you are satisfied with the way your investments are being managed. If you have the slightest doubts or questions, get on the telephone immediately.

IS YOUR PENSION SECURE?

Another asset you certainly want to watch over carefully is your pension plan. Learn the facts about your pension plan. The plan administrator is required by law to provide you automatically with the Summary Plan Description, the Summary Annual Report, and Survivor Coverage Data. You also are entitled to receive annually an Individual Statement of Benefits. Be particularly sure you obtain and verify this information at the time of your retirement. Don't take anything for granted or on hearsay.

KEEPING YOUR RECORDS

Monitoring your assets and keeping your financial records in order doesn't mean your house must be jammed with crates of paperwork. Some records you can toss in the garbage, at least after they have served their usefulness. Some, however, you must keep for a lifetime. Here is a review:

- *Your will.* Leave the original with your lawyer or executor. Keep a copy at home or in your safe-deposit box.

- *Tax returns.* Save tax returns for six years. If the IRS is charging you with fraud or other violations, of course, you must keep them until all issues have been resolved.

- *Brokerage and mutual fund statements.* Keep for six years.

- *Employee benefits.* Keep all documents related to your benefits permanently on file in your home.

- *Dividend notices.* Save until you receive your annual 1099-DIV from each issuer.

- *Insurance policies.* Current policies should be kept in a safe place at home, where you or someone else can get at them quickly.

- *Real estate.* Deeds, titles and mortgages, and invoices and canceled checks covering capital improvements, should be kept in your safe-deposit box for at least six years after you have sold the property.

- *Stock and bond certificates.* If you trade regularly, keep these at your brokerage firm in a *street name* registration. If you're a long-term investor, place the certificates in your safe-deposit box.

INFORMATION RESOURCES

Retirement folklore is rife with horror stories of substantial fortunes that have been squandered in months, or even weeks. As eternal vigilance is the price of liberty, it is often the price of solvency as well. Fortunately, you need not be alone in your fight to conserve your financial resources. If you have an able advisor or planner, he or she will probably be your best resource for investment decisions. An understanding of your personal balance sheet, and your psyche, are key to many of the decisions you will be called upon to make before and after retirement. But many other important resources also are available:

- *Your employer.* Your employer is a prime source for information about your retirement benefits package. Generally all you have to do is ask. You need not, however, take everything your employer says or does as absolute, or beyond appeal. You may have legal rights that enable you to head off proposed cuts in your benefits, for example.

- *The public library.* Your library offers a wide variety of useful publications on retirement, books on nearly every imaginable aspect of money management and investing, and a knowledgeable staff. You can only gain by using your library.

- *Local agencies.* Many cities and states now have offices that offer useful information about retirement, including tax and other financial breaks, housing, recreational facilities, and health and other community services.

- *Federal agencies.* Detailed information on retirement planning may be obtained by writing to the U.S. Administration on Aging, Department of Health and Human Services, Washington, DC 20201. In addition, the U.S. Department of Labor will supply you with information about pension and other employee benefit programs. Write the agency at 200 Constitution Avenue NW, Washington, DC 20216. Your nearest Social Security office may be contacted for estimates of your retirement benefits. Special postcards are available for requesting social security earnings information.

- *Service Core of Retired Executives.* SCORE, a part of the U.S. Small Business Administration, offers guidance to small business owners. SCORE is located at 1441 L Street NW, Washington, DC 20416.

- *Private agencies.* Private organizations such as the American Association of Retired Persons, the National Council on the Aging, the Employee Benefit Research Institute and the National Council of Senior Citizens, all located in Washington, DC are often more helpful than state and federal agencies.

Don't be reluctant to take advantage of every resource available, beginning with your lawyer, accountant and financial advisor. Their advice does not come without some cost, but generally it's well worth the money. Your banker may be another source of valuable financial guidance, but not as a substitute for the advice of these other professionals. Banks sell financial products that may or may not be the products that will best serve your financial objectives at the time. You should also reach out to knowledgeable friends and business associates. Often they can provide information and perspective that will help you avoid costly mistakes. And don't forget all that free assistance available from federal, state and local governmental agencies and private organizations dedicated to helping you prosper in retirement. You've earned the right.

2

Assembling Your Nest Egg

You should begin planning for retirement in your twenties or early thirties. That has always been true, but it's more important today than ever before. The prospect of further significant increases in the average human life span means that people who will be retiring in thirty or forty years will have to amass a great deal more money than those retiring this year or next. Perhaps the easiest way to begin is by opening a savings or money market account. If your employer offers a payroll deduction plan for the purchase of U.S. savings bond, you should by all means take advantage of that. In addition, invest annually the maximum allowed for Individual Retirement Accounts (IRAs). With many years of prime earning ahead, and the expectation that your income will rise, you can also take some investment risk for greater potential growth. It would be prudent of you, for example, to begin investing in stock mutual funds at a very young age. The most amazing and delightful thing about steady saving and investing, even in modest amounts, is that over the long haul your money compounds again and again, building up to mountainous sums by the time you need it.

Buying a home also should be one of your principal goals in your twenties and thirties. Structure your retirement plan to take this move into account, setting aside enough money to cover your main goals in life before investing in riskier ventures.

As soon as your first child is born, begin saving for his or her college education. U.S. savings bonds are an excellent vehicle for this. Interest earned on the bonds is not taxable if they are used to pay tuition and other direct costs of sending a child to college.

The head of a young family also should have adequate life insurance. Insurance is primarily a way to guarantee an estate for your family when you die, but can also be a type of forced saving, and you pay lower premiums if you take it out when you are young. Various kinds of annuity policies let you build up cash value to be drawn as needed—as a loan for the education of your children, for example, or to provide income or a lump sum when you retire. Many annuity programs are tax-sheltered.

Take full advantage of all tax-sheltered savings, investment and retirement plans available through your employer. You may not be able at first to sock away a lot of money, but get the saving habit and stay with it. At this stage in your life consistency is more important than amount.

By the time you reach your forties you should have an established career and a broad base of assets, savings, investments and a home. Talk with the administrator of your company's pension plan and estimate exactly what you can expect when you retire. Then decide how much more money you will need to supplement that amount. If you can increase your pension by paying in more of your salary, do so. The same advice holds for the 401(k) salary reduction plan designed to help employees accumulate money in tax-sheltered retirement accounts. Many companies match or pay a percentage of employee contributions. Matching company contributions are one of the best deals you will ever find. Take advantage of it as soon as you can. If you haven't yet invested in IRAs, now is the time to do so. If you are self-employed, look into a Keogh plan which allows more money than an IRA to be set aside, tax-free, annually.

Look for ways to shelter your income from taxes. IRAs, 401(k) plans and Keogh plans are some examples. The amounts you invest, the sums contributed by your employer, the interest, dividends and other earnings, and the capital gains on these investments are not taxable until you start withdrawing your money.

Look for ways to shelter your investments from taxes. Tax-advantaged investments include U.S. savings bonds, annuities, universal life insurance, real estate, municipal bonds, tax-free mutual funds, tax-exempt unit trusts and investment limited partnerships.

Make out a will to insure the smooth transfer of assets to your heirs. Consider whether you will want to continue your education as a means to a second career. If you haven't already done so, begin to take better care of your health with regular checkups in anticipation of your active retirement.

By the time you reach your fifties many of your obligations to your family probably have been met. Your mortgage is paid off or nearly so. Your children have finished college. And with a fairly large amount of assets accumulated during years of careful saving, now may be the time to meet with a financial planner to reevaluate your investments. If you have no home mortgage, for example, you may want to consider some of the tax-advantaged investment options discussed above. Periodically, you should take a look at your Social Security account. Check your earnings annually. Keep copies of your income tax returns. Check your local Social Security office to see what they have recorded in your earnings account. Match that against your own records. In cases of dispute, a worker's records are conclusive proof of earnings. Ask for a free Personal Earnings and Benefit Estimate Statement (PEBES). The number to call is (800) 937-2000. Also keep an eye on your company's health benefits plan. With healthcare costs continuing to rise, many companies are making changes in these plans to reduce employee benefits. These changes may require adjustments in your retirement planning. (If you are already retired, however, you may have guaranteed benefits that you can protect, if necessary, through recourse to legal action.)

THE NEST EGG SECURITY BLANKET

The trouble with this maturity business, of course, is that it sneaks up on you with damn little consideration for your feelings, none at all for what you want. You still *feel* sixteen, but the world says you're mature, worn, an older American. You've been ambushed by the years, caught naked on the down escalator in the department store of life with everybody staring. But then you awake from the anxious daydream of unwelcome maturity with a comforting thought: "Thank God I have my nest egg!" Your nest egg is indeed your financial shield as well as your psychic security blanket in later life. The very word is calming, like warm milk in the pit of the stomach, suggestive enough to transport you right back to the womb.

We were taught so well—and compelled to believe in every cell in our body—that if we nurtured our nest egg carefully and it grew apace, our retirement years would indeed be golden. We could be free at last. We could finally thumb our nose at anybody. "Save!" we were admonished. "Invest! Make your money work hard. Build your nest egg. Add a little to it every week, every month. Fondle it in your mind so that you never forget how central it is to your well-being when you eventually retire and leisure is your principal occupation."

The drumbeat of such advice becomes a bit tiresome, to be sure, but it is good advice nevertheless. Why do so few of us really take it to heart? In the summer of 1989 IDS Financial Services, a Minneapolis-based subsidiary of American Express, released a survey of Americans aged thirty-five to sixty-four with household incomes of $30,000. The results of the independent study, conducted by the Daniel Yankelovich Group of New York, were enough to rattle even the most complacent preretiree. The Yankelovich organization reported:

- Having a steady source of income and maintaining current lifestyle in retirement are among Americans' top financial goals. Yet only half the people who say these goals are important say they are doing well at achieving them.

- Half those surveyed say they must work at least part time during retirement to make ends meet.

- Almost three-fourths of the people surveyed expect they will have to lower their standard of living in retirement.

- There is an increased understanding, especially among baby boomers, of the importance of retirement planning.

- Baby boomers are particularly pessimistic about how they'll live in retirement, about the future of Social Security, about inflation eroding their retirement savings and about achieving financial independence.

- Even though half of the people surveyed said they think Social Security will not amount to much by the time they retire, most of them are still counting on Social Security to provide one-fourth of the money they will need for retirement.

- One in four of those surveyed said they are concerned about depending on a child or relative for support.

- On average, the survey group estimated they would need about $36,000 per year in today's dollars to live on in retirement.

IDS financial analysis shows that even those with some savings and some pension would have to save between $200 and $500 a month to generate that income over an entire life span. Baby boomers want a higher retirement income than the older respondents in the survey—$42,000 compared to $32,000—and they also want to retire earlier—sixty compared to sixty-two. But to accomplish that, they would have to save well over $500 a month during their working years.

The obvious truth of the matter is that a great many Americans really cannot afford to retire at sixty-two or even sixty-five. They either have to go on working full time or part time, accept a drastically reduced lifestyle, take money and other kinds of financial assistance from children or other relatives, or all of the above. In many of these situations, however, better utilization of assets and a dollop of common sense can work wonders. There is more than one way to fatten a nest egg. And for those of you who think your own nest egg is anorexic, we are going to discuss a few ideas for putting more meat on its bones. The strategy is to recognize and put into play sources of wealth you may have overlooked in your anxiety about the future. Chart 5 sets out a checklist of the basic pension and retirement plans.

THE VALUE OF A HOME

Owning a home is not as easy as it used to be. Prices have skyrocketed in most parts of the country. Getting the down payment together seems beyond the income of many households. But for those of you nearing retirement today, the story is quite different. You probably bought a home in your twenties, then upgraded once or twice over the years as your income and your family expanded. Now your children are grown and out on their own. Your financial responsibilities have decreased. Your need for living space has shrunk, and you probably have most of the furniture, appliances and other durable goods you need, at least for a few years. You may even own a vacation home, a rental property or two, perhaps also a building lot and some acreage you've been holding for years, hoping that an oil company or a developer would come along and make you rich by paying many times what you invested to buy it.

All this property you have accumulated has enormous cash value. The house you paid $50,000 for in the sixties or early seventies is likely to be worth $300,000 or even more in today's real estate market, depending on its location and condition. The building lot you bought for $15,000 could easily be worth $100,000. The acreage you so cleverly purchased from an old farmer may now be surrounded by suburban housing or commercial establishments and worth a small fortune. And the beloved vacation home in the country or on the lake, for which you paid $70,000 may have a value of over $200,000. So even if your cash savings are fairly meager, and your Social Security benefits and pension from work are nothing to shout about, you are not exactly poverty stricken.

You may indeed have a net worth of anywhere from half a million to a million dollars. (Net worth equals financial assets minus liabilities.) Property,

CHART 5
Guide to Employment, Pension, and Other Retirement Plans
(Participants may have more than one type of plan)

Integrated Plans	
Various Plans	Some of the plans below may take into account the participant's Social Security retirement benefits.
Qualified Defined-Benefits Plans **Tax-exempt by the Internal Revenue Code**	
Flat-Amount Plans	All participants receive the same benefits if they meet the minimum years-of-service requirements, regardless of how much they earned.
Fixed-Benefit Plans	Participants receive predetermined benefits of a stated amount or of a stated percentage of compensation during entire employment or during a specified number of years prior to retirement.
Unit-Benefit Plans	Participants' benefits are based upon a predetermined formula combining both the level of preretirement income and number of years of service.
Qualified Defined-Contributions Plans **(also known as Capital Accumulation Plans)** **Tax-exempt by the Internal Revenue Code**	
Thrift or Savings Plans	As an incentive for employees to save, employers contribute amounts equal to all or part of each participant's contributions.
Money-Purchase Plans	Contributions by employers are based upon fixed formulas. Benefits to participants are based upon investment performance of the plans (accumulated principal, growth in value, and reinvested interest, dividends and other income).
Targeted-Benefit Plans	These are hybrid plans, primarily money-purchase plans, but also combining targeted defined benefits. Methods for determining employers' contributions are different from those in straight money-purchase plans.
Profit-Sharing Plans	Employers contribute specified percentages of profits, which may be a flat percentage on all profits or percentages on a sliding scale of profit levels. Employees may be permitted voluntarily to contribute additionally to their accounts.

Qualified Defined-Contributions Plans (also known as Capital Accumulation Plans) Tax-exempt by the Internal Revenue Code *(continued)*	
Employee Stock Ownership Plans (ESOPs)	These may be bonuses in company stock contributed by employers or they may be employee stock-purchase plans subsidized in part or entirely by employers. One form of the latter are PAYSOPs (Payroll Stock Ownership Plans).
401(k) Salary-Deferral Plans	A portion of an employee's compensation is contributed to the plan and the income tax on this amount, and on any matching contribution by the employer, and any earnings on the plan are deferred until distribution.
403(b) Salary-Deferral Plans	These are similar to 401(k) plans, above, except they are for employees of non-profit, tax-exempt employers, such as educational, charitable foundation, and religious organizations. They evolved from Tax-Sheltered Annuities (TSAs) for teachers.
SEP Plans	In Simplified Employee Pension (SEP) Plans, employers make contributions directly to employees' own Individual Retirement Accounts (IRAs).
Deductible Employee Contributions (DEC) Plans	DEC plans are a variation on SEPs, above. Employees make their IRA contributions to their employers' established retirement plans, rather than into IRAs separately maintained by these employees.
Individual Retirement Accounts (IRAs)	Employees establish and maintain IRAs for themselves and their spouses. Income taxes on some contributions and on growth in value and reinvested earnings in these accounts are deferred until withdrawal in accordance with tax regulations.
Keogh Plans	Self-employed individuals establish and maintain these plans, which are similar to IRAs.
Non-Qualified Plans Not tax-exempt by the Internal Revenue Code	
Various Plans	These plans may be structured in many ways. They are established and maintained by employers to provide incentives for employees and to single out accomplishments and provide additional benefits for selected employees. Employers are not required to report to the government on coverage and operation of these plans.

Source: SPYF p. 288–9.

Note: The trend in recent years has been more to defined-contributions plans and less to traditional defined-benefits plans. With defined-contributions plans, employers are not obligated to provide guaranteed benefits as they are with defined-benefits plans. Such plans adversely affect employers if investment performance falls short of this commitment.

however, is not a liquid asset. You can't spend it for food, clothing, shelter and medical care. What you can do, of course, is sell some or even all your real estate, invest the proceeds wisely and live in relative comfort and financial security for the rest of your life. Even if your home has great sentimental value, and is the sacred gathering place for the family on holidays, you don't need it anymore. Nor do you need the foolish encumbrance of sentimentality at this stage in your life. One of the more important imperatives in planning for your retirement is to clear your mind of as much emotion as possible and deal with your financial condition as it is, not as you might like it to be.

If you are like many other retired or soon-to-retire individuals, you may well be weary of the upkeep on a big house. Buy or rent a smaller, less expensive retirement home and make a new, happier life for yourself. When you begin to feel weepy and nostalgic about the old homestead, think about all the money you have in the bank. You've heard it before: nothing makes you feel as good as money in the bank.

The rate of appreciation on your vacation home, building lot and other raw land has probably slowed dramatically. And while it might be nice to hold on to the country house, if you can afford it, a second home in retirement is an extravagance, definitely not prudent for most and not essential to your happiness. Rent a vacation home for a month when you feel the urge to be in the country. Or take a real vacation, explore America, go on a white-water boating trip down the Colorado, drive through the wine country of California or the south of France, spend a couple of weeks on a Greek isle, climb a small mountain in Nepal. Live a little. It can't hurt. Incidentally, February through June are the prime months for selling vacation homes.

Again, if you need the money to add to your nest egg of investments, you should also consider disposing of your rental properties. You probably bought them with retirement in mind in the first place. Wait for an active real estate market to develop in your area before listing the properties, where feasible, but don't hesitate to cash in. If, however, managing the rentals is no burden to you, and your financial return from the units is equal to that you would receive from investing the money in other assets, it may be just as well to hold on to them. It's a matter of personal preference.

We are not suggesting that you sell anything you really love and don't urgently need to convert to cash for building your investment nest egg. Further, if you require sheltering of some of your income in retirement, owning mortgaged property may be one of your better options. There may also be tax reasons for not selling your property, or for spreading sales over several years. It all depends on your individual financial situation. Consult members of your family, your banker, accountant, lawyer and other trusted financial advisors before committing yourself to any course of action that will fundamentally reorient your assets. It would be poor judgment to do anything else.

THE USES OF REVERSE MORTGAGES

While a so-called reverse annuity mortgage is not, strictly speaking, a nest egg builder, it is a method of using your property to add to your income in retirement. (A reverse annuity mortgage, or RAM, may also be called a reserve account mortgage, reverse equity mortgage, home equity conversion mortgage, or a variety of similar names, some proprietary to individual lenders.) If you own a home with little or no mortgage balance, a reverse mortgage is at least worth investigating. The Federal Housing Administration (FHA) recently launched a national pilot program that could expand the use of reverse mortgages by providing mortgage insurance for banks, thrifts and other lenders who participate in the program.

Like any other kind of mortgage, a reverse mortgage is a loan against the value of your property. The mortgage lender makes a monthly payment to you, the property owner, and in return takes a proportionate share of equity in your home. The lender's equity share grows with each payment to you the borrower. The mortgage is paid off, along with interest, in a lump sum at the end of a fixed term or when the borrower moves, sells or dies.

Say your home is fully paid for and has a current market value of $120,000. Your RAM makes available to you $96,000—80 percent of this $120,000 value. You get $750 every month until you have received this $96,000 combining principal paid to you and interest on these loans. If your interest rate is 10 percent, you would receive $750 a month for 8.5 years (102 months). At that time you would have accumulated $61,200 in loans and $35,461 in interest—a total of $96,661. A 10 percent annual interest rate is 0.833 percent each month. This 0.833 percent would be accumulated on your first month's $750. In the second month 0.833 percent interest would accumulate on both your first and second payments from the lender, and also on your first month's accumulated interest. Some RAMs are linked with an insurance policy to pay off debt accumulated to that date if you die before maturity (which in the above example is the $96,000). If there is no such linkage, your estate would repay the debt. To protect you if you live to maturity, you should be sure your original RAM loan agreement guarantees to refinance your home (at then-current rates) when you reach your limit.

Have the prospective lender or lenders you're talking with show you various possibilities for monthly payments, interest, tenure (usually a maximum of fifteen years) and terms. Ask whether you can receive a larger payment if you agree to share a percentage of the home's appreciation with the lender.

A reverse annuity mortgage involves risk so you should consider it very carefully before you decide to do it. Have your property's value appraised. Determine how a RAM might affect your income taxes and Social Security and pensions. Are changes in your will required to reflect the RAM? How much will RAM insurance premiums cost you? What are the RAM's closing costs? Are you required to maintain the property as specified by the lender?

Reverse mortgages can be attractive to some older individuals because eligibility is based on equity in their home, rather than income. Usually, reverse mortgages, including those insured by the FHA, are restricted to persons sixty-two years of age or older. A reverse mortgage, however, should not be the only solution considered by older homeowners in need of cash for living expenses. Hefty upfront fees make those loans insured by the government expensive in the short term. If you expect to move within three years, most experts suggest that you avoid a reverse mortgage. As an alternative, you may want to consider the possibility of carving out a rental apartment in your home (if local zoning laws permit).

In general, reverse mortgages are recommended as a last resort. If you live to maturity you are saddled with a large debt rather than owning a paid-up home. To qualify for the FHA program, you must meet with an FHA-certified counselor to discuss the program as well as other financial options. Loan payments received under a reverse mortgage are not taxable, nor do they affect eligibility for Medicare or Social Security. They may affect Supplemental Security Income or Medicaid payments, however, because these programs are based strictly on need. To get the names of participating FHA-program lenders in your area, call (800) 245-2691. To obtain a complete list of participating public-sector and private reverse-mortgage lenders, send a stamped, self-addressed business-size envelope to the National Center for Home Equity Conversion, 348 West Main Street, Marshall, MI 56258.

DISCOVERING OTHER RESOURCES

In addition to the real estate that you may be able to sell to fatten your nest egg, think about your other assets that may be marketable. We have a friend who several years ago bought a nonworking farm in upstate New York from an Australian media mogul. Along with 120 acres of land, the Greek revival main house, pond, swimming pool, babbling brook, tennis court, garage, pool house, garden house and other amenities, the wealthy seller threw in at no cost to the buyer two tractors, one of them a large John Deere, a collection of farm and garden tools and implements, a case of fine old French Bordeaux, a lot of beautiful furniture and several creditable oil paintings. When he recently sold the property, our friend engaged a local auctioneer to dispose of all these items, adding over $50,000 to his take on the buildings and land. About a year before placing the property on the market, he also hired a lumber company to selectively thin his forest land, reaping $30,000 from that transaction. He felt a bit guilty that he could not be as generous with his buyer as the media mogul had been with him, but only when he was not thinking about the portfolio of additional investments he acquired with the extra money.

Another friend showered his wife with expensive jewelry when the couple was in their thirties and forties and he was a managing partner in a thriving business. When the time came for him to retire, however, none of his children wanted to step in and take over. The business had to be closed and its few hard assets divided among several owners, including his two brothers and a sister. One of the things he did to save himself, in addition to selling his expensive suburban house and moving to a smaller home in a warmer climate, was to sell most of his wife's fine jewelry. One piece alone, a large diamond ring which he had purchased in the 1950s for $10,000, brought over $80,000. By adding the total take from the sale of the jewelry to his investment portfolio, and by working part time at his old occupation, our friend has been able to live nicely if not lavishly in retirement. His decision to get rid of the jewelry was practical and necessary under the circumstances, and his wife seemed just as happy with new costume jewelry. She admitted, in fact, that she had always lived in fear the high-priced jewelry, especially the diamond, would be stolen. Relieved of that psychological burden, she was happy her jewels would contribute to a new lifestyle for herself and her husband. The husband, meanwhile, found working in New York City a few days each month just the right break from his retirement routine of gardening, golfing and socializing. The monthly trips also allowed him to spend time with his children and grandchildren.

COLLECTIBLES

When looking for things you can sell to build up a retirement nest egg, make sure you don't overlook collectibles you may have acquired over the years. Stamp and coin collections, even comic book and baseball card collections, can be worth a great deal of money. A desire to see once again the Superman comic books they read as a child will cause otherwise rational people to pay top dollar to recapture a bit of their past. Comic books have been around, in one form or another, since the early years of this century, but the ones commanding the highest prices are those that were published from the early 1930s through the end of World War II. This period, with a bit of leeway on both sides, is known in collecting circles as the Golden Age. There's also a Silver Age, spanning the middle 1950s and early 1960s. If you do find a cache of old comics in the attic or the back of a closet, their value will depend in part on their condition. Old comics are usually graded as either good, fine or mint. According to Bob Overstreet's *Comic Book Price Guide,* the bible of the industry, the most valuable comic book in America is *Marvel Comics #1.* Published in the fall of 1939, it has a present-day value of between $3,000 and $20,000, depending on its condition. *Action Comics #1,* which gave Superman to the world, is second in line, with a current value of $2,800 to $14,000. Even some fairly recent comic books have appreciated rapidly.

If you have a certain toy model of the *Lusitania* gathering dust somewhere in the house, get it out immediately. It could be worth upwards of $28,000. A French bisque doll once sold for $38,000. A Chicago lawyer is reported to have paid $30,000 for a political button of James Cox and Franklin Roosevelt. And a rare Honus Wagner baseball card once fetched a record $27,000. How about a copy of a Chicago newspaper bearing the headline "Dewey Defeats Truman"? Today it's the single most valuable newspaper of the twentieth century, with a selling price of over $1,000. The point is this: don't overlook anything that may have value when adding to your retirement nest egg.

Those candlesticks you bought for $150 in London decades ago with more copper than silver showing? Don't toss them out. They may be Georgian silver, two hundred years old and now worth about $4,000. The young artist you knew years ago who once sketched your sleeping dog on a wet after-noon: if he's now famous you may own a valuable work of art; if he died young and notorious, very valuable. Even many of your wedding gifts prob-ably have appreciated in value over the years.

If you do find an interesting and potentially valuable item stored away in the attic, garage or barn, have it appraised by several dealers in the field. But don't take the word of only one appraiser, especially if he or she brushes the item aside as practically worthless, then offers to take it off your hands for a song. That could be a tipoff that your exotic discovery can be sold for much more money than you've been led to believe. It happens all the time, so caution is the watchword.

MISSING MONEY

Now what about your "missing money"? You don't know of any, you say? Well consider this: you left your first job back in the late 1950s and in the intervening years have made three geographic moves in as many other jobs. In 1990 you retired with the feeling that your financial life was in good order. But you have forgotten that on your first job you were part of the pension plan. Pension was not a word you thought much about in 1958. Yet you are entitled to collect whatever monies are owed you. The pension administrator of your first company may have tried and failed to find you, both because of the mileage and the years between then and now. So your money reverted back to the pension fund, where unclaimed checks remain.

Pension administrators are required to notify the U.S. Social Security Administration of any beneficiaries they cannot locate. When the beneficiary applies for Social Security, therefore, he or she will be told about the private pension money waiting to be claimed. If you do recall being in such a plan and are now retired but haven't received a check, contact your former em-ployer. You will then be put in touch with the firm's pension administrator. If the company has gone out of business, a local bank may be acting as the pension fund trustee. You should also be aware that the federal govern-ment's Pension Benefit Guaranty Corporation acts as trustee for about 700 terminated plans. Any retiree can write or call to find out if a plan is under government trusteeship. If your plan is still ongoing, however, the pension benefits agency can't help. Chart 6 will assist you in keeping track of your retirement plans.

While you are remembering jobs past, give a thought to any bank accounts you might have left behind. In the excitement of a job, location or other life change you might have forgotten a relatively small savings account. These unclaimed assets end up in the state's coffers by a process called *escheatment*. (This law is not in effect in Colorado or the District of Columbia.) Under the escheatment process, banks, insurance companies and other holders are required to turn abandoned property over to the state after a certain period of time. It may be one year, or up to fifteen. The average is five years.

The states are supposed to make an effort to locate the owner, whose claim almost always supersedes escheatment. If the owner dies, the legal heirs inherit the abandoned property. Even after the account has been escheated, banks retain records of the transaction, so the account can be traced. If you now remember a long-forgotten bank account, contact the bank first. Better yet, see if you can locate your old bankbook. This will make claiming much easier for you and the bank. If that bank is no longer in existence, contact the treasurer's office in the state in which it was chartered or headquartered.

Just how much money any or all of these ideas will add to your retirement nest egg will vary from person to person. One of our purposes has been to get you to think creatively about the possibilities. Another is to suggest that you must face the future honestly and with determination to take the steps necessary to insure your financial security in retirement.

A MAN WITH A SOLUTION

Ben Coulter, president of First Financial Planners Inc., in Jupiter, Florida, is both a CPA and a Certified Financial Planner (CFP) who understands a great deal about the problems of acquiring a nest egg large enough to insure adequate income in retirement. As an exercise that might be helpful to people in roughly the same financial boat, we recently asked Ben to tell us how he would approach the dilemma of a hypothetical acquaintance.

Call her Ellen Rogers. Slim, attractive at age fifty, mother of two grown children, employed as office manager by a solid, medium-sized company, Ellen appears to be doing well financially. Yet when the topic of retiring comes up, a faint hint of desperation clouds her face. Ellen's husband died in his late forties, leaving her the mortgage-free family home worth about $225,000, plus $200,000 in cash resting in money market accounts. She spends most of her salary—$52,000 a year—on living expenses, and insists

---

CHART 6
Form to Copy for Recording Each of Your Retirement Plans

Type: ☐ IRA ☐ 401(k) ☐ Pension Plan ☐ Keogh ☐ SEP
☐ Annuity ☐ Other

Description and Details of Above (Payments, Key Dates, Benefits, etc.) _____
_____
_____
_____
_____

Names of Holder(s) _____
Account Number _____Date Started _____
Institution _____
Name of Plan _____
Address _____
City _____State _____Zip _____Phone ( ) _____
Location of Holders' Records _____
Other Information _____
_____
_____
_____
_____

---

on retiring in twelve years at age sixty-two. She lives well now, and would like to continue living well when she retires.

On hearing Ellen Rogers' story, Coulter reached for his calculator.

"Assuming that she will need income of $4,000 a month in today's dollars, and assuming an average annual inflation rate of 5 percent over twelve years," he said, "she will need $7,200 a month ($86,400 a year) to maintain her lifestyle when she retires in the year 2002. Are you sure she has no other financial assets?"

"She's maxed out on Social Security, and she has a company retirement plan that will throw off $32,000 a year at age sixty-two," we responded.

"We can work with that," said Coulter. "Assuming Social Security benefits rise at the rate of 4.5 percent a year between 1990 and 2002, her income from that source will be about $19,000 a year. That plus her $32,000 in pension income add up to $51,000. She needs $35,400 in investment income in the year 2002 to reach her retirement-income objective of $86,000."

"Any hope of that?" we asked.

"Yes, but we do have to turn the $200,000 cash legacy her husband left her into $500,000 by the year 2002 to make it work," Coulter noted. "Taking inflation into account again, a total annual investment return of about 8 percent on half a million dollars ($40,000 a year), added to her Social Security and pension benefits, will bring her to the $86,400 goal with a little to spare."

"How are you going to do that?"

"I'll get back to you with suggestions," he said. And the following day, Coulter was back on the phone.

"In order for Ellen Rogers to accumulate $500,000 by the time she retires in twelve years, I would recommend that she invest her $200,000 as follows," the financial planner told us.

Following are Coulter's recommendations:

$20,000   Kemper Money Market-Government Securities (for working or emergency capital) at an interest rate of roughly 8 percent

$30,000   American Funds Group (stock mutual funds, for staying ahead of inflation)

$15,000: Washington Mutual Investors Fund
Total return in 1989: 28.97 percent
Five and ten-year average total return:
20 percent per year

$15,000: American Mutual Fund
Total return in 1989: 25.24 percent
Five-year average: 18.1 percent per year
Ten-year average: 18.4 percent per year

$50,000   Single-Premium Deferred Annuity (for safety and tax deferral)

$25,000: Western Reserve Life Multi-Plan
at a first-year interest rate of roughly 8 percent

$25,000: United Pacific Life Prosperity
Five-year guaranteed interest rate: about 8.8 percent

$50,000   American Pathway II (variable annuity for growth, income and tax deferral), sponsored by Sun Life and Anchor National. Includes a death benefit to at least the amount purchased less withdrawals.

$25,000: Growth

$25,000: Growth and Income
Total return Jan. to Nov., 1989: 28.03 percent

$50,000   Best of America IV (variable annuity), sponsored by Nationwide Life. Has same death benefit as American Pathway to age 75.

All initially into money market, then invested by dollar-cost averaging as follows:

$2,000/month: Fidelity Equity Income
(conservative, low volatility)
Growth in 1989: 15 percent

$2,000/month: Twentieth Century Growth
(more aggressive)
Growth in 1989: 27.6 percent

Other financial planners no doubt would come up with other investment ideas, perhaps equally as productive, for our hypothetical friend Ellen Rogers. Economic conditions and financial markets can also change rapidly, dictating the selection of investment opportunities different from those favored by Ben Coulter at the time we conferred about Ellen. (You may have noted that Coulter did not include in his calculations the value of Ellen's home. This was deliberate. The home is an additional cushion if the portfolio does not quite meet expectations.)

The main lesson of the Ellen Rogers exercise is to show that it is almost never too late to try and build a bigger nest egg of investments for your retirement. Unfortunately, most Americans are all talk and no action when it comes to doing that. Even those who do plan have little idea how much money they will need. Don't you be one of the know-nothings. Make up your mind right now to act.

3

Social Security

A CHANGE OF ATTITUDE

Many Social Security beneficiaries have complained bitterly since the early 1980s about the quality and availability of the personal service offered by the agency. The problems have been blamed on huge staff reductions at the agency and on excessive workloads imposed on remaining employees, which impair their morale and thus their efficiency. But the new Social Security commissioner, Gwendolyn S. King, is apparently moving to halt workforce reductions and to shore up the spirits of her remaining employees, which number in the tens of thousands.

In noting Social Security's unique role in our society, King has promised to give better service to the public as well as to protect the integrity of the Social Security Trust Funds. She has also set forth a hopefully attainable statement of her goals and objectives as commissioner. These include paying benefits promptly, serving the public with compassion and courtesy, assuring that those who need or desire personal face-to-face service have ready access to that service, providing prompt resolution of claims and reaching out through public information programs to make sure beneficiaries are fully aware of their rights under all Social Security programs.

KING'S SUPPLEMENTAL SECURITY INCOME INITIATIVE

Another indication of the new approach at Social Security is Commissioner King's attempt to enroll poor people in the Supplemental Security Income (SSI) program. Her initiative stands in sharp contrast to the miserly attitude of former President Ronald Reagan, whose administration made little if any effort to find the estimated 1.8 million aged, blind or disabled poor people who are eligible for the program but not participating. To be eligible for SSI benefits you must be sixty-five or older. Blind means the vision in your better eye is 20/200 or less, or you have a visual field of twenty degrees or less. Disabled means you have a severe physical handicap or mental condition that keeps you from doing any substantial work, and medical evidence shows it is expected to last at least twelve months or result in death.

Supplemental Security Income beneficiaries may also be eligible for food stamps, Medicaid and social services. Single people in the program receive up to $368 a month in federal benefits, while couples receive up to $553, and many states supplement the federal benefits. SSI beneficiaries must show that their resources, such as real estate, cash, bank accounts, stocks and bonds, are not more than $2,000 for an individual and not more than $3,000 for a couple. However, Social Security does not count your home and some personal belongings when it is calculating assets.

If you are receiving only Social Security, your annual income cannot exceed $4,656 for an individual and $6,876 for a couple. For those whose only income is from their work, earnings cannot exceed $9,852 a year for an individual and $14,292 for a couple.

Created during the administration of Franklin D. Roosevelt as part of the "New Deal" Roosevelt had promised the American people, Social Security comprises a protection package that includes retirement, survivors, and disability insurance. It almost certainly won't meet all one's financial needs in retirement. Instead, for most of us, it's a vital floor from which to build, together with our savings, investments, insurance, real estate and other financial assets. More than thirty-nine million Americans currently receive monthly Social Security benefit checks.

ELIGIBILITY REQUIREMENTS

To be eligible for Social Security benefits, you must first have credit for a certain amount of work under Social Security. These credits may have been earned at any time after 1936. Your earnings under the Railroad Retirement Act may also be creditable, but generally only if you have less than 120 months of railroad service.

All employees and self-employed people earn Social Security credits the same way. In 1990 you received one credit of coverage for each $520 of earnings, up to a maximum of four credits based on annual earnings of $2,000 or more. This includes gross wages paid and net self-employment income. The amount needed to earn a credit will increase automatically in future years as average wages increase. If you stop working under Social Security before you become insured, credits for the earnings reported for you will remain on your Social Security record. You can add to them if you return to work some time in the future. No benefits based on your earnings can be paid to you or your family until you have enough credits to become insured, and no one can be fully insured with less than six credits (one-and-a-half years of work). If you have credit for ten years of work, however, you can be sure that you will be fully insured for retirement benefits, although it doesn't guarantee that you will receive the maximum benefit available the day you apply. That is available only to those workers who have paid the top Social Security tax during the 10-year period immediately preceding their retirement at age sixty-two.

If you retired at sixty-two in 1990, you need thirty-nine credits to be fully insured. In 1991 or later, you will need forty credits. You also are fully insured if you have one credit for each year of work after 1950 up to the year you reach sixty-two. In counting the years after 1950, a person born in 1930 or later would omit years before age twenty-two.

BENEFITS TO SPOUSES AND CHILDREN

Social Security benefits also are paid to spouses and children of retired workers. Those who are eligible include: (1) unmarried children under eighteen (or under nineteen if full-time elementary or high school students); (2) unmarried children eighteen or over who were severely disabled before age twenty-two and who continue to be disabled; (3) wife or husband sixty-two or over; (4) wife or husband under sixty-two if she or he is caring for a disabled child under sixteen or a child who is receiving a benefit based on your earnings. Benefits also can be paid to a divorced spouse at sixty-two if the marriage lasted 10 years. In cases where the divorce has been in effect for two years, that rule applies even if your former spouse is not retired and not receiving benefits.

NEARLY ALL JOBS ARE COVERED

Almost all jobs in the United States are covered by Social Security, although special rules apply to some types of work. If you work as a domestic employee in a private household and one employer pays you $50 or more in a three-month calendar quarter, your wages are covered by Social Security. If you are hired to do farm work, including domestic work on a farm, your wages are covered by Social Security if your employer spends more than $2,500 during the year on agricultural labor or spends less than $2,500 but pays you at least $150 in cash. Most federal employees hired on or after January 1, 1984, are covered by Social Security.

If you are self-employed, your income is covered if you have net profit of $400 or more in a year. Even if your actual net earnings are less than $400, your self-employment income may count for Social Security. If in doubt, check with any Social Security office. A church or qualified church-controlled organization can elect exemption from Social Security taxes if it is opposed to paying them on religious grounds. If employed by such an organization, you are still covered by Social Security if you earn $100 or more in a year. However, you are considered self-employed and your earnings represent self-employment income even if they are less than $400. Chart 7 shows how you can apply to Social Security, long before retirement time approaches, to confirm that your Social Security records are in order.

MEDICARE

The two parts of Medicare—hospital insurance and medical insurance—help protect people sixty-five and over from the high costs of healthcare. Disabled individuals under sixty-five who have been entitled to Social Security disability benefits for twenty-four or more months also are eligible for Medicare, as are insured workers and eligible family members who need dialysis treatment or kidney transplant because of permanent kidney failure.

Medicare is handled by the Health Care Financing Administration, not by Social Security. But the people at Social Security offices will help you apply for Medicare and will answer your questions about the program. The hospital insurance part of the program helps pay the cost of inpatient hospital care and certain kinds of follow-up. The medical part helps pay the cost of physician services and some other medical items and services. If you are eligible for Social Security or Railroad Retirement benefits either as a worker or family member, you also are eligible for hospital insurance protection at age sixty-five.

You should apply for Medicare three months before your sixty-fifth birthday even if you plan to continue working. That way your protection will start the month you reach sixty-five. When you apply for hospital insurance,

---

CHART 7
Your Social Security Earnings and Benefit Estimate
Are Your Social Security Records Correct?

The Social Security recordkeeping system, like any other recordkeeping system, is not infallible. Your earnings could end up in someone else's account or fail to be recorded at all. This would mean less insurance for you now and lower retirement benefits later.

To avoid this, obtain a "Request for Earnings and Benefit Estimate Statement" (form SSA-7004) from your local Social Security office, fill it in, and mail to the specified Social Security Administration center listed on the form.

You will receive a free statement which shows your Social Security earnings history, tells you how much you have paid in Social Security taxes, estimates your future Social Security benefits, and provides some general information about how the program works.

---

you will be enrolled automatically for the medical insurance part of Medicare unless you tell the agency you do not want it. People over sixty-five who have not worked long enough to be eligible for hospital insurance can obtain this protection by enrolling and paying a basic monthly premium of $175 (per person) through December 1990. If you do that, you must also enroll in the medical program, with a monthly premium of $28.60 (per person) through the end of 1990.

HOW YOUR BENEFIT IS FIGURED

The amount of your monthly Social Security retirement benefit is based on your earnings covered by Social Security, and the number of years used in figuring your average earnings depends on when you reach sixty-two. While all your earnings up to the maximum covered under Social Security are considered, they are adjusted to take account of changes in wage levels since 1951. These adjusted earnings are averaged together and a formula is applied to the average to obtain a benefit rate. This is important because average wages in the U.S. economy change greatly over a 30-to-40-year working life. Once a person starts receiving benefits, his or her benefits will increase automatically as the cost of living rises (except in rare cases of legislatively mandated benefit freezes). See Chart 8 for increases in Social Security benefits.

You can retire as early as sixty-two, provided you are fully insured under Social Security, although your monthly benefit will be permanently reduced. Benefits also are reduced for a spouse if he or she begins receiving benefits before sixty-five and is not caring for an entitled child. The amount of reduction depends on the number of months you will receive benefits before age sixty-five. By starting benefits early you may receive about the same total over your lifetime, but in smaller amounts to compensate for the longer period you will presumably be receiving them. The normal retirement age today is sixty-five. Beginning in the year 2000, the age at which full benefits are payable will be increased in gradual steps to age sixty-seven. This will affect people born in 1938 and later. Reduced benefits will still be payable at sixty-two, but the lifetime reduction will be larger than it is today.

SOCIAL SECURITY RETIREMENT AGE BY YEAR OF BIRTH

Year of Birth	Normal Retirement Age
1937 or earlier	65
1938	65 and 2 months
1939	65 and 4 months
1940	65 and 6 months
1941	65 and 8 months
1942	65 and 10 months
1943–1954	66
1955	66 and 2 months
1956	66 and 4 months
1957	66 and 6 months
1958	66 and 8 months
1959	66 and 10 months
1960 and later	67

If you work for a nonprofit organization that was mandatorily covered by Social Security beginning in 1984, you may be able to receive retirement benefits with fewer credits than shown in the table above. If you were *both* fifty-five or older and an employee of the organization on January 1, 1984, you need only the number of credits shown on the table below. The credits must have been earned *after* January 1, 1984, and this special rule does not apply if you declined coverage when it was offered by your employer.

NONPROFIT ORGANIZATION EMPLOYEES 55 OR OLDER

Your Age on January 1, 1984	*Credits You Need*
55 or 56	20
57	16
58	12
59	8
60 or older	6

IF YOU DON'T APPLY, NO BENEFITS

Before you can receive Social Security payments, of course, you must apply for them. This should be done as soon as possible after you decide to claim benefits. If you plan to retire before age sixty-five, it is important to apply for monthly benefits no later than the last day of the month you want benefits to begin. In general, benefits payable for months before age sixty-five can begin no earlier than the month you apply, and you also must be eligible from the first day of the month. Inquire at the nearest Social Security office a few months *before* you reach sixty-five about your entitlement to Medicare hospital and medical insurance, which are available to persons sixty-five or over even if they continue to work. If you wait until the month you reach sixty-five to apply for the medical insurance you will lose at least a month of protection.

PENSIONS AND SOCIAL SECURITY

Knowing the amount of money you will receive from Social Security, and how cost-of-living increases will affect this amount, should have an important bearing on your financial planning.

This guideline will serve as a yardstick to help you ascertain, along with your company personal pension payouts, what you might expect as annual cost-of-living increases in Social Security benefits.

CHART 8
Increases in Social Security Benefits Through 1989

The annual cost-of-living increase in Social Security Benefits has been based since 1975 on the change in the Consumer Price Index (CPI).

Effective Dates of Increases	Social Security Increases
January 1990	4.7%
January 1989	4.0%
January 1988	4.2%
January 1987	1.3%
January 1986	3.1%
January 1985	3.5%
January 1984	3.5%
July 1982*	7.4%
July 1981*	11.2%
July 1980*	14.3%

- The 1989 increase raised the *average monthly payment for a retired worker* to $537 in 1989 from $516 during 1988.

- The *maximum monthly benefit* for a worker who retired in 1988 at age 65 rose to $899 from the prior $838.

- Average monthly benefits for *an aged couple, both getting benefits,* increased from $883 to $921.

- Average monthly benefits for *a widowed mother and two children* increased from $1,070 to $1,112.

- Average monthly benefits for *a disabled worker, spouse and children* increased from $902 to $943.

- Average monthly benefits for *all disabled workers* increased from $509 to $529.

- Another increase enabled *retired people aged 65 to 69* to earn $8,880 without sacrificing benefits, up from $8,400 in 1988.

- Social Security beneficiaries *under age 65* could earn $6,480 without penalty.

- The maximum *Federal Supplemental Income* (program for the aged, blind or disabled) increased from $354 to $368 for an individual and from $532 to $553 for a couple. (Most recipients of Supplemental Security Income also received Social Security benefits.)

Note: Benefits are rounded down to the next dollar, so most people received an increase slightly smaller than the rate of inflation.

Source: SPARN 6/89.

*In 1983 the increase was delayed for six months as one of the means to help Social Security out of a financial crisis.

If you apply for retirement benefits after you reach sixty-five, back payments can be made for up to six months. You can apply for benefits up to three months before you become eligible, either by phone or personal visit to a Social Security office. Several proofs may be needed when you make your application, so take them with you. They include: (1) your Social Security card or a record of the number; (2) birth certificates for you and your children (other documents may be used if your birth was not recorded); (3) evidence showing your recent earnings (last year's W-2 or a copy of last year's self-employment tax return), and (4) proof of the worker's death, if you are applying for survivor benefits. But don't delay your application because you lack these proofs or evidence. The people at the Social Security office can tell you about other evidence that can be used.

DIRECT DEPOSIT YOUR SOCIAL SECURITY CHECKS

You should also bring your checkbook or savings passbook so that Social Security can arrange to have your checks deposited directly into your account. Direct deposit is the government's preferred method of paying benefits. It is safe and more convenient for you and more efficient and economical for the government. Of course, if you don't have a bank account, or do not want to take advantage of direct deposit, you can receive your checks through the mail. Either way, your benefit should arrive about the same day every month, usually on the third. If the third falls on a Saturday, Sunday, or legal holiday, you will generally receive your check on the last banking day before then. Each check covers benefits for the previous month. A check you receive July 3, for example, is for the month of June. If you receive your benefit by direct deposit, it will probably never be late, Social Security says. But if you receive it by mail, it can sometimes be late because of mail delays. You should allow at least three full days from the third of each month for the check to arrive. Contact Social Security if you don't receive it by the sixth day of the month. Don't endorse the check until you are standing in front of the person who will cash it. If you sign ahead of time and then lose the check, anyone who finds it can cash it. If a check is lost or stolen, contact Social Security immediately. The check can be replaced, but it takes time. To be safe, cash or deposit your checks as soon as you can.

It is especially important to tell Social Security about any change in your mailing address even when you receive benefits by direct deposit. That's because you want to be sure you receive any letters from the agency that may affect your benefits. If you decide to change your bank account, or move from one financial institution to another, keep the old account open until the first benefit is received in the new account. Usually it takes from one to two months for Social Security to process an account or bank change. If you receive a check you know isn't due, take it back to any Social Security office, or mail it to the U.S. Treasury Department, Division of Disbursement, at the address on the check envelope. Enclose a note telling why you are returning the check.

HOW YOU WILL BE CONTACTED

Social Security will normally use the mail when it wants to contact you, although occasionally an agency representative may come to your home. Before talking with the person, ask for identification. Remember that no one from Social Security will ever ask you for any money to have something done. That is the agency's job. And if you ever doubt anyone who claims to be from Social Security, call the Social Security office and ask if they sent a representative to call on you.

EARNINGS TEST

A basic purpose of Social Security cash benefits is to help prevent dependency by providing continuing income to a worker and his or her family when their usual income is cut off or reduced because of retirement. The annual retirement earnings test theoretically measures whether a loss of earnings has occurred and it applies to everyone who receives Social Security retirement or survivors benefits, except those who are seventy or older. In 1991, you will receive full benefits for the year if your earnings do not exceed the annual exempt sum of $9,720 for people sixty-five through sixty-nine, and $7,080 for people under sixty-five. When your earnings rise above the exempt amount, $1 in benefits will be withheld by Social Security for each $3 of the earnings overage. Only your earnings from employment or self-employment count. Income from savings, investments, pensions or insurance does not count.

THE EFFECT OF ADDED EARNINGS

If you return to work after you start receiving retirement benefits, your added earnings may result in higher benefits. Social Security will automatically refigure your benefit after the additional earnings are credited to your record.

For each month you delay receiving benefits, beginning with the month you are sixty-five, and ending with the month you are seventy, you will receive an extra amount in benefits when you do retire. The rate of the delayed retirement credit varies according to your year of birth. For some people it may be only 1 percent, but starting in 1990 and later, the credit will be gradually increased until it reaches 8 percent in the year 2009.

TAXABLE SOCIAL SECURITY BENEFITS

Up to one-half your benefits may be subject to federal income tax for any year in which your adjusted gross income, plus nontaxable interest income, and one-half your Social Security benefits, exceeds a base of $25,000 for an individual, $32,000 for a couple filing jointly, and zero for a couple filing separately if they lived together any part of the year. The amount of benefits subject to tax will be the *smaller* of (1) one-half the benefits, or (2) one-half the amount of combined income (adjusted gross income, plus nontaxable interest, plus one-half of total benefits) in excess of the base amount.

At the end of each year, you will receive a "Social Security Benefit Statement" (Form SSA-1099) in the mail showing the amount of benefits you received. The statement is to be used only for completing your federal income tax return if any of your benefits are subject to tax.

Most people who are neither residents nor citizens of the United States will be taxed by having up to 15 percent of their benefits withheld. If you are subject to this tax and you become a U.S. resident or citizen, you should notify any Social Security office. If you have taxable income, you may want to consult Internal Revenue Service Publication 554, *Tax Benefits for Older Americans,* and Publication 915, *Tax Information on Social Security.* Special rules apply to people outside the United States. If you go abroad for thirty days or more while you are receiving benefits, your absence from the country may affect your right to benefits. Ask at any Social Security office for a copy of the booklet, "Your Social Security Checks While You Are Outside the United States."

YOUR RIGHT TO APPEAL

It is Social Security's duty to make sure that every eligible applicant for benefits receives them on time and in the right amount. When the agency makes any decision about your right to receive benefits, or your level of benefits, it will send you a written notice. If you don't agree with that decision, you have the right to appeal. That means you can ask the agency to look at your case again, and eventually you can take your case to federal court. There are four steps in the appeals process and generally they must be taken in order. They are: (1) reconsideration; (2) hearing by an administrative law judge; (3) review by the Appeals Council, and (4) federal court review. You have sixty days to make an appeal from the date you receive notice of a decision. An appeal must be in writing and any Social Security office can and will help you prepare it. You have the right to be represented by an attorney or other qualified person of your choice in dealing with the Social Security Administration at any step in the appeals process. For additional information about this, ask for a copy of the fact sheet, "Social Security And Your Right to Representation."

RECONSIDERATION

Reconsideration is a complete review of your claim by someone who did not take part in the original decision. All the evidence you submitted with your claim will be looked at again, and you also may submit added evidence. There are special rules if you have been receiving benefits because you are disabled and the agency decides that you have medically improved. You may meet with a disability hearing officer and explain in person why you believe you are still disabled. You also may ask Social Security to continue paying benefits while the decision process on your appeal is underway, although you may have to return the money if you lose. Keep in mind that you have only ten days from the date you receive notice to make your request for continued benefits. Special rules also apply if you were receiving Supplemental Security Income checks and the agency decides you are no longer eligible or that your payments should be reduced. Here again, you may continue to receive payments if you ask for reconsideration within ten days of the date of notice, but you may have to pay the money back if your appeal is rejected.

ADMINISTRATIVE HEARING

If you don't agree with the decision after reconsideration of your case, you may ask for a hearing by an administrative law judge. This judge works in Social Security's Office of Hearings and Appeals and had no part in the initial decision or the reconsideration in your case. The hearing is usually held within seventy-five miles of your home, to make it as convenient as possible for you and your representative to attend and argue your case in person. The administrative law judge will explain what has to be decided and may question you and any witnesses you bring to the hearing. You or your representative also may question the witnesses, provide new information, submit a written statement about your case, and look at the information the judge will use to make his or her decision. If you do not want to attend the hearing, you must notify Social Security of your decision. But if the judge believes your presence is necessary for any reason, you may have to be there anyway. The judge probably won't decide your case on the day of the hearing, but you will be notified of it in a timely manner.

APPEALS COUNCIL HEARING

If you still take issue with that decision, you may ask for a review by the Appeals Council, which is part of the Office of Hearings and Appeals. The council considers all requests for review, but can deny a request if it believes the decision by the administrative law judge was correct. In the event the Appeals Council decides your case should be reviewed, it will either make a decision itself or return the case to an administrative law judge for further review. Either way, you will be notified.

FEDERAL COURT REVIEW

Your only recourse from a negative decision by the Appeals Council is to file a lawsuit to overturn the decision in federal district court.

4

Insurance

SPREADING THE RISK

The purpose of insurance is to spread the risk of misfortune among a large group of people who are willing to pay something to avoid it, or at least to ameliorate the consequences for themselves and their families.

Insurance coverage exists for every purpose under the sun, or so it seems. There's life, liability, umbrella liability, disability, auto, homeowners, renters, healthcare, long-term healthcare, consumer credit, mortgage and municipal bond, to name only some of the more important forms. In this chapter, however, we will examine just three major types:

1. Life—in its many inventive variations and permutations.
2. Homeowners—covering all kinds of property losses from theft to hurricanes to fires.
3. Automobile—what you need and how to hold costs down.

Healthcare insurance is the subject of a separate chapter. Some other insurance variations, including consumer credit policies and municipal bond insurance, we also discuss elsewhere. If you're retired, you don't need and probably couldn't get disability insurance, so we're ignoring that. But we do talk about annuities in this chapter. They are insurance company products.

LIFE INSURANCE

The logical place to begin this essay is with life insurance. Nearly two of every three Americans are covered by some form of life insurance, and of all the types of insurance we pay for over a lifetime, the cost of our life insurance is likely to be highest.

The primary purpose of life insurance is to minimize financial hardship resulting from a person's death, and most people buy it with the following in mind:

- Cash for immediate needs—expenses for final illness and burial, taxes and debts.

- Readjustment money—interim funds for family members who will need time to make important decisions about moving or looking for a job.

- Replacement income—funds to help replace the deceased's paycheck or other regular contribution to the family's welfare.

- Income for retirement, college costs or other future financial needs.

As a protection device, life insurance provides an immediate estate. It helps ensure that when you die your family will have the financial resources it needs to protect your home and car and provide the income needed to run a household.

A life insurance policy is a contract between you and an insurance company. In return for your payment of premiums, usually at regular intervals such as monthly, quarterly, or annually, the contract requires that the company pay someone you name—your beneficiary or beneficiaries—a certain amount of money when you die. Your survivors can use the insurance proceeds as they see fit. The money is not subject to federal or state income tax, although it may be subject to death or estate taxes.

Insurance companies sell either *nonparticipating* or *participating* policies. Traditional nonparticipating policies have fixed premiums based on what the company believes it will cost to provide the insurance protection. However, some newer policies of this kind carry premiums that may be changed from time to time or that may not even have to be paid at regular intervals. Participating policies have somewhat higher premiums with a built-in cushion to allow for fluctuations in company earnings and expenses. At the end of the year, the company computes its actual costs and refunds any portion of the premium it does not need. This refund is called the policy dividend, and is not taxable.

TERM AND WHOLE LIFE POLICIES

Life insurance is an essential part of your financial planning. Congress has recognized the importance of life insurance by giving it a special tax status. Death benefits are not subject to income tax and the cash value increase in a whole life policy accumulates tax-deferred. There are two principal types of life insurance—*term life* and *whole life*. Term life policies, like fire insurance, provide temporary protection only. Whole life policies provide lifetime death protection and also accumulate cash value which is available upon surrender of the policy or can be borrowed against during the life of the policy.

Term insurance is the simplest kind of policy. It provides death protection for a specified and finite period of time—usually one, five, ten or twenty years, or up to age sixty-five. A term policy pays a benefit only if you die during the period covered by the policy. If you stop paying premiums, the insurance coverage ends. If you have a renewable term policy, you will not have to provide evidence of insurability to renew the coverage, but your premiums will increase because you are older. A 30-year-old nonsmoker buying $100,000 worth of one-year renewable term insurance with a premium-waiver disability benefit may pay a premium of about $200 the first year, if a man, and $190, if a woman. Women pay less because on average they live several years longer than men. Here is how the policy premium might increase:

Age	Man	Woman
40	$ 310	$ 280
50	$ 580	$ 460
60	$1300	$1000

Some term insurance policies are convertible to whole life without the need to provide evidence of insurability, but the premium increases at the time of conversion. Whole life premiums generally remain level for the rest of your life. Term insurance is initially cheaper than other types of policies for the same amount of protection. It is particularly recommended for young families with small budgets who need a large amount of insurance protection.

Whole life insurance, also known as straight life, ordinary life, permanent life, or cash value, is protection that can be kept in force for as long as you live. An important feature of whole life in most cases is its cash value. Cash value builds over the years on a tax-deferred basis. If you cancel your policy, you can receive the cash value in a lump sum. You only pay taxes if the cash value plus any policy dividends you have received exceeds your total premium payments at the time you cancel. Each policy contains a table that enables you to determine its cash value, although values between policy anniversaries have to be interpolated. Cash value has a number of beneficial uses:

- You can borrow the full amount of your policy's cash value from your insurance company. These loans generally carry a low rate of interest. Cash value thus becomes a contingency fund for emergencies or new opportunities. The loans need not be repaid, although any amount outstanding will be deducted from the face amount of the policy at the time of death.

- Automatic premium payment provisions in many policies protect you if you fall behind. If you have authorized such a provision, your insurance company will draw from the cash value of your policy to prevent an inadvertent lapse.

- If you wish to stop paying premiums, the accrued cash value can be used to fund a paid-up policy that provides a reduced level of protection, or the policy can be continued as term insurance for a specific period of time.

- In many cases you can use the cash value to purchase an annuity that provides a guaranteed monthly income for life.

- You can give the policy up completely and your insurance company will pay you the cash value.

Finally, here's a way life insurance can help you get the most from your company pension plan. When you retire, you generally must choose from two monthly payment options. You can choose the maximum initial monthly benefit, but in that case when you die your spouse (if still alive) receives nothing further; or you can choose a somewhat lower initial monthly benefit, in which case after you die your spouse receives a monthly check for half or two thirds of the amount you received. This latter *joint and survivor* option is actually a form of life insurance, purchased by you to insure that your spouse will continue to receive an income in the event you die first. An alternative is to buy—at the time you retire—a permanent life insurance policy that can be turned into a monthly benefit for your spouse if you die first. Then you can take the maximum initial benefit from your company, knowing that your spouse will receive the same benefit—a benefit provided by your permanent life insurance policy.

There are several variations of whole life insurance:

- Modified life carries a premium that is relatively low in the first several years but rises in later years. It is tailored for those who want whole life insurance but wish to pay lower premiums when they are younger and have less income.

- Limited-payment whole life provides protection for the life of the insured, but premiums are payable over a shorter period of time, such as twenty years, or until your death. Because the premiums are payable over a shorter period, premium rates are higher than for traditional whole life insurance.

- Single-premium whole life provides protection for the duration of your life, in exchange for the payment of the total premium in one lump sum at the time of application.

- Combination plans are policies which combine term and whole life insurance in one contract. Frequently, premiums for combination plans do not increase as you grow older.

Universal life is a relatively new form of insurance. Generally, a universal life policyholder may pay premiums at any time, in virtually any amount, subject to certain minimums and maximums. You can change the amount of insurance more easily than under traditional policies. In a universal life policy, the amount of cash value reflects quite directly the interest credited to it from time to time by the company. Instead of a guaranteed premium or maximum premium, as in other policies, a universal life policy contains a guaranteed minimum interest rate that will be credited, and guaranteed maximum mortality charges for the death protection. Universal life got off to a fast start in the 1980s when prevailing interest rates soared and insurance companies were advertising rates in the 12 to 13 percent range. Universal life's market share currently is about 25 percent, compared with 55 percent for whole life.

Excess interest whole life contains some features of universal life. It requires regular premium payments, but its cash value growth or premium level depends quite directly on the interest rate credited each year by the company. If the early premium payments are quite large and market conditions are favorable, premium payments on excess interest whole life policies may be temporarily reduced to zero a few years from issue.

Variable life insurance predates universal life by several years. (In the

United Kingdom it is called equity-linked life insurance and has been available for decades. As a security, with cash values invested in an account somewhat akin to a mutual fund, it is subject to the registration requirements of the Securities and Exchange Commission. Under a variable life policy, death benefits and cash values fluctuate according to the investment success of the account, which is managed by the life insurance company. As a policyholder you have a chance to obtain higher cash values and death benefits than with nonvariable policies. Conversely, you also assume the risk of poor investment performance (although a minimum death benefit may be guaranteed). Life insurance agents selling variable life must be registered representatives of a broker-dealer that is licensed by the National Association of Securities Dealers and registered with the SEC. If you are interested in this type of policy, be sure your agent gives you a prospectus. It contains extensive disclosure about the variable life policy, including sales costs, risk charges for expense and mortality guarantees, and asset charges, which compensate the insurer for its costs in managing the investments.

Adjustable life insurance is a hybrid of whole life and term. With most of the flexibility of universal life, it allows you to change the policy as your needs change. For example, if you want to increase or decrease your coverage you can either change your premium payments or change the length of time the policy is in force. If you increase your death benefit, however, you may be asked to provide evidence of insurability, sometimes including a physical examination by a doctor.

HOW MUCH DO YOU NEED?

In considering how much life insurance you need, the first question you should consider is whether you need any at all. James H. Hunt, a director of the National Insurance Consumer Organization, offers the following advice:

> If you're single with no dependents, you should think twice before buying, because you don't need life insurance for a spouse or child you don't have. It's better to take care of your own immediate insurance needs—a first-class health plan, plus a disability income plan to provide for yourself if you become disabled. (On the other hand, buying life insurance early can be a good way to get started

on a life insurance program and avoid having to pay more later if your insurability deteriorates.)

If you're married without children, whether you need life insurance may depend on whether your spouse works. If both of you have roughly the same income, each has an interest in the other's income. In theory, each needs life insurance equal to the present value of the other's future income after deducting taxes and those expenses of living that disappear at the death of that person. When only one spouse works, the question is whether the other spouse will be able to work at comparable wages; if not, the breadwinner needs life insurance to protect his or her mate.

If you have children or other dependents, such as aged parents, you probably need life insurance in fairly substantial amounts.

Children do not need life insurance. But if the death of a child would terminate support payments, life insurance may be indicated if the family's expenses would go down by less than the lost income.

Hunt points out in "Taking the Bite Out of Insurance," a guide published by the consumer group, that most life insurance agents are trained by their companies to estimate your life insurance needs, but results will vary widely because there is no standard formula and because agents apply the theory with differing skills. He adds: "We prefer a simple rule of thumb: Buy an amount of life insurance equal to five times your annual income. This rule gives answers reasonably close to those based on theoretical formulas for the typical life insurance family—one wage earner with two or more young children. While not precise, such a rule also recognizes the practical reality that few families will buy as much life insurance as the formulas indicate they should have."

The American Council of Life Insurance, an industry group, says the five-times-annual-income formula may not be appropriate for all families because no two families have exactly the same needs. If you can identify your responsibilities for others, your monetary resources and, in the event of your death, who should be protected financially and in what amounts, you will make a wiser insurance purchase, the council adds. Chart 9 is a worksheet to assist you in determining your life insurance requirements. After you have identified these factors, you can determine how much insurance you need by consulting a good life insurance agent.

SELECTING AN AGENT

Word of mouth is often a good way to select an insurance agent. Friends and acquaintances will no doubt be able to recommend several. Collect the names and then shop around. A life insurance agent is an important person in your life and you should be satisfied with his or her reputation. All states require that agents be licensed to sell life insurance, but some are obviously more reliable and competent than others. Professional designations help. If the agent's business card indicates he or she is a CLU, for Chartered Life Underwriter; ChFC, for Chartered Financial Consultant, or LUTCF, for Life Underwriters' Training Council Fellow, you can assume the agent has devoted considerable time to the study of life insurance and family financial services. Local membership in the National Association of Life Underwriters suggests the agent subscribes to both the professional and ethical standards of that industry organization. Make sure your agent is willing and able to discuss various types of policies and other insurance-related matters, and makes a sincere effort to get you the right type of insurance at a cost you can afford. Make sure also that your agent reviews your coverage from time to time. If you're not convinced that a particular agent understands your needs and provides you the service you want, find another agent.

The American Council of Life Insurance says your chances of making a good life insurance buy will be increased if you use a special cost comparison index developed for that purpose. Be aware that the price of a given type of policy can vary from one company to the next, and companies are not equally price competitive for all policies. One company may offer the best policy for 25-year-olds, but not for 50-year-olds. The cost comparison index provides you with a number that reflects the price of the policy. A policy with a smaller index number is likely to be a better buy than a comparable policy with a higher index number. Your agent or life insurance company can give you more information about the index. In addition, the following rules should be kept in mind:

- Cost comparisons can only be made between similar life insurance plans.

- Index number comparisons should only be made for your age, for the kind of policy you intend to buy and for the amount of insurance you plan to purchase.

- Future dividend results, current-interest credits and the like cannot be known at time of purchase, yet all influence the index number.

- Small differences in index numbers might be offset by other policy features, or differences in the quality of service you get from the company or agent.

- Base your decision not only on a low index number but also on whether the policy meets your needs, whether you can afford the premium and whether you understand its cash values, if any, its illustrated dividends, if any, and its death benefits.

- Do not use the index to determine whether your current policy should be replaced by a new one. The index only applies to comparisons of new policies.

The National Association of Insurance Commissioners and many state insurance departments have prepared buyers' guides to help you understand life insurance terms, benefits and relative costs. If you have questions about companies or policies, you may also wish to check with your state insurance commissioner's office.

After receiving a life insurance policy, read the contract carefully and ask the agent (or the company, if you have bought direct) to explain any language you do not fully understand. These contracts are legal documents and you should be familiar with what they promise. You have ten days in which to change your mind about your policy. If you decide you don't want it after all, the company will return your premium without penalty.

If you already own life insurance, think twice if anyone suggests that you replace it. Before you give up this protection make sure you are still insurable. Remember that you are now older, and a new policy will cost more because of your age. An existing policy may have provisions that are not duplicated in some new ones. The insurance council recommends that you ask your agent or company for an opinion about the new proposal, so you hear both sides of the matter.

The American Council of Life Insurance suggests ten rules you should remember when buying life insurance:

CHART 9

Your Check List to Determine How Much Life Insurance You Need

Whom do you want to protect with your life insurance? ☐ Spouse ☐ Children
☐ Children from a prior marriage ☐ Parents ☐ Other: _____
To what extent do you want to protect them? ☐ Provide for their current lifestyle
☐ More modest lifestyle ☐ More affluent lifestyle
How long do you want to protect each? _____

Lump-Sum Benefits and Expenses When You Die		Income and Expenses (After Your Death) of Those Whom You Want To Protect	
Lump-Sum Benefits	*Lump-Sum Expenses*	*Their Income*	*Their Expenses*
☐ From health insurance for expenses of a terminal illness	☐ Cemetery plot (not prepaid)	☐ New working income (after taxes and pay deductions)	☐ Fixed expenses (household, utilities, transportation, insurance premiums, education, child care, pets, etc.)
☐ From your current personal life insurance coverage	☐ Funeral costs (not prepaid)	☐ From interest, dividends, net rents, etc. from assets owned by them (some of which may have even been inherited from you)	☐ Variable expenses (food, beverages, clothing, grooming, medical [unreimbursed], contributions, recreation, etc.)
☐ From your current employment and other group life insurance coverage	☐ Costs of an expensive terminal illness (not covered by health insurance)		
☐ Death benefits from your pension, profit-sharing, deferred-income, and other plans	☐ Tax, probate, attorney, accountant, any other estate expenses	☐ From your personal, employment, government, and other insurances and plans that pay in installments rather than in lump sums (see first column)	
☐ From Social Security, veterans', and other government sources	☐ To pay your existing debts not collateralized or covered by redemption insurance		

| □ Other: _____ | □ Transitional funds to help tide your beneficiaries over as they adjust after your death | □ Interest, dividends, or other income from investment of the amount left over, if any, after deducting lump-sum expenses (second column) from lump-sum benefits (first column) | □ Special: _____ |
| | □ Other: _____ | □ Other: _____ | |

Calculations

After filling in the check list above, you can prepare your worksheet, entering the dollar amounts for each item you checked.

- If your lump-sum expenses (column two) exceed your lump-sum benefits (column one), you need additional life insurance with lump-sum proceeds to pay the difference.
- If your beneficiaries' expenses (column four) exceed their income (column three), you need additional life insurance to provide the difference (from income paid by the policies, or from income resulting from investment of lump sums paid by the policies).
- The two items above show you need more life insurance. But you may be paying for more life insurance than you need if your calculations show significant excesses of both lump-sum benefits over lump-sum expenses and your beneficiaries' income over their expenses.

Redetermine periodically or when circumstances change substantially (such as children on their own and no longer dependent). Your periodic redeterminations should take into consideration keeping pace with increases from inflation.

Source: SPYF p. 88–9.

- Understand and know what your life insurance needs are before any purchase, and make sure that the company you choose can address those needs.

- Buy your life insurance from a company that is licensed in your state.

- Select an agent who is competent, knowledgeable and trustworthy.

- Shop around and compare costs.

- Buy only the amount of life insurance you need and can afford.

- Ask about lower premium rates for nonsmokers.

- Read your policy and make sure you understand it.

- Inform your beneficiaries about the kinds and amount of life insurance you own.

- Keep your policy in a safe place at home and, in addition, your company's name and your policy number in a safe-deposit box.

- Check your coverage periodically or whenever your situation changes, to be sure it meets your current needs.

All of this is sound advice, and most of it comes straight from the insurance industry itself.

ANNUITIES

An annuity contract is the opposite of a life insurance contract. With an annuity, you pay toward the day benefits will be provided to you, not your survivors. But annuities are written by insurance companies and deserve mention in the context of this discussion. They can effectively guarantee that you'll have regular income, no matter how long you live. Annuities are popular with people who are not sophisticated investors or don't want the responsibility of more complex investments. You still need a certain amount of savvy to invest in annuities, but it's not as worrisome as buying stocks. Buyers look for guaranteed interest rates, a high return, flexibility, service and, above all, security.

An annuity may be immediate, starting almost as soon as you pay the premium, or payments may begin at a later date you designate. The premium may be a single lump sum payment, or it may be made in installments over time. Although your purchase is usually made with after-tax dollars, you need pay no income tax on the accumulated interest until payouts begin.

You can choose a guaranteed rate of interest through a *fixed annuity*, or you can put your principal into an equity account and accept a variable rate of interest. With a *variable annuity*, accumulated value and monthly benefits will vary according to the underlying investment performance, although there may be a guaranteed minimum return. You may have a choice of investment vehicles—a stock, money market or bond mutual fund. Even with a fixed annuity the accumulated value and monthly payout may change in accordance with the interest rate credited by the company each year, subject to a guaranteed minimum. Once purchased, both types should be held for the long term, if possible. Annuities are not good short-term investments.

Your annuity payout choices are these:

- *Straight life* provides payments to you for your lifetime.

- *Refund* pays somewhat less per month, but provides that total payouts will at least equal the purchase price. If death occurs before the money is paid out, your beneficiary will receive the balance.

- *Joint and survivor* provides payments for as long as either you or your designated survivor lives.

- *Certain period* makes payments for your lifetime with a guaranteed minimum number of years.

When you go shopping for an annuity, ask about the interest rate currently being credited. Can the rate change? How often does it change? Is there a bailout option that permits you to cash in the annuity without penalty if the interest rate drops below a specified figure? What penalties are there for early liquidation? Are there guaranteed maximum withdrawal charges over a period of years? How much can you withdraw at any one time without a penalty? Ask also about front-end load charges or annual administrative fees. How much are they and how will they affect your return?

Before handing over your money to buy an annuity, check out the issuing company. As a general rule, look for a company that has a good reputation. You can read the financial history of the company in *Best's Insurance Reports* or in reports issued by Moody's or Standard & Poor's. Consider only companies with the highest ratings.

HOMEOWNERS INSURANCE

Let's turn now to homeowners insurance, which is one of the most important forms of casualty insurance. Every home should be insured, even if it's an apartment and you insure just the contents. Begin by estimating what it would cost to rebuild your house, at current prices, should it be destroyed. An insurance agent or professional appraiser can help you determine that value. Whether you've just bought your home or owned it for several years, take a careful look at your homeowners insurance policy. You could be underinsured if your policy isn't keyed to current costs. Unless your policy has inflation-guard provisions, check the amount of your coverage once a year.

Next, make an inventory of the contents of your home. Include furniture and important personal belongings. Keep store receipts and note dates of purchase. Videotape or take still photos of each wall in each room with cabinet or closet doors open. Take individual photographs of your most important possessions, such as works of art, silverware, antiques, jewelry and expensive pieces of furniture. Note serial numbers of major appliances. Store a copy of your inventory and photographs in a safe place away from home.

Why an inventory? Try this test. Sit in your kitchen and make a list of everything in your living room. Now check on how many items you missed. No one really expects to lose furniture or other belongings in a fire, a burglary or a tornado. But such events do occur. If disaster struck your home, would you be able to report exactly what you lost to police, the Internal Revenue Service, or to your insurance company? A thorough inventory of your household furnishings and personal belongings can help:

- Determine the value of your belongings and personal insurance needs.

- Establish the purchase dates and cost of major items in case of loss.

- Identify exactly what was lost. Most people can't recall items accumulated gradually.

- Settle your insurance claim quickly and efficiently.

- Verify losses for income tax deductions.

To obtain a home inventory form, send a self-addressed, stamped envelope to Insurance Information Institute, Consumer Affairs, 110 William Street, New York, NY 10038, and ask for "Taking Inventory."

Homeowners policies generally provide a package of protections, including:

- Repair or replacement of your house, garage and other structures, such as a tool shed, and personal belongings.

- Claims and lawsuits against you and members of your household for injury or property damage.

- Additional living expenses, should damage to your home force you to live temporarily in a hotel and eat in restaurants.

Furniture, clothing and most other personal belongings are covered for their actual cash value—their original cost minus depreciation due to wear and tear—at the time of loss. Another kind of policy provides replacement-cost coverage—what it would cost to replace the lost items without subtracting anything for depreciation—for relatively new personal property. However, both kinds of policies provide only limited coverage for furs, jewelry, silver and other valuables, including small boats. You may wish to protect your investments in such valuables with a personal articles floater or a boat policy.

Some homeowners policies cover more perils than others. But most policies cover damage caused by snow and ice, or the freezing of plumbing, heating and air-conditioning systems. None cover floods, earthquakes, war, or nuclear accident. Flood coverage is available through a special government program, and earthquake coverage is sold by many insurance companies.

The liability coverage provided by your homeowners policy applies at home or elsewhere to legal obligations resulting from injuries or damages caused by you, a member of your family or even a pet. It includes the cost of defending you if you are sued. This coverage does not apply to liability resulting from the use of an automobile, but it does apply to your liability as an owner of a small boat.

Your homeowners insurance will pay for any increase in living expenses when you can't live in your home because of damage caused by any of the covered losses. For example, if your home is badly damaged by fire, you may have to live in a hotel and eat in restaurants while it is being repaired. Your insurance company will reimburse you, up to the limits stated in your policy, for the difference between these expenses and your normal living expenses.

Renters or tenants insurance is similar to homeowners. Some tenants assume that their personal belongings are insured against loss or damage by the landlord's insurance policy, but that is not true. Your landlord probably has insurance on the house or apartment building, but it does not include coverage for your personal property. Nor does the landlord's policy cover your liability to others—someone else's injury or damage for which you may be held responsible. For example, a visitor could slip and fall in your apartment, suffer a head injury resulting in vision problems—and sue you for hundreds of thousands of dollars. Tenants insurance is inexpensive and no renter should be without it. Complete the checklist in Chart 10 for your required homeowners or tenants insurance.

Burglaries are among the more common causes of losses by homeowners and renters and knowing a burglar's three worst enemies—light, time and noise—can help you protect your home from crime. A burglar won't find your home an easy mark if he's forced to work in the light, if he has to take a lot of time breaking in, and if he can't work quietly. Take the time to "case" your house or apartment, just as a burglar would, with the following questions in mind:

- What is the easiest entry? How can I make it more burglar resistant? Consider trimming trees and shrubs near your doors and windows, and think carefully before installing a high wooden fence around your back yard. High fences and shrubbery can add to your privacy, but privacy is a burglar's asset. You may want to trade a little of your privacy for a bit of added security. Force any would-be thief to confront a real enemy—light. Make sure at least several of your exterior lights are mounted out of reach.

- How can I slow a burglar down? A thief who can be delayed even four or five minutes is apt to give up and try for another, less difficult location. Simple security devices, including such ordinary equipment as nails, screws, padlocks, door and window locks, grates, bars and bolts, can discourage intruders and keep them from entering.

- How can I make the burglary of my home an unpleasantly noisy business? Many types of alarm systems are available, with detectors to be mounted on doors and windows, but deciding how much home protection you need and can afford is a personal judgment. Ask your police department or sheriff to have someone survey your home and advise you about suitable protection.

CHART 10 **Do You Have Enough Homeowners/Tenants Insurance?**		
Type of Coverage[1]	**Amounts of Coverage**[2]	
	Present Amount	*(After Reviewing) Amount You Should Have*[3]
For Dwelling and Other Structures	$	$
For Personal Property[4]: For destruction or loss of furniture, clothing, and other general contents	$	$
For destruction or loss of valuables, such as: money; securities; collectible coins; stamps; gold, silver, platinum objects; jewelry, furs; fine arts; silverware, goldware, pewterware	$	$
For destruction or loss of personal computers	$	$
For Loss of Use of Home: For cost of living away from your home while it is being repaired	$	$
For Personal Liability: For bodily injury and property damage	$	$
For Medical Payments to Others: For persons, other than you and members of your family, injured on your home's premises	$	$
For Damage to Others' Property: By you or members of your family	$	$
For Compensation: For liability, medical payments, and disability payments to domestics employed by you on a regular basis at your home	$	$
Other[5]:	$	$

1. Type of coverage may vary by individual states.

2. Representing the full amount or a percentage of the cost, the depreciated value, or the replacement value?

3. Keep in mind that you might increase both the amount and the deductible so that your premium cost may not be higher.

4. On your home premises only or both at home and away from home?

5. "Other" may include coverage for perils not usually covered, such as flood or earthquake, or resulting conditions, such as collapse.

If any of your valuables, such as a painting, a collection of silver picture frames or an antique chair, are easy to see from outside, consider rearranging your furnishings to make your home less inviting to a thief. Outside doors should be metal or solid hardwood, and at least one-and-three-quarter inches thick. Sliding glass doors present a special problem because they are easy to open, but there are locks designed for them. A broomstick in the door channel can help, but don't depend on it for security. A peephole or a wide-angle viewer in your front door is safer for identifying visitors than a door chain. Deadbolt locks are best. They usually are locked with a key from the outside and a thumb turn on the inside. The key cylinder should be pick resistant. Ask your hardware dealer for a reputable brand or buy your locks from a locksmith. Key locks are available for all types of windows. Double-hung windows can be secured simply by pinning the upper and lower frames together with a nail which can be removed from the inside. For windows at street level, consider iron grates or grilles. For windows opening onto a fire escape, metal accordion gates can be installed on the inside.

Here are some home-security habits you should practice:

- Establish a routine to follow in making certain that doors and windows are locked and alarm systems are turned on.

- Avoid giving information to unidentified telephone callers, or announcing your personal plans in want ads or public notices, such as giving your address when advertising items for sale.

- Notify police if you see suspicious strangers in your neighborhood.

- Handle your keys carefully. Don't carry house keys on a key ring bearing your home address or leave house keys with your car in a commercial parking lot. Don't hide your keys in "secret" places outside your home—burglars usually know where to look.

- Remember special vacation tips. Leave blinds in their usual position. Have mail and packages picked up, forwarded or held by the post office. Lower the sound of your telephone bell so it can't be heard outside. Arrange to have your lawn mowed or your walk shoveled. Stop newspaper deliveries. Use automatic timers to control lights in your living room and bedrooms. Tell police and dependable neighbors when you plan to be away.

If you discover a burglar in your home, run away and call police if you can. Lock yourself in a room if you can't escape. If you find yourself face to face with the intruder, stay calm and cooperate as much as possible.

The registry of insurance, Chart 11 will allow you to see, quickly, the insurances covering your home(s).

AUTO INSURANCE

Auto liability insurance is required in nearly all states. The six basic types of coverage are:

- Bodily injury liability—provides money to pay claims against you and the cost of your legal defense in the event your car injures or kills someone.

- Property damage liability—covers claims against you if your car damages another person's car or other property.

- Medical payments—covers medical expenses resulting from injuries to you or your passengers.

- Uninsured motorist—pays medical expenses resulting from an accident with an uninsured or hit-and-run driver.

- Comprehensive—covers "acts of God and nature," such as fire, flooding, hail, theft and some other calamities.

- Collision—pays for damages to your car when you hit another car or some other object.

- Umbrella liability coverage—pays legal bills and damage awards if you are sued. Umbrella supplements basic auto and homeowners coverage and can boost a $300,000 basic policy to $1 million.

About half the states have no-fault insurance systems, where there are restrictions on liability lawsuits and where personal injury protection is required or optional. In others, coverage for medical costs for you and your passengers is optional.

When it comes to auto insurance, being a smart shopper is the best policy. The rates of companies operating in the same state may vary as much as

CHART 11
Registry of Insurance on Your Home(s)

The form below (describing insurance coverage on your home[s]) supplements the general *"Registry of Insurance"* form.

Reproduce the form below. Fill in and attach as the "Description of Coverage" section of the related *"Registry of Insurance"* form you complete.

Description of Coverage

	Home	*Second Home*
Amount on Home		
Amount on Contents at Cost		
Amount on Contents at Replacement Value		
Extra Coverage on Specified Property Such as Jewelry, Furs, Etc. (record item and amount of coverage)		
Personal Liability (record amount of coverage)		
Other Coverage (specify coverage and amount)		

100 percent. Ask agents, brokers or insurance companies for price comparisons. Also check rates with your state insurance department. In addition, there are a number of things you can do right now to lower your insurance premiums:

- *Deductibles.* While savings vary from company to company, increasing your deductible is an excellent way to lower premiums. Raising your deductible from $200 to $500 could reduce your collision premium by 15 to 30 percent. Raising it from $200 to $1,000 could reduce the premium by about 40 percent.

- *Collision/comprehensive.* You may want to drop collision and/or comprehensive coverage if you have an older car worth less than $1,000.

These optional coverages usually aren't cost effective on old, worn-out autos.

- *Desirable cars.* Before you buy a new or used car, keep in mind that premiums usually are much higher for autos that are more expensive to repair. Autos that are favorite targets for thieves, such as sports cars or luxury cars, also cost more to insure.

- *Multi-car policies.* If you have more than one car in your household, you can save 15 to 20 percent by insuring all of them on a single policy with the same company.

- *Younger drivers.* It's usually cheaper to insure teenagers who are infrequent drivers of the family car on the parents' policy rather than separately. There is another discount if young drivers insured on the parents' policy are away at school (100 miles or more).

- *Mature drivers.* Drivers who are fifty or older may qualify for discounts of 10 to 20 percent, depending on the insurance company and how much you drive.

- *Passive restraints.* You may be able to obtain discounts of 10 to 30 percent on some coverages for automatic seat belts and/or air bags. These savings apply to the medical portions of the policy.

Other discounts are available for an accident-free driving record, car pooling, driving a limited number of miles in a year, antitheft devices, buying your auto insurance from the company which insures your home, being a woman who is the only driver in the household, and being a farmer.

Auto insurers often send you information about some of their discounts when it's time to renew your policy. Look over this material and ask your agent about other discounts. The worksheet in Chart 12 will help you work out your car insurance requirements.

For additional information about insurance, contact one of the following organizations:

National Insurance Consumer Helpline
Telephone: (800) 942-4242

CHART 12
Do You Have Enough Automobile Insurance[1]?

Type of Coverage[2]	Amounts of Coverage	
	Present Amounts	*(After Reviewing:) Amounts You Should Have[3]*
Bodily Injury Liability: For death, injury, suffering inflicted on one or more people by your car	$[4]	$
Property Damage Liability: For property accidentally damaged by your car	$	$
Medical Payments[5]: For injury sustained by you and your passengers in your car and on you as a pedestrian by a car	$[6]	$
Uninsured Motorist's[5]: For your medical bills if you are the victim of an uninsured motorist, a hit-and-run driver, and, in some states, the victim of an underinsured motorist	$	$
Collision[7]: For cost of repair of damage to your car or its cash value, whichever is less	$	$
Comprehensive: For theft, glass breakage, fire, flood, and additional adversities other than collision damage, wear-and-tear, and mechanical problems	$	$
Other	$	$

1. Be sure you know how your coverage is affected if your state has no-fault insurance.
2. Type of coverage afforded may vary by individual states. Also, get in touch with your state insurance commission for car insurance minimum legal requirements and for information on car insurance companies.
3. Keep in mind that you might increase the deductible as well as the amount of coverage so that your premium cost may not be higher. Also, be sure your premiums reflect discount possibilities that may be available, such as safe driving and for multiple car ownership.
4. Is there a maximum amount payable to any one person in any one accident? A maximum amount for all injuries occurring in any one accident?
5. In reviewing the amount of your coverage in your auto insurance, also consider the protection afforded by your regular health-insurance and disability-income insurance policies.
6. Are medical benefits paid promptly without determining who is at fault?
7. Some policies are available which provide replacement cost; benefits are higher, but, of course, so are premium costs.

CHART 13
Registry of Insurance

Date: _____

Reproduce this form. Fill in for each insurance policy.
Keep one copy of each completed form in your safe deposit box.
Keep one copy at home.

Type of Insurance	☐ *Life* ☐ *Health* ☐ *Home* ☐ *Auto* ☐ *Other:*
Name(s) of Insured	
Name(s) of Owner(s) of Policy	
Policy Numbers	
Effective Dates: From: To:	
Insurance Company Location Phone #	
☐ Individual Policy: ☐ Agent: ☐ Group Policy Name of Employer or Organization Location Phone #	
Location: Original Policy Copies	
Premium: Amount Payments Due	
Description of Coverage (Benefits/ Beneficiaries	
Other Information	

Extension Service
U.S. Department of Agriculture
Washington, DC 20250

Consumer Information Center
General Services Administration
Washington, DC 20405

The National Association of Life Underwriters
1922 F Street NW
Washington, DC 20006

Insurance Information Institute
110 William Street
New York, NY 10038
Telephone: (800) 331-9146

National Insurance Consumer Organization
344 Commerce Street
Alexandria, VA 22314

National Consumers League
815 15th Street NW
Washington, DC 20005

To help you keep track of your insurance policies, including their effective dates, locations, coverages, premium due dates and the like, use an insurance registry like the one in Chart 13.

5

Healthcare

Aside from the fear of running out of money, Americans in retirement worry most about adequate healthcare, and for good reason. As our bodies age, it's natural and inevitable that more and more things go wrong. If it isn't high blood pressure, it's erratic, unsatisfactory bowel movements. If it isn't brown spots on the skin that need to be removed, it's an aching back or stiff joints, or bladder infections, or some other large or small affliction. Even when nothing actually hurts, there are various aggravating reminders that we are no longer thirty something. The eyes require stronger spectacles. The ears need amplifiers. The nose refuses to smell with its old flair, and the taste buds lose their old subtlety. Even the memory component of the brain goes on vacation at odd, inconvenient times. And the teeth—they absolutely yearn to fall out, or to make one's periodontist the richest man on earth.

So, generally, the longer we live the more we need doctors and nurses and hospitals to keep us repaired and on the road. We can and do rail against it, as we might rail against sudden rain on a picnic in the park, but we can't do much about either. To complicate matters, we are less able financially to pay the cost of maintaining our health. Our one and only defense, indeed, is health insurance sufficient to just about every possible eventuality. That's why some depth of knowledge about this type of insurance is so vital.

GROUP HEALTH

If you work for a company of any size, you are probably covered by a group health insurance plan paid for at least in part by your employer. If fully retired, or working only part time, of course, you must foot the bill yourself. The protection provided by group insurance varies with each plan.

Some provide medical coverage only, but a growing number also include dental coverage as well. If you have group health insurance, check with your employer or union to see exactly what benefits are provided. If your plan does not cover all your health insurance needs, including hospital, physician, prescription drug and medical appliance costs, you should consider supplementing the group plan with an individual policy. Or, if your group policy will pay only $200 a day toward a hospital room, when the daily cost in your area is $500, and only half the going rate for surgical procedures, you may want to add to your coverage. Buying individual insurance allows you to tailor a plan to fit your needs from the insurance company of your choice. Shop carefully, however. Costs vary considerably from company to company. The same is true of major medical coverage. If your policy maximum is $100,000, you should be looking for an individual policy that will increase your coverage to several times that. Some experts say major medical coverage of $1 million is not excessive. Complete Chart 14 to see if your present health insurance is adequate. Keep in mind that in addition to health insurance, you will require disability income coverage as a replacement for lost earnings, which we will discuss further in the chapter.

If you lose your job, you may also lose any group health insurance you have unless you take the proper steps. Under the Consolidated Omnibus Budget Reconciliation Act of 1985 (COBRA), group health plans sponsored by employers with twenty or more employees are required to offer continuation of coverage under the group plan for terminated or laid-off workers and their dependents for a period of up to eighteen or thirty-six months. An employee or dependent qualifies under COBRA if coverage is lost for any of the following reasons:

- Employment is terminated or there is a reduction in the number of hours of employment for reasons other than gross misconduct.

- The employee dies.

- A spouse divorces or is legally separated from the employee.

- An employee becomes eligible for Medicare.

- A dependent no longer is considered a dependent child under a parent's health insurance policy.

The employer, however, is not required to pay for this continued coverage and may charge you up to 102 percent of its cost. If you do lose your health

CHART 14
Do You Have Enough Health Insurance?

Date: _____

Health Care	Estimated Average Costs	Approximate Benefits Provided by Coverage* in $ or % of column 1	Approximate Additional Benefits Coverage You May Need in $ or % of column 1
IN HOSPITAL:			
Room and board (daily)			
Intensive care (daily)			
Special nurses (per shift)			
Drugs			
Medical supplies and appliances			
Radiology			
Laboratory tests			
Surgical (per types of operations):			
Surgeon			
Anesthesia			
Operating room			
Physician (visiting)			
Maternity (doctor, etc.)			
OTHER FACILITIES:			
Ambulatory			
Psychiatric			
Alcohol and Drug			
Emergency			
Convalescent/Rehabilitation			
Nursing			
OTHER SERVICES:			
Ambulances			
Other medical transport			
Home care (drugs, supplies, appliances and services)			
Dental			
Psychiatric			
Physiotherapy			
OTHER EXPENSES:			

*Estimate maximum number of days.

insurance because COBRA does not apply, there are steps you can take to protect yourself until you find another job. Employ this basic strategy:

- Find out exactly how long your insurance will continue after your last day of work. It may be until the end of the month or possibly longer, depending upon your employer's policy. If you are married and your spouse is employed, see if you are able to obtain coverage through his or her employer.

- Next, check to see if you can convert your group coverage to an individual policy. Keep in mind that your benefits may not be as good as they were under the group policy, and that the individual policy will cost more. If converting your group coverage doesn't appeal to you, and if you are healthy, not yet eligible for Medicare and you want more complete protection, you might consider an interim or short-term health policy. Some companies write interim coverage that runs until you are again eligible for group coverage through a new employer. Such policies are frequently written for two to six months, may be renewed once during a 12-month period, and typically include payments toward hospitalization, intensive care treatment, inhospital doctor visits, surgical expenses and sometimes nursing home care. Outpatient diagnostic X-ray or laboratory procedures and ambulance coverage also can be included.

With the outrageously high cost of healthcare today, it makes sense to be as well insured as you can afford to be. The practical approach is to look at health insurance protection on three levels: basic, major medical, and disability.

BASIC PROTECTION

Basic protection includes benefits that pay toward daily room and board and regular nursing services while in the hospital, and for certain hospital services and supplies, such as X-rays, laboratory tests, drugs and medication. Basic protection also pays toward the cost of surgical procedures performed in and out of the hospital, doctor visits and, in some cases, such additional services as diagnostic tests. Basic protection policies have their built-in limits, however, including the following:

- If your policy covers only part of the daily cost of your hospital room, or your surgery, you must pay the remainder out of your own pocket unless you have other insurance.

- If your insurance entitles you to *service benefits*, a plan designed to pay bills in full, payment is made based upon what are considered *reasonable* charges. You may have to pay any costs determined to be not reasonable.

- While most insurance policies and Blue Cross will cover a lengthy hospital stay, some policies do not give such protection. You must review your policy to see precisely what protection it does offer. In fact, review it before you buy it.

It's also smart to review your health policy once a year. Benefits change and your needs change. Here is a list of the items you should check:

- What are the deductibles?

- What percentage of the hospital bill does your insurer pay?

- What caps are imposed on benefit payments and what will you have to pay out of your own pocket?

- What percentage, if any, does the policy specify for drugs, medical supplies and equipment such as wheel chairs? Even bedpans cost.

- What are the allowances for inpatient services, outpatient services, mental care?

- Does the policy cover dental expenses?

- Is there provision for home healthcare services? Which services? What are the caps?

- How much are the premiums? What percentage are you required to pay and what percentage will your employer pay?

MAJOR MEDICAL

Major medical insurance is the second level of healthcare coverage. It provides protection against the cost of lengthy, high-cost illness or injury by helping to pay for just about everything prescribed by your doctor. And although it can take over where your basic coverage leaves off, you can also buy major medical alone to cover the bulk of your medical expenses. You may even want to consider major medical first in your health insurance planning, since it offers the most protection.

While major medical insurance has very high maximum benefit amounts, it also carries a deductible—an amount you must pay before your benefits begin if you have just that policy and no basic protection. In addition, under a major medical plan you would typically be responsible for a coinsurance payment of 15 to 25 percent of covered expenses, although many such policies feature a stop-loss provision under which you must pay up to a certain amount and no more. For example, a stop-loss clause may specify that after you have paid, say $2,500 out of your own pocket, the insurance company will pay 100 percent of all remaining covered medical expenses. Make sure you understand the deductible and coinsurance features of any major medical plan you are considering, and get answers to these basic questions:

- Who is eligible for coverage under my policy?

- Will the policy still cover me after age sixty-five?

- What conditions or illnesses are covered and which are not?

- How do premiums compare from policy to policy?

DISABILITY INCOME

Disability income is the third level of health insurance to be considered. It provides for a regular cash income, usually a percentage of your former earnings, in case of disability caused by illness or injury. The Health Insurance Association of America says there are a number of key facts you should know about individual disability policies:

- Many require that you be totally disabled before benefits begin. Benefits for a partial disability are sometimes provided, but in some cases only if the partial disability follows a period of total disability for the same reason.

- Different insurers have varying definitions of disability. For example, some policies define it as merely being unable to do your regular work. Others are much stricter. Some require that after a certain period, perhaps two years, you must be unable to engage in any gainful occupation for which you are reasonably suited by education, training or experience.

- Policies pay benefits starting anywhere from a week to one year after the onset of disability. The longer you are willing to wait, the lower your premium.

- Disability policies pay benefits for as few as thirteen weeks to as long as a lifetime. The shorter the benefit period, the lower your premium.

- Don't expect to insure yourself for your full salary. The most an insurer will allow is two-thirds to four-fifths of your salary including benefits. While you are disabled, however, your expenses for taxes, transportation and clothing should diminish.

When you go shopping for disability insurance, ask for noncancelable or guaranteed renewable coverage. Either will protect you from being dropped by your insurer if your health becomes poor. Consider long-term coverage—to age sixty-five or seventy-two—if you are still gainfully employed. The possibility of being disabled permanently makes this coverage worth considering. Buy both accident and sickness coverage. Some policies pay only in cases of disability due to an accident. You want to be insured for illness, too. When buying a policy always remember that you may already have some form of disability insurance through your employer, and that your state pays workers' compensation benefits for job-connected disability. Finally, there is Social Security. You are eligible for benefits in the sixth month of disability as long as it has lasted or is expected to last at least twelve months, and you are under age sixty-five. Be warned, however, that the Social Security Administration's definition of disability is strict. Complete Chart 15 to ascertain your disability requirements.

PAYING FOR HEALTHCARE

The traditional method of providing—and paying for—healthcare is called fee-for-service. Under this system, you pick your own doctor, hospital, outpatient clinic, etc., and pay for their services as required. Today, however, a number of other options are available which are generally less expensive. Health maintenance organizations (HMOs) are one example. Depending on the group, an HMO usually covers everything from medical to dental to vision care, including medications, for one annual fee and some minor copayment charges. Copayments generally run no more the $5 to $10 a visit. HMO subscribers must use specialists and hospitals assigned by the group, and most sharply limit visits to specialists. Some HMOs, including the Blue Cross plans, often disallow outside specialist visits altogether.

Preferred provider organizations (PPOs) are a second alternative to fee-for-service. Your employer sets up a PPO by striking a deal with a group of physicians, a hospital or an insurance company to provide a list of doctors and a hospital you can call upon for healthcare by paying one low premium. If you use the doctors and facilities on the PPO roster, most of your health-care expenses will be covered. If you choose a doctor not on the list, you'll be reimbursed only to the extent of the discounted fee the PPO doctor receives. You pay any difference out of your own pocket. The opportunities for joining a PPO as an individual are limited, but some Blue Cross/Blue Shield PPOs have made individual memberships available, and other insurers may do so as well.

An independent practitioner association (IPA) is a third healthcare option. In an IPA you are allowed to keep your own family doctor, but must use specialists within a given group. Both PPOs and IPAs are obviously akin to HMOs but offer you a bit more flexibility. The downside is that they usually cost more than conventional HMOs and may also have fewer doctors enrolled.

Within all three groups there is a bias toward outpatient surgery rather than hospitalization as a means of containing costs. A federal study also has revealed a tendency among HMO and certain other group practitioners to treat disease symptoms, bypassing the extensive diagnostic workups that are a part of routine care under the fee-for-service system. In place of extended psychotherapy, the groups lean toward short-term crisis intervention and use fewer specialists. Membership in an HMO-style group may also mean that you must wait longer for nonemergency visits and elective procedures. Nevertheless, a patient with serious medical problems will be competently treated by most groups, experts say, even though you may get a lot less hand-holding by your doctors in the process.

HMOs emphasize a team approach to the practice of medicine. Doctors work closely with physician assistants and nurse practitioners who perform many of the routine tests and exams ordinarily handled by physicians in fee-for-service settings. So if you require a great deal of personal attention from your doctor, you may not be happy with HMO care.

Summing up the pros and cons of HMO membership:

- You'll receive total healthcare with no deductibles and only minor copayment charges for doctor visits.

- You'll be assigned a primary-care doctor, but are free to ask for a transfer to another group physician if not satisfied.

- You'll have access to group specialists and diagnostic procedures only if your doctor recommends them.

- Emergency care will always be available.

- When traveling you're covered only for emergency medical care on a temporary basis.

- Most surgeries will be performed on an outpatient basis or with short hospital stays, and you'll provide a great deal more of your own post-operative care.

To give yourself the best shot at competent HMO care, select a group that practices at a hospital associated with a medical school. These hospitals demand top-notch training for all their doctors. Before signing up, however, ask about doctor caseloads. A load of about 1,500 persons (not families) is considered manageable. Ask also about the availability of board certified specialists in the group, and whether specialist visits must be authorized by your primary-care physician.

Check your insurance coverage carefully before turning for help to non-traditional therapies such as acupuncture, biofeedback, hypnosis and the like. By venturing outside the medical mainstream you may be stepping into a jungle of insurance-payment problems, confusing treatment choices and questionable medical advice. Even in cases where office-visit fees charged by alternative healthcare providers are much lower than those charged by traditional doctors, your out-of-pocket cost could end up higher because you won't receive reimbursement by your insurance carrier.

The primary exception to that rule is chiropractic treatment of back pain. Medicare, union health plans, most group insurance plans, some Medicaid, some Blue Cross and Blue Shield policies, some HMOs, and some individual insurance contracts cover this form of alternative treatment because chiropractors are now licensed in every state, which makes them by law "eligible renderers of medical care."

Some group plans will reimburse you for acupuncture, biofeedback and hypnosis, if the service is rendered by a physician or under the direct supervision of a physician. And keep in mind that insurers' positions on al-

---

CHART 15
Will You Have Enough Income If Disabled?*

1. MONTHLY AVERAGE OF TOTAL LIVING EXPENSES
WHILE DISABLED .... $ _____
This amount should be adjusted as follows:
a. Increased because of related unreimbursed health care
expenses .... _____
b. Reduced because of waivers of premium clauses on
health and life insurance during period of disablement
(check policies) .... _____
                                    TOTAL $ _____

2. MONTHLY AVERAGE OF SUBSTITUTE INCOME WHILE DISABLED THROUGH ILLNESS OR INJURY	Monthly Benefits		
	Immediate**	*After 6 Months*	*After 2 Years****
Group Disability Insurance (Benefits tax-free if you have paid premiums; taxable if your employer pays premiums.)........	$ _✓_	$ _✓_	$ _✓_
Social Security (Benefits begin with sixth month. Dependents also qualify for certain benefits. Consult Social Security Office.)..	___	___	___
State Disability Plans.......................	_✓_	_✓_	_✓_
Workers' Compensation	_✓_	_✓_	_✓_
Veterans Administration	_✓_	_✓_	_✓_
Personal Disability Insurance (Benefits tax-free)...................................	_✓_	_✓_	_✓_
Spouse's Income	___	___	___
Savings and Investment Income (Interest, dividends, rents, etc.)	___	___	___
Legal Settlements Because of Disabling Accident......................	___	___	___
Other	___	___	___
TOTAL MONTHLY SUBSTITUTE INCOME	$ ___	$ ___	$ ___

CHART 15 (continued) Will You Have Enough Income If Disabled?*			
3. SHORTAGE OR OVERAGE (EXPENSES LESS INCOME)	$ ____	$ ____	$ ____
4. BORROWING POWER (Using borrowed or withdrawn funds from life insurance, employee pension, savings, etc.)	____	____	____
5. ADDITIONAL DISABILITY INCOME COVERAGE NEEDED (Item 3 minus Item 4)	$ ____	$ ____	$ ____

*If you are under age 65, the odds are far greater that you'll suffer a disability serious enough to keep you away from work for more than three months than that you will die.
**Waiting period may be up to or more than 90 days.
***You may want to consider effect of inflation on your needs.
√ = Check with appropriate issuer of insurance.
ALSO CHECK IF YOUR GROUP/PERSONAL DISABILITY INSURANCE: Has a benefits cost-of-living adjustment? Is guaranteed renewable? Charges a higher premium for your occupation? Provides benefits only if you're unable to perform your own occupation—or if you're not able to engage in any occupation? Covers partial disability? Does a period of total disability have to precede partial? Affords benefits if you work part-time?

Source: from SPARN 3/89.

ternative medicine sometimes change. A Blue Cross/Blue Shield advisory board meets regularly to review alternative therapies and decide whether they should be upgraded to "accepted." To be safe, check with your insurance representative before you visit an alternative practitioner. If you're told the service is covered, get the approval in writing. Customers all too often are told the cost of a service is reimbursable, but when their claims are rejected they have no proof that they were given prior approval.

The best way to find a reputable practitioner is through a referral from a medical doctor. If that doesn't work, ask your friends and acquaintances for their recommendations. Alternative medicine seems to attract more than its fair share of fanatical adherents. Avoid practitioners who insist they have all the answers, or a sure cure, and urge you to break off all other treatment or visits with other physicians. Also beware of those who preach to you about complicated theories and elaborate diagnoses. A quality healer will make sure you understand the treatment and the principles behind it. A criticism often leveled at alternative practitioners is that many attempt to make you dependent, seducing you into costly, long-term therapy under a pretense that a cure is complicated and takes time. To avoid this, refuse to contract for a preset number of visits, don't pay in advance for an entire course of treatment, and be wary of anyone who won't give you some idea of when you can expect results.

Following are sketches of the most common alternatives:

- Chiropractic—for back pain, leg pain, stiff necks and slipped discs. Chiropractic is based on the theory that spinal vertebrae can entrap and damage nerves if not properly aligned. Treatment consists of the chiropractor applying manual pressure to joints or vertebrae, or manipulating vertebrae into place by a sudden maneuver known as "cracking." A good chiropractor will give you advice on special exercises and other preventive measures. Many chiropractors work on hospital staffs with private doctors.

- Biofeedback—for treating stress-related conditions, including some migraines, insomnia, some cases of high blood pressure, and asthma. Biofeedback equipment provides data on bodily responses by measuring skin temperature or muscular tension. Biofeedback theory asserts that you can learn to use your mind to control these responses through relaxation techniques. Its goal is to teach you how to relax in everyday situations.

- Acupuncture—for relief of pain from migraines, tendonitis, arthritis and backaches. Its basic premise is that specific body points influence the functioning of organs and the central nervous system. In treatment, hair-thin stainless steel needles are inserted into acupuncture points, which lie within the layer of muscle below the skin. Acupuncture is a complete healthcare system in China, where it is used to treat everything from emotional disturbances to digestive disorders. It is primarily employed in the United States to treat pain.

- Massage—for reducing soreness from workouts, relieving muscle tension, and combating feelings of stress. Four types of massage are practiced in the United States. Swedish massage, the most popular, is performed while you are lying down, undressed, and is characterized by five different strokes. Oriental shiatsu, for which you remain dressed, involves a series of downward vertical pressures. Reflexology, also oriental in origin, is a foot massage which practitioners claim has a salutary effect on the whole body. Aromatherapy may combine both Swedish and shiatsu strokes and incorporates oils infused with essences of herbs or flowers. These are said to be capable of affecting your mind and emotions when inhaled and absorbed by your skin.

- Hypnosis—for behavior modification, often to help people stop smoking, drinking or overeating, and to eliminate phobias. By creating a state of mind in which usual methods of thought are suspended, the hypnotherapist communicates suggestions to your unconscious that hopefully will have an impact on your conscious responses when you're awake. The classical hypnotherapist induces a trance using a metronome, pendulum, bright light or soothing sound, then makes direct suggestions for behavior change (e.g., "stop smoking"). Other approaches involve indirect suggestions guiding you to memories or associations that may help you overcome your problem. Experts say that if a problem is susceptible to treatment by hypnotherapy, there should be some positive response by the sixth session.

- Nutritional counseling—for correcting dietary problems such as overweight, gout, diabetes, ulcers, constipation, elevated cholesterol and high blood pressures. By restructuring your eating habits, this theory proposes, you can control conditions such as obesity, improve your overall health and reduce the risk of some diet-linked diseases. Beware of any nutritionist who overemphasizes or sells vitamin or mineral supplements.

- Herbalism—for treating sore throats, some toothaches, digestive ailments, low-level infections and sinus problems. Herbalists argue that natural substances fight bacteria, viruses and pain, with fewer side effects. The herbalist recommends a remedy based on your symptoms. Remember that some herbs can be dangerous if taken incorrectly or in excess.

LONG-TERM HEALTHCARE

The most crucial insurance purchase you may make in your life could be coverage for long-term nursing home and home care. Unless you are very rich, you probably need it. But what to buy and when are more difficult questions which you can answer only by thoroughly investigating the available solutions. The subject is so new that insurers have little data on which to go. They are unsure how to price their policies, including provisions for inflation, or what you might require. And there is a hue and cry among insurers, regulators and consumer advocates over what should be offered. Contrary to popular belief, neither most private insurance policies nor Medicare provide the coverage you need. Medicaid, the welfare program that does cover long-term care, requires the recipient to "spend down" to the poverty level to become eligible. Even private insurance designed to complement the two federal programs may not pay for long-term custodial care. Yet, the U.S. General Services Administration reports that 8 million Americans over sixty-five already need some form of long-term care, and the American Association of Retired Persons says half of all Americans will need nursing home care during their lifetimes. The problem is acute for another reason: The cost of nursing home care, which now runs from about $24,000 to $36,000 a year in most parts of the United States, can be as high as $50,000 a year in some locales—enough to impoverish.

Private insurance can help. Unlike Medicare, which limits coverage to 150 days in a skilled facility, most nursing home policies offered by insurers cover care in skilled, intermediate or custodial facilities. You select the per diem benefits you want, typically ranging from $40 to $100, and the waiting period you desire. Premiums are based on your age when buying the policy and the benefits you choose. A newer form of insurance, at-home care, is becoming more popular. It pays the cost of long-term care at home for people who might otherwise have to enter nursing homes. These policies cover at-home services ranging from dressing and bathing to housekeeping and shopping. Usually, no prior admission at a hospital or nursing home is required.

Don't wait until you need it to buy long-term care insurance. The premiums are lower the younger you are. Also consider the possibility you might become disabled at a preretirement age. Know the company you're dealing with and check its A.M. Best & Company rating. Your state insurance commissioner can help. Shop around. There are wide variations in coverage and in prices. Read and compare policies. Don't take the agent's word for it. Check specifically the waiting period before policy benefits begin, the amount paid per day, and the duration of the benefits. Check the kinds of nursing homes and home care services available in the area where you live to determine whether they meet the requirements defined in your policy.

For a copy of "Coming of Age," an excellent brochure produced by John Hancock Mutual Life Insurance Company, write to Marketing Communication, T-33, John Hancock, P.O. Box 111, Boston, MA 02117. The brochure contains useful information on long-term care, an explanation of the role of insurance and a list of sources for assistance. You also may obtain a copy of "The Consumer's Guide to Long-Term Care Insurance" from the

U.S. Department of Health and Human Services by sending 50 cents to Consumer Information Center, Dept. 460-T, Pueblo, CO 81009. For a thorough analysis and critique, including policy comparisons, see the May 1988 issue of *Consumer Reports* magazine. You should find a copy in your local public library, or send $5 to Reader's Service Division, Consumers Union, 256 Washington Street, Mount Vernon, NY 10553.

The National Association of Life Underwriters reports that long-term care policies are increasingly available. A survey by *Life Association News* identified more than fifty companies that offer the policies, seventeen that offer group policies, and several that offer long-term care riders. To check the availability of these policies in your area, call your local Association of Life Underwriters. You should find the listing in your telephone directory. The association will send you a copy of its survey of long-term care policies if you send a self-addressed, stamped #10 envelope to: NALU, Dept. PR-SP, 1922 F Street NW, Washington, DC 20006.

Also, Chart 16 has been designated to assist you to determine the appropriate structure of your potential long term care needs.

MEDICARE

Medicare is a federal health insurance program for people sixty-five or older and certain disabled persons, and is operated by the Health Care Financing Administration of the U.S. Department of Health and Human Services. Social Security Administration offices across the country take applications for Medicare and provide general information about the program. Medicare insurance comes in two parts. Part A, *hospital insurance*, helps pay for inpatient hospital care, some inpatient care in a skilled nursing facility, home healthcare and hospice care. Part B, *medical insurance*, helps pay for doctors' services, outpatient hospital services, durable medical equipment, and a number of other medical services and supplies that are not covered by the hospital insurance part of Medicare.

Part B of Medicare—the medical part—has premiums, deductibles, and coinsurance amounts that you must pay yourself or through coverage by another insurance plan. Part A—the hospital part—has deductibles and coinsurance, but most people do not have to pay premiums. The amounts you pay are set each year, according to formulas established by law. New payment schedules begin the first day of each year.

Generally, people age sixty-five and over can get premium-free Medicare

---

CHART 16
Are You Satisfactorily Covered for Long-Term Care?

- It is estimated that one in five Americans will spend some time in a nursing home.
- Estimated average confinement time is 2.5 years.
- Present average cost of a nursing home is $26,000 per year.
- An estimated 20% to 25% of the elderly are currently confined to their homes with regular care from others than relatives.

Use this checklist to appraise any (A) insurance policy or (B) other protection (a) you now have or (b) are, or will be considering adding:

1. If an insurance policy, how does "Best's" rate the insurer?
2. Does the insurance policy or other protection cover (A) "custodial"- and (B) "intermediate"- type nursing homes as well as (C) "skilled"?
3. Also cover (A) home health care agencies (service providers, supplies, and equipment) and (B) adult day care centers?
4. Insurer's "care coordinator" required to locate and approve (A) facilities and (B) services?
5. Exclusions for (A) existing conditions (B) pre-existing conditions (C) former conditions?
6. Exclusions for mental and nervous disorders, such as Alzheimer's disease?
7. To qualify for benefits: (A) Do you have to enter the nursing home directly or within a maximum period from hospital discharge? (B) Enter into a custodial or intermediate nursing home from a skilled? (C) Enter into home care or adult day center care from a hospital or nursing home?
8. How long is the "deductible" ("waiting," "elimination") period (when your benefits begin after confinement starts)?
9. How long will benefits continue: (A) maximum period(s) of confinement or (B) maximum dollar amount(s)?
10. If "discharged" from a confinement period, but resumed in the future: (A) New deductible period? (B) Prior confinement count toward maximum benefits?
11. What expenses are covered?
12. What expenses are not covered?
13. (A) Are benefits a fixed dollar amount for each qualifying day? If so, how much? (B) Or do benefits vary for different kinds of care?
14. Are benefits adjusted (fixed or variable percentage) each year for inflation? If so: (A) How much each year? (B) For how many years?
15. "Duplicate benefits": How do other plans you may have affect benefits of this policy or protection (other than a policy)?
16. Oldest age permitted to buy this policy or other protection?
17. (A) Guaranteed renewable or (B) "conditionally" renewable? (If conditions, what are they?)
18. What are the premiums or other costs? (Some premiums are a set amount with benefits and conditions the same for all. Others will have variable premiums based upon conditions (such as age) and benefits that you specifically select [such as deductible period, how long benefits continue, amount of benefits, and the like].)
19. Are the premiums you start with (A) fixed for as long as you continue to pay the premiums or (B) can they be increased if increased for all policyholders or holders of other protection (other than a policy)?
20. Are premiums waived ("waiver of premiums") while benefits are received?

Source: SPYF p. 86.

hospital insurance benefits, based on their own or their spouses' employment. These are the qualifying conditions:

- You receive benefits under the Social Security or Railroad Retirement system.

- You could receive benefits under Social Security or the Railroad Retirement system but did not file for them.

- You or your spouse had certain government employment.

You also can get premium-free Medicare hospital insurance benefits under age sixty-five if you have been a Social Security or Railroad Retirement Board disability beneficiary for more than twenty-four months, and generally if you receive continuing dialysis for permanent kidney failure or have had a kidney transplant. If eligible for the hospital insurance, you can enroll for Part B medical insurance, pay the required premiums and receive benefits. Even if you are not qualified by work credits for Medicare coverage, you may be able to buy into the protection. Check with Social Security about how to accomplish a buy-in.

You should receive a Medicare card in the mail when you turn sixty-five if you are getting Social Security or Railroad Retirement benefits. But you must file an application for benefits if you have not applied for Social Security or Railroad Retirement, if government employment is involved, or if you have kidney disease. Be sure and file your application immediately to avoid delays in receiving benefits.

The Medicare card shows your coverage and health insurance claim number, sometimes referred to as your Medicare number. It has nine digits and a letter. On some cards there may also be a final number following the letter. Your full claim number must be included on all Medicare claims and correspondence. When a husband and wife both have Medicare, each will receive an individual card and number.

- Always show your Medicare card when you receive services that Medicare helps pay for.

- Write your health insurance claim number, including the letter, on any bills you send in and on any correspondence about Medicare.

- Carry your card with you whenever you are away from home.

- Immediately ask Social Security to get you a new card if you lose yours.

- Use your Medicare card only after its effective date.

- Never let anyone else use your Medicare card.

If you believe you have received poor quality healthcare by an inpatient hospital, hospital outpatient department, or other provider under Medicare, you may tell your story to a Peer Review Organization (PRO), which has a duty to investigate written complaints from beneficiaries or their representatives. You may also complain to the PRO in your state if you feel you were improperly refused admission to a hospital or forced to leave too soon. Ask for a written explanation of any such decision.

PROs are groups of practicing doctors and other healthcare professionals who are paid by the Federal government to review the care given Medicare patients. Each state decides, for Medicare payment purposes, whether care is reasonable and necessary, is provided in the appropriate setting, and meets the standards of quality accepted by the medical profession. PROs have the authority to deny payments if care is not medically necessary or not delivered in the most appropriate setting.

Medicare hospital insurance helps pay for inpatient hospital care if all of the following four conditions are met:

- A doctor prescribes inpatient hospital care for treatment of your illness or injury.

- You require the kind of care that can only be provided in a hospital.

- The hospital is participating in Medicare.

- The Utilization Review Committee of the hospital or a Peer Review Organization does not disapprove your stay.

If you meet these conditions, Medicare will pay for up to ninety days of hospitalization in each benefit period. A benefit period is a way of measuring your use of hospital services. Your first period starts the first time you enter a hospital after the effective day of your Medicare insurance. The period ends when you have been out of the hospital for sixty consecutive days. There is no limit to the number of benefit periods you can have for hospital and skilled nursing facility care. However, special limited benefit periods apply to hospice care. A hospice is a public or private agency engaged in providing pain relief, symptom management and supportive services to the terminally ill.

During 1991, Medicare pays for all covered services from the first day through the sixtieth day except the first $592. This is the hospital insurance deductible. From the sixty-first through the ninetieth day of each benefit period, Medicare pays for all covered services except for $148 a day. This daily charge, which you must pay, is labeled hospital coinsurance.

MEDICARE MEDICAL INSURANCE

Medicare medical insurance helps pay for doctor's services, outpatient hospital care, diagnostic tests, durable medical equipment, ambulance services and many other health services and supplies which are not covered by Medicare hospital insurance.

You must pay an annual deductible of $100 (in 1991) in approved charges for covered medical expenses. You are required to meet this deductible only once during the year, and it can be met by any combination of covered expenses. There is no separate deductible for each different kind of service you receive.

After paying the annual deductible, you also must pay a share of the Medicare-approved charges for most services and supplies. This share is called coinsurance, and the standard amount is 20 percent of your bill.

Doctors and other healthcare professionals may sign agreements to become Medicare participants. This means they agree in advance to accept assignment on all Medicare claims. By "taking assignment," your doctor or supplier agrees to accept as total payment for services the fees established as reasonable by Medicare. In addition, all doctors and suppliers must fill out claim forms for you and forward them to Medicare for payment, whether or not they take assignment. Medicare reimburses your doctor or supplier 80 percent of the Medicare-approved charge (you pay the other 20 percent as your coinsurance share), after subtracting any part of the $75 annual deductible you have not met.

Participating providers include hospitals, skilled nursing facilities, home health agencies, comprehensive outpatient rehabilitation facilities, and providers of outpatient physical and occupational therapy and speech pathology services. They are required to submit their claims directly to Medicare.

For additional information about Medicare, write: Consumer Information Center, Department 59, Pueblo, CO 81009. The following free publications are available:

- Guide to Health Insurance for People with Medicare (512W).

- Hospice Benefits Under Medicare (513W).

- Medicare and Prepayment Plans (515W).

- Getting a Second Opinion (545W).

- Medicare and Employer Health Plans (602W).

- Medicare Coverage of Kidney Dialysis and Kidney Transplant Services (603W).

Allow six to eight weeks for delivery.

MEDICAID

Medicaid is a healthcare program offered by state governments for low-income people. You may be eligible for Medicaid if you are receiving public assistance or Supplemental Security Income, or if you meet the criteria for disability under the Social Security Act and have limited assets such as money and property. To obtain more information about eligibility requirements, call the nearest Medicaid office. You will find the agency listed in your local telephone directory.

There are definite limits to the amount of so-called reserve assets (money and property) you can own and still receive Medicaid, ranging from $3,000 for an individual to $5,900 for a family of seven. However, a number of items are not taken into consideration in figuring these limits, including: your home; term, group and other insurance that has no loan value; automobile; clothing; personal effects; furniture and appliances. If you are aged, blind or disabled, certain other assets also may be exempt. Your local Medicaid office can give you details. All other persons may reserve assets as follows:

Number in Family	Allowable Reserves
1	$3,000
2	4,650
3	5,200

ALLOWABLE INCOME UNDER MEDICAID

Medicaid applicants living at home are allowed income up to the amounts below:

Number in Family	Annual Income
1	$5,000
2	7,300
3	7,400
4	7,500
5	7,600
6	7,700
7	7,800

For families larger than seven, the annual income exemption is increased by $700. Keep in mind, however, that single individuals, some parents and childless couples between the ages of twenty-one and sixty-four, not blind or disabled, must meet public assistance eligibility requirements to receive Medicaid. The above chart does not apply to these persons.

Medicaid payments are made directly to the individual or medical facility which provides your healthcare.

If you are eligible for Medicaid, you may go to healthcare providers in your state who take part in the program. Ask about this before you receive any services. Otherwise, you may be stuck paying the bill. However, once a Medicare provider accepts you as a patient and sees your card, he or she must accept payment from Medicaid as payment in full for all covered services. You should not receive a bill. And if a service is not covered by Medicaid, the medical provider is obligated to tell you so in advance.

AVOID THE MEDICAID TRAP

Middle-income Americans abhor the prospect of having to impoverish themselves to become eligible for Medicaid, particularly long-term nursing home care. Fortunately, with careful planning and the help of a good lawyer you can conserve some of your assets. The strategy is spelled out in a book by Arnold D. Budish, a Cleveland-based attorney. Published by Henry Holt

& Company at $22, *Avoiding the Medicaid Trap* can be ordered by calling (800) 247-3912, or be found at many bookstores. The book is an eye-opener, recommended for anyone who may one day have to place a family member in a nursing home. It may also be of help to many attorneys who lack expertise in the field of practice known as *elderlaw*. Following are a few of Budish's key suggestions for asset preservation:

- Place money in exempt assets—pay off your home mortgage, make necessary home improvements, buy needed household goods and/or personal effects, upgrade equipment for a small productive family business, set aside funds for burial plots and funeral costs.

- Transfer assets to children, spouse, and/or others—make gifts of exempt assets to children or others whom you trust to help you in a financial emergency; make gifts of non-exempt assets directly to children or others more than thirty months before entering a nursing home; pay children for services they have provided; optionally, transfer your house to children while retaining a life estate interest.

- Make a durable power of attorney, which can guarantee that you and your loved ones will not spend any more than about $60,000 on a nursing home. No one should ever lose more.

6

Estate Planning

IT'S MORE THAN WRITING A WILL

Poor estate planning can cost your family tens of thousands of dollars in unnecessary taxes and probate expenses, as well as endless weeks, months, even years of heartache and discontent. Yet, it's not uncommon even for well-to-do individuals who ought to know better to neglect or ignore this vital duty to those they cherish. A principal reason is that estate planning is often considered unpleasant because it invokes the specter of death. An acquaintance of ours, a healthy 80-year-old widow, refuses even to write a will because she can't bear to think about the possibility of death. She also professes not to "give a damn" about what happens to her money when she passes on, even though she has enjoyed many long years of love and devotion by the members of her large, closely-knit family. Because of her selfish megalomania, her considerable estate, worth upwards of $5 million, will be decimated by taxes and internecine warfare when she dies. Don't let this happen to your family.

Good estate planning involves much more than writing a will and filing it away. Good estate planning does not even start with making out a will. Your will should be viewed as only one part of your estate plan, which in turn is part of your overall financial plan. Both depend on keeping detailed records of what you own and a sensible program for managing these assets.

Estate planning is not something you should attempt on your own. There are simply too many complex variables to be considered. And unless it's your profession, you'll plan only one estate—your own—in a lifetime. You should therefore seek the help of trusted advisors who can help you avoid the many common estate-planning mistakes that others have made before you. A lawyer can help you draw up a will and set up trusts. Consult your accountant for advice on tax planning. Ask your financial advisors for assistance with appropriate investments.

THE MOST COMMON ERRORS

Stephen R. Leimberg, author, lawyer, and professor of taxation and estate planning at The American College, Bryn Mawr, PA, says the most glaring estate planning errors are these:

- *Lack of a master strategy game plan.* Do-it-yourself estate and financial planning is the closest thing to do-it-yourself brain surgery.

- *Lack of adequate records.* This can drive your executor crazy—and lead to thousands of dollars of needless expense.

- *Leaving everything to your spouse.* Do you intend to subject the estate to a second tax wallop? Can the surviving spouse manage the inherited assets?

- *Improper disposition of assets.* Will the wrong assets go to the wrong persons in the wrong manner or at the wrong time?

- *Improper use of jointly held property.* Jointly held property can become a nightmare of unexpected tax and nontax problems.

- *Improperly arranged life insurance.* Proceeds are often made payable to a beneficiary before he or she is capable of handling it, or in the wrong manner—outright instead of over a period of years. Leimberg says you also should name two contingent or backup beneficiaries.

- *Lack of liquidity.* Anticipate the executor's need for cash—for taxes, debts, family expenses and a laundry list of other required payments.

- *Wrong choice of executor.* The person who administers the estate must—with dispatch, often without compensation, with personal financial risk and without conflict of interest—perform tasks which are complex, time consuming and technically demanding. Is your executor capable?

- *Failure to make a will or update a will.* Update your will whenever there is a change in your needs or those of your beneficiaries.

BEGIN ESTATE PLANNING EARLY

Your estate planning should begin as soon as you begin accumulating financial assets—life insurance, savings, real estate, stocks and bonds, pension rights, employee death benefits and Social Security. And each important change in your financial situation should also be factored into your estate plan and discussed with your family and financial advisors. For example, if you are about to be pushed into a higher tax bracket, you may want to transfer more of your assets into tax-exempt securities. The birth of a grandchild may require a change in your will. Assuming responsibility for elderly parents may prompt you to set up trusts that would provide for their living expenses and healthcare should anything happen to you. An impending divorce would no doubt prompt you to revise your insurance policies and pension plans.

Fully seven out of ten people in the United States die without making a will. Many wrongheadedly think they lack sufficient assets to warrant a will. Others simply put it off until too late. Yet, the importance of a will cannot be overemphasized. Failure to execute one can only be viewed as a gross disservice to your family. Without a will, you abdicate control, leaving your family's future in the hands of rigid state intestacy laws, courts and lawyers. The distribution of your estate and even child guardianship decisions are made for you, not by you, beginning with the selection of your executor. This court-appointed person will be someone who is a stranger to your family, someone with no particular concern for your financial assets or the welfare of your loved ones. You also invite the likelihood of having part of your estate distributed to individuals you yourself would not have chosen and even to people you did not know. If you married a second or third time, and wanted to leave more of your property to your children that your last wife, the laws of the state will frustrate that desire. If you were a single parent with minor children, the court has authority to appoint their guardian, which again might be someone you would not have preferred. If you die intestate, you cannot leave gifts to friends or charities. If the state concludes you have no kinfolk close enough to qualify as heirs, your property will go to the state itself. Finally, your estate and, indirectly, your heirs can end up paying a whopping federal estate tax bill. The brackets range from 37 percent on estates worth more than $600,000, up to 50 percent on those worth millions of dollars. A number of states also impose an estate tax, while others levy an inheritance tax. Estate taxes are generally deducted from the assets in your estate. Your heirs owe inheritance taxes on the share of your estate they receive.

THE PURPOSES OF A WILL

The functions of a will are to distribute your assets in the manner you choose, provide adequate cash to your executor and heirs during the probate process, protect your family's lifestyle, ensure that assets are well managed after your death, and preserve your estate from excess taxation. Avoid easy assumptions. Husbands don't always die before their wives, even if they are older. A wife should have a will, even if her only property is that which she holds jointly with her husband and will inherit anyway. State laws governing dying intestate apply to women as well as to men. And even if a wife doesn't independently own real estate or stocks and bonds, or have a substantial bank account, she may have furs, silverware, crystal, antiques and works of art that should be distributed in a will to avoid friction and bickering in the family.

A will has been described as a kind of legal science fiction. The testator, or will maker, and his or her lawyer must make decisions in the present that will take effect at some unknown time in the future. But how can a person foresee every eventuality? One approach is to make a highly detailed will, with alternative arrangements to cover a variety of possible events. Another is to tailor the will to your current circumstances, then revise it as your situation changes. The latter course is probably the most sensible. If you remarry, for example, you may need to update your will to include your new spouse. Or you may want to make a change reflecting the changed financial circumstances of beneficiaries. Experts say a common mistake people make is to leave everything in equal shares to spouse and children. Suppose, however, that one of your offspring makes a lot of money, while others struggle along. You might decide to leave a larger portion of your estate to the children who need it more. If your executor—the person you have selected to carry out the provisions of your will—becomes incapacitated or otherwise unsuitable to take on that responsibility, you must change your will accordingly. If you move to another state, have a local attorney check your will for compliance with the laws of the new state.

LIFE EVENTS REQUIRE WILL CHANGES

Here is a quick checklist of life events which generally require changes in your will:

- When you move to another state.

- When you change your mind about how you want to divvy up your property.

- When a child or grandchild arrives—unless your will already takes this into account.

- When you marry, separate or divorce.

- When your net worth changes substantially.

- When one of your beneficiaries dies.

- When tax laws change in a way that affects your estate or financial plan.

- When state or federal trust laws are changed.

- When you add or lose major assets; for example, your valuable coin collection is stolen.

Very simple will changes can be executed by codicil or amendment to the original document. To be valid, however, a codicil must be signed, dated and witnessed in the same manner as the will itself. Do not mark up or modify the document in any way without observing the legal requirements of the state in which you live. To do so is to risk having the court declare the will invalid when it goes to probate. If major changes are necessary, ask your attorney to draw up a completely new document.

THE LANGUAGE OF THE WILL

The language of your will is important. In a recent symposium on writing wills in New York, experienced surrogate (probate) judges offered the following advice:

- Make sure the will is written in clear, concise language. Say what you mean, and mean what you say.

- Avoid complicated bequests, if at all possible: life trusts, for example, that transfer property to a second heir after the first heir dies. Life trusts can lead to both tax and property title problems, the judges point out.

- Be accurate. The simplest mistake can lead to a dispute that may have to be settled in court.

- Get the correct names and addresses of all those receiving property, to avoid expensive delays in locating beneficiaries.

LEGAL FEES

The legal fees for drawing up wills are usually based on the time required for the job. Many attorneys, however, will do a simple will for a flat fee of around $250. If married, you and your spouse should normally employ the same lawyer. This saves time and money and allows for close coordination of will provisions. If your will is more complicated, and particularly if it involves the creation of trusts, you should shop around for an attorney who is experienced in the handling of trusts and estates of your size. Your own lawyer may be perfectly capable, but may lack the specialized, up-to-date knowledge required for preparing complex trust documents. Any mistakes will prove costly to your heirs, especially in the area of taxation.

When you finally go to work with your lawyer, don't waste his or her costly time. Come prepared to be clear and specific about your intentions and bring a complete list of your assets, including significant personal possessions. When the will is completed and trusts established, ask an estate or financial planner, or your accountant, to check it out for loopholes that could cause your heirs trouble later.

NEGOTIATE FEES WITH YOUR LAWYER

Many people worry about the cost of probating a will. But Attorney John Coulter of Coulter & Polhemus, Poughkeepsie, New York, says a lawyer's fee for probating an estate can be negotiated by the estate executor in advance. "If you think a fee of 5 percent, or $10,000, is too high for probating an estate valued at $200,000, you should speak out," Coulter says. "In many instances your lawyer will be willing to reduce the fee to 3 or 4 percent."

You can also ask your lawyer to charge the estate on an hourly basis, but that can be a trap if hourly fees exceed a set percentage. If your lawyer is agreeable, discuss a slightly higher hourly fee with an absolute limit not to exceed a negotiated percentage.

"Most of the disputes over lawyers' fees occur when the executor is suddenly presented with legal bills that may represent a year of work for a lawyer, but seem astronomical to the heirs," adds Coulter. "The best thing to do is put it all on the table up front."

THE "RIGHT-TO-DIE" WILL

A regular will distributes the maker's property, but there's a complementary type which is increasingly popular among older Americans—a "living" or, more accurately, "right-to-die" will. This will directs, within the laws of your state, how you are to be treated in the event you become terminally ill or mentally-incompetent. You may refuse medical treatment under certain circumstances, or reject specific treatments when medical authorities and family agree there is little hope for your recovery. For example, if you are in terrible pain and/or early death appears certain, you may refuse life-support systems. Since laws on the validity of living wills vary—some states do not recognize them at all—you should consult your attorney on the law in your state of residence.

DIVIDING YOUR PERSONAL PROPERTY

The task of dividing up your property and personal valuables in a will requires careful thought, although many people take the easy way out. They leave half to their spouses and divide the other half equally among their children. Usually, if the estate is substantial, the first clauses in a will make specific bequests—a certain valuable, say, an antique car or a painting to a friend or lover, a cash or other gift to a long-time employee, a donation to a charity or your alma mater. Spouse, children and other relatives—your primary beneficiaries—then get various portions of the remaining assets. The specific legacies must be paid out first. Take care not to make so many of these that little is left to your principal heirs. Your purpose, after all, is to help the members of your family maintain or enhance their lifestyles. If you give more to some of your children than others, it's also a good idea to explain in the will why you did so.

SPECIAL PROVISIONS

Your will should also make provision for payment of burial and other expenses, along with any debts and taxes that become due upon your demise. If you have minor children, name a guardian for them. Designate an executor to manage and settle your estate. Specify all the trusts you want established for your children or other relatives, and name trustees for each. You may also want to instruct beneficiaries in the handling of certain assets, such as a stock portfolio, although you should not be so rigid in these that adjustments can't be made as changed circumstances demand. Finally, you may choose to set forth the funeral arrangements you prefer. For instance, a specific instruction that you want a simple service, followed by cremation, will relieve your family of having to make these decisions. (Chances are, however, that your will won't be read until after the funeral. It's better to leave such instructions with a family member.)

WHERE TO KEEP YOUR WILL

Do not keep your completed will in a safe-deposit box. Many states seal these boxes upon a person's death, denying access, until a personal representative of the estate has been appointed by the probate court. If your will or your insurance policies are in the box, your family may have real problems. For one, they may be denied access to cash or proceeds from insurance policies that are needed to pay burial expenses and meet immediate financial obligations incurred by the estate executor. To avoid the problem, keep your will in a safe-deposit box owned by a trust you create, or place both the will and your insurance policies in your spouse's safe-deposit box, and vice versa. About half the states allow you to deposit your will with the probate court, where it will be kept safe until needed. You could also leave it in your lawyer's office, provided he or she has a well-organized, safe, fireproof storage system. A home safe or a heavy, theft-proof, fireproof filing cabinet may also be used.

KEEP YOUR FAMILY INFORMED

Make certain your spouse and adult family members know where your will is kept, who has been named executor, and where to find your life insurance policies. Your executor and family members should also be aware of the family's assets and outstanding debts, your employee benefits, and how to collect them. In addition, they must know where your bank accounts, joint accounts and real estate properties are.

By filling in the worksheets in Chart 17 and updating them periodically, you're on your way to getting your affairs in order. You should then duplicate the material and forward a copy to your executor or a trusted family member.

PLAN YOUR ESTATE TO AVOID TAXES

One of the principal goals of estate planning is to avoid death taxes altogether by removing assets from your taxable estate, or at least to make certain the government gets as little as possible. There are generally two ways to accomplish these ends—giving money away and setting up irrevocable trusts. Under current law, you can give $10,000 a year to one or more relatives or other persons—anyone you like—without paying a gift tax. Your spouse also can give $10,000 a year to the same individuals, for a total of $20,000. Larger gifts are subject to a transfer tax paid by the donor rather than the recipient. The Uniform Gift to Minors Act also allows you to give cash, securities, life insurance policies, annuity contracts or other qualifying assets to a child. The assets are managed by a custodian until the child reaches maturity at age 18 or 21, depending on where you live.

TYPES OF TRUSTS

A trust is a legal arrangement through which you give property to a trustee to manage and use for the benefit of a chosen beneficiary. It allows you to direct how the funds are to be spent and when the principal should be distributed. The two main types of trusts are *testamentary* and *living* or *inter vivos*. A testamentary trust is established in your will and goes into effect when you die. Living trusts become effective any time you choose during your lifetime. Wallace L. Head, an official of Arthur Andersen & Company, the accounting firm, points out that living trusts serve a number of useful purposes.

- To transfer management of financial affairs to an individual or institution thought to be more expert at shepherding assets, particularly certain types of investments.

- To avoid probate. Assets owned by a living trust—a "revocable funded living trust," to be exact—do not flow through probate at the grantor's death, since the trustee is responsible for distributing these assets in accordance with the trust document. Heirs thus have early access to trust proceeds.

- To avoid public disclosure of the total value of an estate, or how its assets are distributed among heirs. Unlike a trust, a will is probated in court and is a public document.

- To avoid probate-process delays in transferring a deceased's property to beneficiaries.

- To avoid gaps in the management of financial resources when an individual becomes incapacitated.

- To convey assets to a person whose identity the grantor wants to shield: a lover or illegitimate child, for example.

Living trusts may be revocable or irrevocable. Under an irrevocable type, you surrender all rights to the assets involved. You cannot terminate the arrangement, move assets in or out, or use them in any way. You are locked in for life. The great advantage of irrevocable trusts is that they offer tax savings. When you (the grantor) give up control of the trust's assets for life, they are removed from your taxable estate, assuming you live for three years after it is created.

Under a revocable trust you maintain complete control, can reclaim trust assets anytime you choose, and they remain part of your taxable estate.

A trust can be created for a wide variety of special purposes. Here are a few examples:

- A life insurance trust receives proceeds from your life insurance policies when you die.

- A "sprinkling" or "spray-powder" trust distributes income and prin-

CHART 17
Registry of Your Documents and Records
For your financial and estate planning
Inventory date: _____

Items	Where Documents and Your Records are Located			
	Documents		**Your Records**	
	Originals	*Copies*	*Originals*	*Copies*
ASSETS				
LIQUID ASSETS				
Bank Accounts:				
Checking:				
Savings:				
Money Market:				
Certificates of				
Deposit:				
Other:				
Life Insurance:				
Employee Plans:				
Cash in Stockbrokerage				
Accounts:				
U.S. Savings Bonds:				
Annuities:				
Miscellaneous:				
MARKETABLE				
INVESTMENTS				
Mutual Funds:				
Stocks:				
Corporate Bonds:				
Government Securities:				
Other Investments:				
NON-MARKETABLE				
INVESTMENTS				
IRAs, Keoghs, SEPs,				
Similar Plans:				
Investment Real Estate:				
Limited Partnerships:				
Business Interests/				
Partnerships:				
Loans to Others:				
Collectibles for				
Investment:				
Other:				

| | Where Documents and Your Records are Located | | | |
| | Documents | | Your Records | |
Items	Originals	Copies	Originals	Copies
CHART 17 (continued)				
PERSONAL ASSETS				
Residential Real Estate:				
Autos, Other Vehicles:				
Jewelry, Furs, Furnishings, Collectibles:				
Other:				
LIABILITIES				
Charge Accounts:				
Credit Card Balances:				
Other Bills to be Paid:				
Mortgages on Investment Real Estate:				
Mortgages on Residential Real Estate:				
Loan Notes:				
Margin Accounts:				
Balance Due on Installment Payments:				
Borrowed from Employer or Against Employee Benefit Plans:				
Income and Other Taxes Due:				
Other:				

cipal according to the needs of beneficiaries and the judgment of the trustee.

- A Craven trust is established to provide lifetime support for a disabled child or an infirm, elderly parent. If preservation of assets is an objective, a Craven trust allows you to do so, since beneficiaries receive income from the trust, not principal.

	Where Documents and Your Records are Located			
CHART 17 (*continued*)				
Items	**Documents**		**Your Records**	
	Originals	*Copies*	*Originals*	*Copies*
VITAL PAPERS Will:				
Letter of Instruction upon Death:				
Cemetery Deed:				
Papers Covering Funeral Arrangements:				
List of Executor and Other Persons to Contact upon Death:				
List of Advisors:				
List of Beneficiaries:				
Safe Deposit Boxes:				
Birth Certificate:				
Citizen Papers:				
Marriage Certificate:				
Divorce Decree:				
Separation Agreement:				
Adoption Papers:				
Custody Papers:				
Social Security Card:				
Social Security Papers:				
Military Service Papers:				
Business Agreements:				
Tax Returns:				
Other:				

Source: SPARN 4/89.

- An accumulation trust permits you to specify that income accumulate for a given period of time before the beneficiary begins receiving payouts.

- A Clifford trust, also known as a boomerang trust or reversionary trust, can be used to accomplish a specific objective, such as income for a child or grandchild's college education. If a Clifford trust exists for 10 years or more, it qualifies for some tax benefits. The assets of a Clifford trust eventually revert back to its creator.

- A spousal remainder trust allows you to provide income for one or more beneficiaries, including a spouse, for a period of not more than 10 years. At the end of its term, a designated beneficiary receives the trust's principal, which is not reversible to the grantor. Don't use a spousal remainder trust if you think there is a chance you and your spouse may separate or divorce before the trust matures. Ask your lawyer or accountant about the tax advantages of this type of trust.

- A charitable income trust provides income to a charity for a certain period of time. At the end of the term, the principal then goes to one or more beneficiaries.

- A charitable remainder trust specifies that income shall go to a named beneficiary for a period of time, after which the remaining assets are distributed to a charity.

Chart 18 displays the fundamentals of estate planning.

CHOOSING AN EXECUTOR

The executor of your estate should be chosen with care, since his or her responsibilities are often difficult, time-consuming, frustrating and potentially costly. For example, the executor of a taxable estate is personally liable for failure to file an estate tax return and pay the taxes on time. Courts have cited executors for overdistributing assets, or distributing assets before setting aside sufficient funds to meet tax payments. Potential problems also arise when heirs get to choose items from the estate, and they all want the same thing. Then the executor may have to choose, opening the way to charges of favoring one heir over another. Among the major tasks the executor must perform are these:

1. Probate the will and be officially designated as executor.
2. Find out what the deceased owned, and collect any money due the estate.
3. Pay outstanding debts and claims against the estate.
4. Invest the estate assets wisely until they can be distributed according to the will. Failure to handle assets as would an "ordinary, prudent person" can lead to lawsuits which may force the executor to make up losses out of his or her own pocket.

5. Collect insurance proceeds and deal with trusts and other assets that are not controlled by the will.
6. Distribute property according to the deceased's wishes.
7. Make sure that all estate and inheritance taxes are paid.
8. Make sure that the affairs of the estate are formally settled to the satisfaction of the court supervising the estate.

Many executors, as family members, get involved in tasks outside the usual parameters of the executor's role, such as helping to plan the funeral. The executor can advance funds for the funeral or reimburse family members who paid for it.

The executor should keep detailed records of every transaction. Whenever possible, get advance written consent from all adult beneficiaries for each transaction.

Additional reminders for executors:

- File a last income tax return for the deceased.

- Obtain an Employer Identification Number for the estate by filing IRS Form SS-4.

- File annual tax returns for the estate until it is completely settled.

- Send a bank search letter to financial institutions where the deceased had accounts.

- Open a bank account for the estate itself as soon as possible.

- Inform the Social Security Administration to stop paying benefits, if the deceased received benefits.

- Cancel credit cards, magazine subscriptions and similar obligations.

- Transfer title to any automobiles the deceased may have owned.

- Arrange for appraisals of assets that require them, including artwork, furniture, antiques, jewelry and collections of stamps, books and rare coins.

CHART 18	
Fundamentals of Trusts for Estate Planning	
Who's Who and What's What In A Trust	The **grantor** (also known as trustor, creator, donor, settler) is the person that creates the trust by a legal agreement. The grantor turns over assets (principal, property, corpus, trust fund, trust estate) to the trust. These assets might include cash accounts, life insurance proceeds, bonds, stocks, mutual funds, real estate. The **trustee(s)** manage the assets in the trust. The **beneficiary** receives income and/or assets from the trust.
Some Possible Advantages	● Some trusts afford tax benefits (which may include taxes on estate, on inheritance, and/or on income) to you as grantor, the beneficiaries, or both. ● You provide professional management of your assets rather than managed by inexperienced beneficiaries. ● You can control periodic distribution of your assets after your death. ● You can provide for the living expenses and education of dependent children without giving them control of substantial assets. ● You can insure that the bulk of your estate will remain intact if you want the principal eventually to go to your children and are concerned your surviving spouse will be unable to safeguard it.
Some Possible Drawbacks	● Your intentions may be thwarted after your death if inadvertently your trust(s) are not set up properly. ● Your beneficiaries' circumstances may change so greatly after your death that flexible as your trust(s) may have been, they may not be able to fully reflect the evolved needs. ● The administrative costs of running your trust(s) may offset some or many of the benefits.
Inter Vivos (Living Trusts)	These trusts are established while you are still living. Assets in a living trust are not subject to probate; thus your beneficiaries have quick access to the assets after your death and your family finances are not publicly disclosed.
Testamentary Trusts	Created by your will to become effective after your death, relevant assets flow through your will through probate and *then* into your testamentary trust(s).
Revocable Trusts	You retain the right to alter or cancel a revocable trust at any time while in effect during your lifetime. For example, you may add to the principal or withdraw assets from it or change benefits or beneficiaries. There are no tax savings with revocable trusts.

CHART 18 (*continued*)	
Irrevocable Trusts	You transfer assets permanently to an irrevocable trust, surrendering your rights to this property. You cannot change or terminate an irrevocable trust (except under certain circumstances with the agreement of the beneficiary). This type of trust can help you on federal income and estate taxes.
Unilateral Trusts	A unilateral trust is complete in itself.
Reciprocal Trusts	(or cross trusts) are related to one or more other trusts.
Simple Trusts	are required to distribute all of their income for the current year and are taxed differently than complex trusts.
Complex Trusts	are not required to distribute all of their income for the current year and are taxed differently than simple trusts.
Fixed Trusts	You cannot add to the principal, which is set at inception.
Flexible Trusts	You are able to add to the trust's principal; the trustees are not locked into specific investments, but can allocate assets.
Open-Ended Trusts	An open-ended trust is set up to go on indefinitely.
Targeted Long-Term Trusts	These trusts have a predetermined expiration date. At that termination time, all undistributed income and assets then in the trust are distributed to the beneficiary or beneficiaries in accordance with the terms of the will.
Types of Trusts Distributions	• Fixed (predetermined) dollar incomes to beneficiaries from income a trust receives, for a specified period or lifetime. • Variable percentage incomes to beneficiaries from income a trust receives, for a specified period or lifetime. • The beneficiary receives specified portions of the principal (by predetermined dollar value or percentage of value at the times of distributions). This results in a reduction in subsequent estate income.

Source: SPARN 8/89.

Note: For legal, tax and other advice on forming a trust, consult with an attorney, accountant, financial planner, estate planner, or other professional experienced in working on trusts for estate planning.
In addition to the basic trusts listed above there is a large variety of trusts available for special and specific circumstances. It is advisable to be very clear as to how you wish your trust set up, and to consult with an estate planner on these requirements.

If your estate is more complex than passing on a house, bank accounts and insurance policies, you should obviously consider naming the trust department of a bank or a lawyer as your executor. Many estate planners feel that banks perform better than attorneys because they have access to various experts. This is particularly useful if the estate includes collectibles.

Essential to estate planning is to know exactly what you have and where it is.

Part II

Investing for Retirement

7

Bonds

Government and investment-grade corporate bonds are a prudent, time-honored investment for retired persons seeking income and capital preservation. When you buy a bond you are essentially loaning your money to a government agency or a corporation. That's why bonds are called debt issues. Essentially, bonds are IOUs. The issuer is obligated to pay back the full purchase price when the bond comes due on its specified dates of maturity. Meanwhile, the issuer pays you, the bond owner, a fixed rate of interest, usually twice a year, for the use of your money—thus the term fixed-income investment. A bond also is a senior security. Corporate bond holders must be paid before shareholders receive dividends.

TREASURY SECURITIES

U.S. savings bonds are the most widely held form of this investment product. They make excellent gifts for children, especially when earmarked for a child's college education. Bonds can be purchased or redeemed at almost any bank or thrift institution in denominations as small as $50. The most painless method of buying savings bonds is through a payroll savings plan where you work. The cost to you of a $50 bond is $25, one-half its face value. For safety, federal government bonds are unbeatable. They are backed by the full faith, credit and taxing power of the United States. You're also protected if interest rates rise. Every six months, the yield on savings bonds is fixed at 85 percent of the yield on five-year treasury notes for the previous half-year. In addition, the interest rate on savings bonds you hold for at least five years can never be less than 6 percent, even if other interest rates drop below that level. The interest on your savings bonds is exempt from state and local taxation, and you can defer payment of federal taxes until you cash them in. If your family's adjusted gross income is less than

$60,000 a year, and the bonds are used to pay your children's college tuition and other designated educational expenses, they are exempt even from federal taxes. Graduated tax breaks also are available to families with adjusted gross incomes of up to $90,000. The principal disadvantages of savings bonds is that you cannot use them as collateral for a loan, nor can you cash them in for six months after purchase. No individual may purchase EE savings bonds with a face value of more than $30,000 ($15,000 actual cost) in any single year.

Regular treasury bonds are the benchmark against which all other types of bonds are judged. Like EE savings bonds, these bonds also are super safe, for the same reasons. Treasury bonds require ten years to reach maturity, although they are highly liquid and can be traded in the secondary government securities market at any time. Shorter-term treasury issues are called bills or notes. You can buy and sell treasury bills, notes and bonds through banks and brokers for a small fee, typically no more than $50. You also can buy them in person or by mail from the U.S. Treasury or from Federal Reserve banks, without paying a fee, through the Treasury Direct Book-Entry System. The process is relatively simple and well worth the effort if you plan to hold your bonds or other treasury securities to maturity. There are twelve Federal Reserve banks with twenty-five branches in major cities across the country. Despite the savings of direct-purchase, however, if you plan to trade the securities before maturity, buy through a bank or brokerage that participates in the secondary government securities market.

Joseph Robinson, who handles original treasury issues for the Federal Reserve bank in Atlanta, points out: "To trade the securities in your treasury direct account, you will have to transfer them to your bank or brokerage account." The time consumed by this process may cost you a profitable selling opportunity. Assuming you have never made a direct purchase of treasury securities, several factors will influence what you buy and how and when you pay.

For example, T-bills, notes and bonds differ in several important respects, including date and frequency of issue, minimum purchase required, and term. Term is simply the number of weeks, months or years that must elapse before the security matures and pays you its face value. A *bill* is a short-term obligation of the U.S. Treasury. Bills mature in 13, 26 and 52 weeks. They can be rolled-over, or automatically reinvested at maturity, for up to two years. The smallest T-bill you can buy is $10,000, with multiples of $5,000 thereafter.

A *note* is a medium-term obligation. Notes mature in two to ten years.

Minimum investment for two and three-year notes is $5,000. The longer-term minimum is $1,000.

Bonds are long-term obligations, with maturities of ten to thirty years. Bonds may be purchased in multiples of $1,000. When buying direct, however, the minimum investment is $5,000. Brokers sell individual $1,000 bonds.

Treasury bills with 52-week maturities are offered on a more or less regular basis every four weeks. For an exact date, contact the nearest Federal Reserve bank. Notes and bonds are sold at various times. All new treasury offerings are announced four-to-six business days in advance. You will usually find sale dates in the business and financial section of your daily newspaper.

Since August 1, 1986, new issues of treasury bills, notes and bonds have been available in book-entry form only. Engraved certificates are no longer issued. Each time you buy a new issue, or one of your old treasuries comes due, you receive a computer-generated statement showing the status of your account.

To buy a security in person, you must submit a tender-offer form to the treasury or Fed bank or branch before the announced date of the offering. If buying by mail and you don't have a tender form, submit a letter with the following information:

- Type of security (bill, note or bond), maturity desired and amount of purchase.

- Your Treasury Direct account number. If you don't have a number, one will be assigned by the Fed on your first purchase.

- A statement that you are submitting a *non-competitive* bid.

- Your name, address, Social Security number and signature.

- Your full bank account name, number and type (checking or savings).

- The name and address of your bank and its nine-digit routing number. If you can't identify this number on one of your checks, ask your bank.

For T-bills, enclose a certified or cashier's check for the face value of your purchase. (The Fed will accept an uncertified personal check for notes and bonds.)

Security prices and yields (the return you'll receive on your principal) are determined at auctions participated in by large financial institutions. If you end up paying less than the face value of a note or bond, the treasury will refund the difference to your designated bank account.

T-bills are sold at a discount based on the rate of interest established as a result of the auction. This discount and your semi-annual interest payments on notes and bonds will also be deposited automatically into your bank account.

Interest on T-bills, notes and bonds is exempt from state and local income taxes, which makes them particularly appealing to residents of high-tax states and municipalities. Chart 19 shows how the daily listing of government bonds and notes looks in your local paper.

MUNICIPAL BONDS

Municipal bonds—*munis* in market parlance—are generally sound investments for high-bracket individuals seeking tax-free income. In fact, since the Tax Reform Act of 1986, they have been one of the few tax-exempt games left in town. Municipal bonds are issued by states, cities and local government agencies and rated for credit quality by Standard & Poor's or Moody's.

General obligation municipal bonds (GOBs) are considered very safe, because they are backed by the issuer's taxing authority. In contrast to general obligation municipal bonds, municipal *revenue bonds* are backed by a stream of revenue from a specific state or municipal project, such as a hospital, sewer district or transportation authority.

For those who want additional safety, insured municipal bonds are also available. Insured municipal bonds offer dual benefits, preserving capital and creating tax-free income, says Michael Applebaum, a vice-president at Shearson Lehman Hutton and a specialist in municipal bonds.

"Insured municipal bonds also have become unusually cheap," Applebaum points out. These bonds are insured against default by a number of independent insurance companies. For example, an A-rated municipality will buy insurance that allows its bond issue to be rated triple-A by a rating agency.

"With insured bonds, the individual investor can pick up some extra protection of principal and interest to go along with the fiscal credit-worthiness of a state or municipality without paying much for it," Applebaum notes.

CHART 19				

U.S. Government Bonds and Notes				
Listings in Your Daily Newspapers				

Name of U.S. Government Agency and the Issue					

Rate	*Maturity*	*Bid*	*Asked*	*Change*	*Yield %*
10.10	Date	110.8	110.22	+ .2	8.26

The listings in most newspapers include U.S. Treasury bonds and notes. Treasury bills are listed separately.

Other listings may include issues of the Federal Home Loan Bank, Federal Land, Student Loan Marketing Association (SallieMae), Federal Farm Credit, Inter-American Development Bank, Asian Development Bank, and the World Bank.

Decimals in "Rate," "Bid," "Asked," and "Change" are 32nds; "110 8/32 is $1,102.50.

"Rate" is yield of face amounts on insurance. "Bid" is price offered to buy: "Asked" is price offered to sell; "Change" is price change (either on bid prices or closing traded prices) between the prior day and this day. "Yield" is based on the current price to maturity. "Maturity" is redemption month ("10" is October).

"It's virtually an ideal risk versus reward situation, especially now that the price difference between lower-rated uninsured bonds and top-rated insured issues has narrowed."

The new situation stems from the Tax Reform Act of 1986, which curtailed the tax benefits of many bonds and restricted the ability of cities and states to issue tax-free revenue bonds. Before tax reform, institutions bought most municipals. But the tax changes made them unattractive to many banks because they could no longer take a deduction for interest expense incurred when they borrowed to buy the bonds. Most tax-exempt bonds are now bought by individual investors or by mutual funds and unit investment trusts that serve the individual.

"The price spread is no longer all that great between, say, an A-rated bond and a bond rated triple-A, because of the insurance premium," says Applebaum. "And insured triple-A municipals are now available with yields of one-tenth to one-twentieth of a percentage point below those of riskier uninsured revenue bonds rated A by Standard & Poor's."

Municipal bonds are increasingly popular with individual investors accumulating assets for retirement. The Federal Reserve says ownership by individuals increased to nearly 40 percent of all municipal bonds outstanding by 1987, compared to only 25 percent in 1980. The upward trend is expected to continue in the 1990s. "One reason you are on a municipal bond buying spree," says M. Kenneth Witover, senior vice-president of Shearson Lehman Hutton, "is that alternative tax-free investments and many tax-advantaged investments have been eliminated."

In the fast-paced investment environment of the 1980s, many innovative products were introduced in the municipal market which are appropriate for retirement accounts. Chart 20 shows how municipal bonds are displayed in your local paper. Here are some of the choices Witover, who is one of Wall Street's leading experts on municipal bonds, says you should be aware of:

- *Prerefunded municipal bonds.* Sometimes known as "tax-free government bonds," prerefunded bonds are backed by an escrow account. Often the escrow account is 100 percent invested in U.S. government securities which give the prerefunded bonds an AAA-rated credit quality. What's more, these tax-free bonds often offer yields as much as a quarter of a point higher than comparable bonds.

- *Premium municipal bonds.* These bonds offer attractive tax-free income because they were issued when rates were higher. In addition to high tax-free income, the high interest coupon provides a cushion against price movements.

- *Tax-free municipal zero-coupon bonds.* These bonds allow your tax-free interest income to be automatically reinvested at a stated rate until maturity. This reinvestment feature allows your investment to enjoy the powerful effect of compounding interest and relieves you of the responsibility of reinvesting your interest income payments.

- *Zero college bonds.* A new type of municipal zero-coupon bond introduced by several states in 1989, college zeros make an ideal gift for a grandchild. They are often available in smaller denominations of $500 to $1,000.

- *Convertible municipal zero coupon bonds.* This innovation in the municipal bond market is likely to become even more popular to finance retirement needs in the next century. Convertible municipal zeros act like a conventional municipal zero until they convert at a specified date to regular municipal bonds that pay tax-free interest semiannually until maturity.

	Coupon			YTM
Debt Issue	*%*	*Maturity*	*Price*	*%*
Municipality Authority Issue	8.000	11-15-Yr.	98⅞	8.10

CHART 20
Municipal Bonds
Listings In Your Newspapers*

"Debt Issue(s)" may include various types of municipal general obligation or revenues notes (shorter maturities) and bonds (longer maturities).

"Coupon %" is the coupon yield: the interest rate when the bond was issued. The "8.000" above is 8%, which was $80 on a $1,000 bond.

"Maturity" is the date on which the principal amount of the debt issue becomes due and payable. Also known as redemption date.

"Price" is the price at which the issue is currently trading in the market. For a $1,000 issue you have to multiply the price by 10; "98⅞" (98.875) would be $988.75.

"YTM" (Yield to Maturity) is the rate of return held to redemption including gain or loss from the current market price.

*Format of listings may vary in different newspapers. Most newspapers will carry these listings weekly instead of daily; and since there are so many issues, will only carry a representative number of issues. Some title the listings "Tax Exempt Bonds" instead of "Municipal Bonds."

Source: SPYF p. 127.

- *Put option municipal bonds.* These offer liquidity, flexibility and tax-free income, and are an excellent, higher yielding alternative to tax-free money market funds. Often their yields are more attractive than after-tax rates available on certificates of deposit (CDs). Typically available in maturities ranging from six months to five years, this tax-free investment allows you to "put" the bonds back to the issuer on a designated date at the same price you paid for them. Many investors buy put option municipal bonds so they can enjoy tax-free income until a future commitment, such as an April 15 tax payment, or until they can determine the direction of interest rates.

The risk of owning uninsured municipal bonds, especially revenue bonds, is that the issuer will default. Who doesn't remember the world-class default by the Washington Public Power Supply System? In general, it's wise to buy only municipal bonds with ratings of A or above. Another risk is that your bonds will be redeemed early. When interest rates drop, issuers often call their old bonds and issue new ones at lower rates. Many municipal bonds are also industrial development bonds backed by corporations rather than governmental agencies. If the company's financial structure weakens, the price of its bonds may drop. Other risks inherent in owning munis:

- Some *private-purpose* municipal bonds are subject to the Alternative Minimum Tax, and some Social Security beneficiaries must effectively pay a tax on them.

- Municipal bonds are less liquid than treasuries, and the market is more volatile. The best way to insure liquidity is to buy the bonds of well known cities or states.

- Small investors pay relatively high brokerage commissions on municipal bonds if they move in and out of the market.

- The minimum bond denomination typically is $5,000, and to be properly diversified you should own five or more different issues, experts say.

CORPORATE BONDS

The once-staid corporate bond market was shaken during the 1980s by takeovers in which investors saw the value of their holdings drop alarmingly. Most, or at least many, of these takeovers were financed with borrowed money—in other words, more bonds. It's not uncommon for an acquiring company to add billions of dollars in bond debt to complete an acquisition. In a few cases, the interest payments on this debt forced companies to the brink of bankruptcy. In other cases they led to reductions in credit ratings, undermining the market value of the company's bonds.

There are in fact two corporate bond markets—investment grade and junk or low grade. Investment-grade bonds are rated BBB − − or higher. Bonds rated BB + or lower are variously termed low grade, high yield or junk. If you are a conservative investor interested in corporate bonds, you may want to consider only investment-grade bonds issued by companies thought to be too large to be swallowed up, or bonds issued by utilities. The state regulatory agencies that control utility companies would almost certainly kill any proposal permitting a utility to issue huge amounts of debt to finance a takeover.

CHART 21								
Corporate Bond Market Listings In Your Daily Newspapers								

52 Weeks			*Curr.*					*Net*
High	*Low*	*Bond*	*Yld.*	*Vol.*	*High*	*Low*	*Close*	*Chg.*
103	98	Smith Corp. 14s 91	14	75	101	100¾	101	+¼

Newspaper listings report the prior day's bond transactions on the bond exchanges and over-the-counter.

Corporate bonds typically are issued in $1,000 denominations, so you have to multiply the interest rate and the market prices and price changes by 10. Thus, the "14s" of Smith Corp.'s bond is 14 percent, which would be $140 annual interest on the $1,000 face value. Smith's "91" bond matures in 1991.

The "High[est]" and "Low[est]" prices at which the bonds traded are shown for the "52 [preceding] Weeks" at left, and for the day at right. The "Close" is the final trade price (101 = $1,010).

"Net Chge." is the change in price if any between the previous day's close (not shown) and the listing day's close ("+¼" = up $2.50).

"Vol." (Volume) is the amount sold during the day ("75" − 75 $1,000 face value bonds).

"Cur. Yld." (Current Yield) "14" is approximately 14 percent on 101.

Source: SPYF p. 126.

Corporate bonds are fully taxable and many of them are subject to premature redemption. How the corporate bond listings appear in the daily paper is shown in Chart 21.

When considering corporate bonds as an investment, experts say you should observe the following rules:

- Limit your bond buying to those listed on an exchange. If you buy bonds that trade over-the-counter, you may have to pay your broker a huge *spread*—the difference between bid price and offer price. If a bond is listed on an exchange, you can learn the asking price in advance

- Give your broker a limit order. Specify the lowest price at which you'll sell or the highest price at which you'll buy.

- Read the offering prospectus. Find out when the bonds are subject to call.

- Concentrate on the issuer's creditworthiness and the bond's total yield or yield to maturity (more about yields later).

- Diversify. Do not invest more than 5 percent of your portfolio in any one issue. Balance riskier issues with safer ones. Diversify maturities.

ZERO-COUPON BONDS

Unlike conventional bonds, which pay out interest twice a year, zero-coupon bonds (also known as strips, because their interest-bearing coupons have been deleted) are sold at a deep discount to face value, and pay no interest to holders until they mature. For example, a zero with a face value of $10,000, maturing in ten years, may cost you less than $3,500, depending on its rate of interest when you buy. EE U.S. savings bonds were the original zero-coupon bonds, and the most favored zeros today are called treasury zeros. These are bonds packaged by brokerage houses and backed by treasury securities. Corporate and tax-exempt municipal zeros also are available in the market. Zeros are particularly useful for accumulating fixed amounts of money for future obligations such as college tuition, and are popular for tax-deferred retirement accounts such as IRAs and Keoghs. Many investors also like zeros because postponed interest helps them avoid using the money, assuring capital growth.

While you are not paid the interest accumulated by a zero-coupon bond until it matures, you are nevertheless required to pay taxes on the annual interest accumulation. But with your zeros in a tax-deferred retirement account, you delay tax payment to a time when you may be in a lower bracket.

The market price of zeros is more volatile than for coupon-bearing bonds, because of their interest-postponement feature. Hold them to maturity, if at all possible. Selling in a down market can be costly.

From the standpoint of the investor, bonds may be compared to dividend-paying stocks in two respects. First, they pay interest, just as blue-chip stocks pay dividends from company profits. Second, they fluctuate in market price, sometimes quite dramatically. For bonds, a bull market occurs when interest rates begin to fall, making your bonds worth more when you sell them. A bear market occurs when interest rates begin to rise and your bonds fall in price. The best time to buy bonds is prior to a recession, when interest rates decline due to a slackening in the demand for credit. The best time to sell is before inflation takes hold in the economy and interest rates soar because of greater demand for money.

BOND YIELDS

Bonds report several different types of yields. The *coupon* or *nominal* yield translates to *rate of interest*. A $1,000 bond with a nominal yield of 10 percent pays you $100 a year in interest—$50 every six months. Second is *current yield*, defined as the bond's current market price divided by its coupon yield (rate of interest). If the market value of your bond has fallen to $500, its current yield would be 20 percent ($100 in annual interest divided by $500). As a bond's price falls, its yield rises, and vice versa. If your $1,000 bond is selling at a premium (more than its face value), its current yield would be less than 10 percent. Assuming you purchased your bond in 1990, and it matures in the year 2000, you will receive its $1,000 face value at that time, no matter what the current market price. Thus, in 2000, your *yield-to-maturity* or *promised yield* is again 10 percent, while your *total return* is 100 percent ($100 a year for ten years). To put the various bond yields into perspective, let's take another example. Say you buy $10,000 worth of bonds paying 8 percent interest. Interest rates suddenly go up and the market value of your bonds drops to $8,000. Your current yield is now 10 percent, but you'll lose $2,000 if you sold, causing your total return to drop to minus 20 percent. Obviously, you should pay the most attention to your bonds' total yield or yield-to-maturity.

The values of short-term bonds and bond mutual funds tend to fluctuate less than long-term issues. If interest rates fall, however, short-term bonds don't offer the same capital gain opportunities as do their long-term counterparts. Many investors who expect interest rates to fall lock in high yields by extending the maturities of bonds they own directly and by buying long-term bond funds. They also shorten maturities when they expect rates to rise. You can anticipate interest rates to some degree by checking the average maturities of money market funds printed in the business and financial section of your daily newspaper. When money fund managers are reducing maturities, they believe interest rates are headed up. That's a clue to weight your bond portfolio short-term. When these managers are extending maturities, they expect interest rates to fall. If they are right, you can maximize interest and market price by extending maturities on your bonds or moving into a longer-term bond fund. You may also want to subscribe to a bond-timing newsletter. The Davis/Zweig Bond Fund Timer, P.O. Box 360, Bellmore, NY 11710, costs $79 a year. Paul Merriman's Fund Exchange, 1200 Westlake Avenue North, Seattle, WA 98109, costs $99.

Maximizers can also take advantage of the special feature that some bonds currently offer. For instance, some bonds pay rates of interest that increase with the profitability of the issuer, with an inflation index, or with an index calculated against short-term treasury rates. These variable-rate issues offer several advantages. First, they provide protection against inflation. Second, they offer the possibility of higher interest from profitable companies. Third, their prices are more stable in an environment of rising interest rates because their interest payments also rise.

Convertible corporate bonds and preferred stock—bonds and stocks that may be converted into the common stock of the issuing corporation—offer investors the chance to participate in price movements of the stock. A hybrid financial product, convertibles have fixed-income streams like bonds, but can appreciate with the underlying shares because they can be converted into common stock. Investors who like a company's common stock generally like its convertibles. Their coupon rate often is higher than the stock dividend, and convertibles usually increase in price as the common stock rises. But even if the stock does not appreciate, the investor is still left with a respectable coupon rate and capital gains potential. The downside to convertibles is that they tend to be issued by small companies with low credit ratings. Analyzing individual convertibles is difficult, investment experts say, so most investors should consider buying them through mutual funds. But shop the convertible mutual funds carefully. The returns they produce vary widely. Guard against individual convertibles that are junk-bond quality, but return only investment-grade yields. You should also realize that convertibles can be risky. If rising interest rates cause both the stock and bond markets to fall into the tank, convertibles may be hit with a double whammy.

INVESTING IN FOREIGN BONDS

Many internationally minded investors prefer foreign bonds issued by governments to those of corporations, and there is a wide range of foreign bonds from which to choose. Japan and West Germany traditionally pay lower interest rates on their bonds than the United States pays on treasuries, because their economies are regarded as stronger. The bonds of many other countries pay substantially higher rates than treasuries because of weaker economies. Yet, foreign bond investors tend to focus less on yields than on currency fluctuations and capital appreciation. For investors, diversification into foreign bonds reduces the impact of a downturn in the U.S. bond market. Another plus: some foreign government bonds pay very high yields with little credit risk. And when the dollar falls in relation to other currencies, your foreign bonds increase in value.

The principal danger of owning foreign bonds is that a rising dollar will depress their value and cancel out high-interest yields. Also foreign bonds are nearly impossible for individuals to research or to buy in manageable quantities. They are fully taxable in the United States, and foreign taxes may be levied as well. A way around some of these drawbacks is to buy shares in an internationally invested bond mutual fund.

BOND FUNDS

Bond funds offer a number of compelling advantages. Minimum investments are low. The funds are professionally managed and diversified. You can't buy part of a bond directly, but as an indirect investor you can buy part of an entire bond portfolio. For additional information on bond funds, see Chapter 9.

BOND PROXIES

Besides bonds, there are bond-like investments known as *bond proxies* or *substitutes*. Among these, *Ginnie Maes*, mortgage-backed securities issued by the Government National Mortgage Association (GNMA), are far and away the most prominent. Other federal agencies, including Fannie Mae and Freddie Mac, also issue mortgage-backed securities, and newer types include Collateralized Mortgage Obligations and Real Estate Mortgage Investment Conduits (REMICs).

Mortgage-backed securities are created by pooling large numbers of individual mortgages held by banks and other financial institutions. Each investor receives a share of all mortgage loans in the pool.

Since they are fully backed by the U.S. government, Ginnie Maes, Fannie Maes and Freddie Macs are very safe. You are virtually certain to be paid the interest promised and to get back your original principal. A disadvantage is that each monthly payment you receive is part interest and part principal. You must keep track of both, for tax purposes, and reinvest small sums each month to maintain the level of your investment principal. In addition, when interest rates are down and homeowners are refinancing their mortgages, your mortgage-backed securities may be returning large portions of principal, which you may have to reinvest at lower rates.

Unlike treasury securities, Ginnie Maes are fully taxable, with no exemption from state and local income taxes.

Industry insiders claim that real estate net leases, one of the lower-risk real estate investments, are *bond-type* deals. Investors own properties ranging from convenience stores to corporate skyscrapers. When a company takes a net lease on a property, it promises to pay all costs of upkeep, plus rent to the owner. Many net leases have automatic rent escalators tied to an inflation index. Others link rents to business volume, so that investors receive larger payouts when a tenant prospers. Net lease limited partnerships generally require minimum investments of only a few thousand dollars. When highly creditworthy tenants are involved, yields compare to those on treasury bonds, and there is a penalty discount for cashing in early.

BUILDING YOUR BOND PORTFOLIO

In balancing your bond portfolio, experts suggest that you select the issues considered least likely to default or swing widely in market value—savings bonds, regular treasuries, investment-grade corporates, investment-grade municipals and Ginnie Maes. Treasuries do better than corporates during economic hard times, because investors worry that companies won't be able to make their interest payments. Other types of bonds and bond substitutes—zeros, junk bonds, convertibles, international bonds and net leases—may add extra yield and diversification, lock in long-term rates, protect against inflation and offer the potential for appreciation. But most involve a bit more risk. If you are retired or nearing retirement, you may want to keep at least two-thirds of your portfolio in the higher-grade issues.

Most financial advisors also recommend diversification among long-, medium- and short-term bond issues. Many investors put half their holdings into bonds maturing in no more than three years, then go as long as necessary with the other half to get the highest yield. If interest rates fall, the yield you have locked in with long-term bonds will be even more valuable, and the market price of those bonds will climb. If rates go up, your long bonds will suffer, but you can liquidate your short-term holdings when they mature and cash in on rising rates. Other investors prefer a *laddering* portfolio structure. In a typical ladder, you invest 25 percent of your portfolio in bonds maturing in two years, 25 percent in four-year maturities, 25 percent in six-year maturities and 25 percent in eight-year maturities. After two years, when your shortest issues come due, you roll the proceeds into new eight-year bonds, maintaining the 2-4-6-8 structure of your portfolio. If interest rates have moved up in the interim, you'll get a higher yield on the new bonds. And, with a quarter of your portfolio always near maturity, you'll be able to cash in those bonds without taking a capital loss, no matter what happens to interest rates.

8

Stocks and Trends

PROTECT YOUR PURCHASING POWER

We already know that as a healthy American retiring today at sixty-two or sixty-five, you can expect to live another ten or twenty years or more. But what does that mean for your retirement planning and your investment portfolio after retiring? "It means above all that you must invest in stocks," many financial advisors say. If you don't, your assets will surely be eroded by inflation. Edward C. Hartman of Moraga, California, a director of the National Association of Personal Financial Advisors, the association of fee-only advisors, is one who believes strongly that equity investments are essential to protecting the purchasing power of your assets.

"When I analyze investment portfolios of new clients who are retired," says Hartman, "a typical recommendation is that they move sizeable sums from fixed-income investments such as CDs and corporate and municipal bond funds to equity-income investments such as equity and balanced no-load mutual funds." His clients first response is shock, says Hartman, "because I am asking them to take money out of investments paying 8 to 12 percent and put that money into investments paying 4.5 to 7.5 percent." But investors must sacrifice some current yield for future inflation protection, in Hartman's view.

As an inflation hedge, Hartman prefers dividend-paying stocks or equity income mutual funds over growth stocks or growth mutual funds. While dividends can go up or down, he points out, they are less volatile than market prices. He cites an example from Safeco Mutual Funds to make his point.

At a constant 5 percent rate of inflation, "annual income of $10,000 would need to grow to $43,219 in thirty years to be able to purchase the same amount of goods it does today. At this rate of inflation, in 30 years today's $1.00 loaf of bread will cost $4.32. And 5 percent inflation is not unrealistic. For the past thirty years the average annual rate of inflation has been 4.7

percent." Some forecasters see an average inflation rate of 4 percent over the next decade, which may turn out to be conservative.

A number of Wall Street experts have expressed views on retirement portfolios which are similar to Hartman's. Among them is the distinguished investment management firm of Neuberger & Berman, which says life expectancies and built-in inflation are causing investors to reevaluate conventional wisdom and include equity investments in their portfolios.

Shearson Lehman Hutton points out that the long-term trend has always been positive for stocks. "When viewed from a historical perspective, stocks have outperformed all other types of investments," the firm tells its clients. "If you are truly a long-term investor, you can bet that in the long run, every declining market will give way to a rising one and bring you to new heights of prosperity." (In this chapter we will show, through illustration, how to follow your stock purchases as displayed in the daily newspaper listings. Chart 22 "decodes" the symbols, and charts 23, 24 and 25 explain the daily listings.)

Safeco Mutual Funds reports that the dividend history of the common stocks included in the Standard & Poor's 500 Index provides an example of rising income through increasing dividends. The S&P 500 is an unmanaged index that tracks the performance of the common stocks of America's 500 largest corporations. Measured through 1987, "the income dividends paid by the S&P 500 stocks increased in 28 of the past 30 years. During this 30-year period the rate of inflation, as measured by the Consumer Price Index, increased a whopping 299 percent. But the increasing dividends from the S&P 500 stocks appreciated 403 percent. A managed portfolio should outperform the S&P 500, although it doesn't always do so.

RIDING THE AGE WAVE

Not long age, Wall Street stumbled across the "age wave," and Thomas Doerflinger, investment strategist at PaineWebber, has written a shrewd analysis of the phenomenon, "Riding the Age Wave to Stock Market Profits," in which he reports that the United States will be profoundly affected by three demographic trends during this decade. They are (1) an increasing life span, (2) declining fertility, and (3) the middle-aging of the baby boomers. Together the three trends are transforming the nation into an older, more mature society. During the 1990s, Doerflinger notes, the number of people aged forty-five to fifty-four will grow by 46 percent.

Doerflinger then proceeds to identify six age-wave generated investment themes for the decade:

CHART 22
Stock Exchange Listings in Your Daily Newspaper
[Explanation keyed to numbers in illustration below]

Most newspapers report the previous day's stock transactions on the New York Stock Exchange, the American Stock Exchange, and other exchanges.

1		2	3	4	5	6	7	8	9	10
52 Weeks				Yld.	P/E	Sales				Net
High	Low	Stock	Div.	%	Ratio	100s	High	Low	Close	Chg.
12	0	XYZ Inds	.55	5.5	10	200	10½	9¾	10	+⅛
30	26	XYZ pl	3.00	10	"	95	28	27	28	+⅝
6	2	XYZ wf	"	"	"	76	3⅛	3	3⅛	+⅛

1. The range of prices at which a stock has sold per share during the 52-week period to date.
   "High" is the highest price at which it sold, "Low" is the lowest.
2. An abbreviation of the name of the company. Securities listed are common stocks unless identified by "pf" for a preferred stock or "wf" for a warrant.
3. Total of the dividends paid per share during the period.
   For XYZ common stock, 55 cents per share.
4. "Yld. %" is the dividend percentage yield. The dividend per share as a percentage of the price of the stock per share.
   For XYZ common stock a 55-cent dividend on a $10 stock would be 5.5 percent.
5. "P/E Ratio" is the price of the stock per share divided by the earnings per share (EPS).
   For XYZ common, a price of $10 per share divided by EPS of $1 would be a 10 P/E ratio (also known as a P/E multiple).
6. "Sales 100s" indicates how many shares were traded during the day. (Multiply the listed amount by 100).
7. "High" is the highest price at which the stock was traded during the day.
   For XYZ common, 10½ is $10.50 per share.
8. "Low" is the lowest price at which the stock was traded during the day.
   For XYZ common, 9¾ is $9.75 per share.
9. "Close" is the last transaction price during the day.
   For XYZ common, 10 is $10.00 per share.
10. "Net chg." is the change in price per share between the close this day and the previous day.
    For XYZ common, the previous day's close was 9⅞ ($9.875); today's 10 close is a net change of " + ⅛" (up 12.5 cents) per share.

- Slower growth for housing.

- Increased savings. As the baby boomers move into middle age, they are likely to begin saving more, boosting the revenues of certain financial institutions while improving the country's anemic savings rate.

- Affluent older Americans will become an increasingly lucrative market. People over the age of sixty-five, and many over the age of fifty, have plenty of disposable income. They have been big winners from the economic trends of the 1980s, including skyrocketing home values in most parts of the United States.

- A rapid increase in the numbers of Americans over age seventy-five. This group will be bullish on health care.

- A baby boomlet in the 1990s. This will increase the demand for toys and children's clothes in the early part of the decade.

- An intensifying labor shortage, which will benefit technology firms throughout the decade.

"A sound and sensible way for individual investors to take advantage of the age wave is to buy the shares of high-quality companies whose businesses will benefit from the graying of America," Doerflinger declares, "companies that have both a consistent record of success and shares that are attractively valued in the stock market."

AGE WAVE WILL HELP SOME COMPANIES

Based on Doerflinger's reasoning, analysts at PaineWebber have identified sixteen companies they think will benefit handsomely from age-wave trends. Not all are rated "buy" or even "attractive" by the firm at any given time, but long-term all are considered well positioned to take advantage of demographic trends. The sixteen companies include:

- Florida Progress, parent of Florida Power, which supplies energy to western and central Florida. The U.S. Census Bureau predicts that Florida, already the fourth-largest state in population, will grow by 31.5 percent during the 1990s.

- TECO Energy, a holding company whose largest subsidiary is Tampa Electric.

- Sun Trust Banks. PaineWebber says this bank is well managed, ultra-conservative, with strong capitalization and excess reserves.

- First Union Corporation, headquartered in Charlotte, North Carolina—"a conservatively managed super-regional bank."

CHART 23							
Over-The-Counter-Market Listings in Your Daily Newspapers							
52 Weeks			*Sales*				*Net*
High	*Low*	*Stock*	*100s*	*High*	*Low*	*Last*	*Chg.*
24	17	Green Mfg. Co	30	19¼	18½	18½	+ ⅛

- Over-the-counter market stock listings are similar to NYSE and other exchange listings.
- Over-the-counter listings indicate daily and yearly highs and lows, closing price (Last) and net change in price.
- Dividends, yields and P/E ratio are not listed.
- Some OTC stocks are traded by NASDAQ, the electronic quotation system of the National Association of Securities Dealers.

- Barnett Banks—"one of the banking industry's most consistent growth machines." Most of its 543 offices are located in Florida.

- AT&T, which is becoming a "high-growth, high-tech company" with an ideal strategic position in its industry.

- Toys "R" Us, which will benefit from the 1990s baby boomlet and from its aggressive automation program.

- Stryker Corporation, which makes medical and surgical products. PaineWebber says Stryker is a small, high-quality growth company with strong earnings consistency and low debt.

- U.S. Surgical, which focuses on wound-closure products and dominates the market in which it competes.

- Medtronic Corporation, a worldwide market leader in heart pacemakers. "With 80 percent of pacemakers being sold to people aged 65 and older, it is a clear beneficiary of increasing longevity," says PaineWebber.

- Merck. As "the biggest and one of the very best pharmaceutical companies in the world, Merck will benefit from the aging of America because several of its most important drugs serve older patients."

- Walt Disney Corporation. According to PaineWebber, "Disney has learned to ride the age wave by producing both movies and 'live' experiences that appeal to an aging population."

- Delta Airlines and AMR Corporation. Observes PaineWebber: "Both seniors and aging baby boomers have plenty of time and money to spend on air travel."

- A. G. Edwards, a tightly managed retail brokerage firm that has offices in forty-six states. Edwards is likely to benefit from baby boomers' savings for retirement and their children's education.

NEW EMPHASIS ON GROWTH INDUSTRIES

Several of the companies PaineWebber thinks will benefit from the age wave also are among those the firm predicts will be helped in the 1990s by a return to emphasis on growth—rather than corporate restructuring—as the stock market's primary investment theme. Which companies are likely to experience quality growth? To provide a partial answer to the question, PaineWebber identified nine industries that—judging from such fundamental economic forces as technological change, demographic trends, Europe 1992, the emergence of a tougher U.S. trade policy, rising living standards in Asia, the U.S. labor shortage, and reforms in the communist world—should grow rapidly in the 1990s.

These industries are: (1) business information; (2) telecommunications; (3) beverages; (4) food; (5) entertainment; (6) specialty retailers; (7) drugs; (8) biotechnology; and (9) pollution control. The PaineWebber analyst covering each of the nine growth industries then was asked to pick the *one* company he or she thinks has the highest probability of growing rapidly through the year 1996.

The analysts' selections:

- *Business information*: Dun & Bradstreet. "D&B is assembling the pieces to be the leader in 'single-source marketing,' " says the firm. "D&B is also well positioned to be the leader in dispensing credit information to the newly integrated European market."

- *Telecommunications*: AT&T. The company's technological excellence, combined with a tougher U.S. stance on trade, will create major overseas opportunities in the 1990s. AT&T has already engaged in a joint venture with Italatel to rebuild the Italian telephone network—a $30 billion project lasting five years. It has also signed a contract to produce equipment for the Chinese market.

- *Beverages*: Coca-Cola. Consumers here and abroad seem to have an insatiable appetite for drinks that are cold, sweet, fizzy and non-alcoholic. And the most widely accepted flavor is cola. In the view of PaineWebber analyst Manny Goldman, Coca-Cola is better positioned than just about any other U.S. consumer firm to benefit from rising living standards abroad.

- *Food*: Kellogg. In the opinion of PaineWebber's Roger Spencer, Kellogg is the best "pure" packaged food company worldwide and is set to grow at a 14 percent pace in the 1990s. Kellogg dominates the U.S. ready-to-eat cereal business with a 41.4 percent market share, and its share is even larger overseas. Kellogg's fast growth is accompanied by high profitability.

- *Entertainment*: Walt Disney Corporation. America's second biggest export industry, entertainment is one of the few businesses in which the United States still has a very powerful global position. Deregulation of television networks in Europe tends to boost demand for American-made programs. Disney is expanding aggressively its theme park division and beefing up its invaluable film library. It also has a proven ability to succeed in foreign markets, and to appeal to older Americans.

- *Growth retailers*: Toys "R" Us. PaineWebber's Margo McGlade believes this firm is one of the best positioned growth retailers for the 1990s. She assigns an 18 percent secular growth rate to the company, with 20 percent annual growth until 1995, and 15 percent for at least the five years thereafter.

- *Drugs*: Merck. Merck's CEO, Dr. Roy Vagelos, one of the world's leading enzyme chemists, believes that Merck can use enzyme inhibition technology to treat maladies in every major organ system. The company has a stable of high-growth drugs that will not come off patent for some years, and leadership in enzyme chemistry may produce more big winners in the next few years. Analyst Ron Nordmann believes Merck will grow at a 25 percent pace through the mid-1990s.

- *Biotechnology*: Amgen/Chiron/Genentech. Analyst Linda Miller says that "based on accelerating strong company fundamentals and a woeful stock performance history, there has never been a better time to invest in biotechnology." The research pipeline is filled with new products which will come to market in the next several years, she adds.

- *Pollution control*: Browning-Ferris. Not unlike the drug industry, pollution control appears to have excellent growth potential, while most newcomers are effectively barred by heavy federal regulation and very high entry costs. Browning-Ferris is steadily gaining market share. The strong trend toward recycling also is bullish for the company. Analyst Bob Miner expects Browning-Ferris to grow at a rate of 15 to 20 percent over the next decade.

Certainly the one thing that Americans produce in abundance and with ease is garbage. Think how often you make a trip to the garbage can, then wonder where it all goes. When it became apparent that the traditional city dump and landfill programs could never handle the mega-tonnage, American ingenuity came into play with the formation of waste-disposal companies. Over the past twenty years or so some of these companies have grown into strong, well managed entities with excellent growth potential.

Waste Management, Inc., the nation's largest waste-disposal concern, has traditionally been among the most favored pollution control stocks on Wall Street. Because of its management, stability and steady earnings growth, many analysts also regard the company as a solid candidate for a retirement portfolio. In addition to Waste Management and Browning-Ferris, other pollution control companies which have enjoyed favor in various quarters on Wall Street include Chambers Development, Inc., which has twenty-five years of landfill capacity (more than any of its competitors); Wellman, Inc., strong in plastics recycling; Safety-Kleen; and All Waste, a leader in petrochemical tank cleaning.

PHARMACEUTICALS REGARDED AS GOOD BET

The wave that rolls toward an older American population is a principal reason pharmaceutical stocks have been in considerable favor on Wall Street. Richard V. Ietor, industry analyst at Merrill Lynch, says he is "generally disposed toward most pharmaceutical companies." The industry is well capitalized and has a reliable earnings history which is not subject to most fluctuations in the economy. One exception is a strong dollar, which drives down profits from overseas sales of drug products.

"This is an industry that spends 12 to 18 percent of its revenues on research," Ietor points out, "and there is a need for many new medications, particularly new medications to deal with chronic diseases which attack the growing population of older Americans."

On the horizon, however, are a couple of potentially dampening effects, Ietor says. One is the fact that pharmaceutical companies have been raising drug prices faster than the rate of inflation for nearly a decade. The other is that third-party drug payments are growing. Both factors intensify pressures to hold prices down by government agencies and private healthcare providers.

Herman Saftlas, industry analyst at Standard & Poor's, says expensive new drug products with new therapeutic qualities tend to lead overall prices higher each year. When a new product hits the market, it is almost invariably priced higher than the product it replaced, causing the drug-price spiral to continue. Like Ietor at Merrill Lynch, among other analysts, Saftlas likes the pharmaceutical group "as a whole." Among major companies in the industry group, in addition to Merck, are Eli Lilly, Bristol Myers, Abbott Laboratories, Upjohn, Marion Laboratories, Squibb, American Home Products, Forest Laboratories, Glaxo Holdings, Shearing Plough, Wellcome, and A. H. Robbins.

ENTERTAINMENT

Investing in entertainment stocks has often been a gamble, with fortunes made, and lost, at the box office. But what was once "show business" has become the "entertainment industry," and the key word—diversification—took on new meaning with the merger of Warner Communications and Time, Inc. Andrew M. Wallach, one of Wall Street's leading media analysts, thinks "all broad-based investment accounts" will be attracted to Time Warner shares. Looking at the filmed entertainment industry as a whole, Wallach expects a substantial rebound in profitability in the early 1990s. Share values in the industry will be helped by a number of factors, including:

- Heightened investor appreciation of entertainment asset values in the wake of the Time Warner deal.

- Strong and improving fundamentals among the filmed entertainment companies.

- A decreasing supply of available entertainment assets in the public and private markets.

Many people retiring today, and many more who retired earlier, have vivid memories of the Great Depression of the 1930s. Some indeed still have nightmares about those terrible times. When such fears are reinforced by today's atmosphere of economic uncertainty (a condition heightened by interludes of outright gloom and doom) it is only natural for investors to look for protection among recession-resistant stocks. Foods, pharmaceuticals and entertainment are three we have already discussed. Utilities is another.

UTILITIES SHINE IN RECESSION

What makes many utilities shine in a recessionary environment? Edward J. Tirello, Jr. of Shearson Lehman Hutton, Inc. says, "This is a semi-monopoly industry—the best utility stocks are like bonds with an increasing coupon." The problem of course is to identify "the best," and for that you should seek help from your broker. A slow rate of economic growth (1 to 2.5 percent), low interest rates and a low inflation rate are among the factors that normally favor utility stocks and fixed-income investments such as bonds. Conservative and retired investors often favor utility stocks because many pay consistent dividends through good times and bad. One caution: be careful about those which have a heavy commitment to nuclear generation.

STOCKS CAN ENHANCE YOUR FUTURE

There are many ways in which you can invest your money, and stocks are riskier than some of the others. But buying stocks in a carefully researched and restrained investment program is surely one of the best ways to enhance your financial future. It's never too late to begin, and you don't need thousands of dollars. Nor do you have to be a financial wizard. A suitable stock investment program can be devised for every budget and every level of risk tolerance. The objective is to use the resources you can afford to risk to achieve your financial goals.

Option	Close	Strike Price	Calls-Last			Puts-Last		
			Jan.	Apr.	Jul.	Jan.	Apr.	Jul.
ABC Corp	20⅜	20	¼	1¾	2½	¹⁄₁₆	⅞	1⅛
ABC Corp	20⅜	25	1¹⁄₁₆	⁵⁄₁₆	⅝	¹⁄₁₀	4½	4¾

CHART 24
Stock Options Listings in Your Daily Newspaper

- "Option" is the name of the stock.
- "Close" is the current price of the stock.
- "Strike Price" is the option exercise price.
- "Last" for "Calls" and "Puts" are the closing trade prices of the options for the day.
- Option contract expirations occur on the third Saturday of each month shown in listings.
- An option gives you the right to buy (call) or sell (put) a stock at a specific price (the strike price) before a specified time (expiration date).
- The cost of an option (the premium) varies; it generally can run from as high as 15 percent of the quoted price of the stock down to 2 percent.

Trading options can be risky.

When you buy a share of common stock you become the owner of a small portion of a corporation. You and all the other shareholders, or stockholders, own the company in common, thus the term *common stock*. Stock owners are entitled to participate in running the company. For every share you own, you may cast one vote for each candidate for the company's board of directors, speak your mind about management's conduct of company business at annual shareholder meetings, and vote on corporate issues that by law require stockholder approval.

The two ways to make money in stocks are through an increase in the market price of each share, known as appreciation, and through dividends paid to you from the company's profits. If a company prospers and grows, the value of its stock is likely to appreciate substantially over the long-term, even though its market price day-to-day may fluctuate. As noted at the beginning of this chapter, a major advantage that stocks have over bonds and other so-called fixed-income investments is that, through appreciation, they offer a way of beating inflation and the consequent loss of purchasing power. The stocks of some of the best companies appreciate in value while also paying handsome annual or quarterly dividends. Chart 25 sets out the dividend listings as displayed in your daily paper.

INVESTING TAKES WORK, PATIENCE

Investing isn't easy work, and it's not likely to make you rich overnight. Success as an investor takes time, knowledge and patience. Here are some rules that will help:

- Determine the basic objective of your stock investment program, and devise a master plan, preferably with the help of a professional financial advisor.

- Know yourself. Decide what kind of investor you really are. Are you suited to taking risks, or would you rather play it safe?

- Don't invest money in stocks that you may soon need for some other important purpose.

- Don't hesitate to invest small amounts of money. In time, these small amounts will add up to a fat portfolio.

- Be impersonal. A share of stock is not a person who applauds your wise decisions or criticizes your mistakes.

- Keep up with developments in the stock market and the economy. Read a number of financial journals and the business section of your daily newspaper.

- Review the share price and operating performance of the companies you own regularly.

- Learn from past mistakes. Most investors remember their successes and forget their mistakes, but you can often learn more from your pattern of mistakes than from success.

Quality—financial strength, profitability and growth potential—is the key to any investment. A quick way to check a company's quality for yourself is to consult the ratings provided by Standard & Poor's, Moody's, Value Line, and other financial services. These services rate corporations on earnings performance and dividend history as well as growth potential. The top S&P rating is A +. The lowest is C. Unless you can afford to speculate, stick with A-rated companies. Also study the analytical reports on companies that financial services offer.

CHART 25				
Dividend Listings in Your Daily Newspaper				
Company	Period	Dividends Reported Amt.	Payable Date	Record Date
ABC Corp	Q	.50	5-1	3-31

- Q is quarterly. Dividends are paid annually or semi-annually. Others are paid irregularly or are special dividends.
- Amt. is the amount paid per share. In this case, .50
- Stockholders as of the Record Date (3-31 = March 31st), will be paid the dividend as of the Payable date (5-1 = May 1st)
- The stocks sells ex-dividend. That is its price is reduced by the amount of the dividend, which is not paid to new stockholders after the record date.
- Listings may also indicate:
  - if current dividends are an increase or a reduction from previous dividends,
  - if they are initial dividends
  - or if dividend is payable in stock.
  - Dividend omissions may also be shown in the listing.

DETERMINING A STOCK'S VALUE

Second only to quality in determining whether or not to invest in a company is the value its stock represents. Value is determined in a number of ways:

- *Earnings per share.* Earnings per share is a fundamental analytical tool because it reduces a company's total financial performance to one number. Earnings per share is calculated by dividing a company's annual net income (income after expenses and taxes) by the number of common shares outstanding. If you can find a company whose earnings per share have increased 10 to 20 percent for five successive years or more, you may have discovered a winner.

- *Book value.* Book value, also known as net worth, is the amount of money each share would represent if the company sold all its assets, paid its debts, and closed its doors. Book value is thus calculated by subtracting debt from the dollar value of assets and dividing the resulting sum by the number of shares outstanding. In evaluating a stock, however, you cannot rely on book value (or any other value) alone. The stocks of growing, successful companies nearly always sell at prices above book value. Asset value can be distorted by plant and equipment that is underutilized or nearing obsolescence. If, on the other hand, the company's stock is selling at a discount to book (less than book), and its asset value is real, the company may be an attractive takeover candidate.

- *Price-to-earnings ratio.* To calculate the price-to-earnings ratio of a company, divide its current stock price by its earnings per share for the past twelve months. A price-to-earnings ratio of twenty tells you that investors are paying twenty times earnings to purchase shares of the stock. To get a true picture of the significance of a company's current price-to-earnings ratio, find out whether it is higher or lower than it was during the past three to seven years. Check also whether it is higher or lower than the price/earnings ratios of other companies in the same industry. If lower, the company's stock may be undervalued. One of the ways to make money in the market is to buy a quality stock when it is undervalued and sell when other investors catch on to the fact, begin buying and cause the price to rise. Some Wall Street analysts devote their professional lives to finding these so-called special situation stock ideas. Says James P. Ruf, special situation analyst at Wertheim Schroder & Company: "Very simply, what I attempt to do is to identify companies where the profitability characteristics are higher, and the valuations are lower, than the market." Typically, Ruf adds, the companies show a return on equity and capital superior to the market, an above-average capability to generate cash flow, a higher-than-market reinvestment rate (rate of return on equity times the earnings retention rate), and implied or theoretical total return above the market, and valuation levels (price/earning, price/cash flow, and price/book value ratios) lower than the market on an absolute and/or relative basis. "Implicit in our strategy is the assumption that, if we are successful in identifying companies with these characteristics, and if indeed the above-average investment returns are sustainable, then sooner or later the market will pay for them. Or, if the market does not, then perhaps somebody else will."

- *Debt to Equity Ratio.* Does the company have a debt-to-equity ratio (liabilities divided by net value) of at least 5 to 1, and total debt that does not exceed 40 percent of capitalization—the total value of its assets?

- *Dividend record.* Has the company paid dividends for at least five consecutive years?

- *Working capital.* Does the company have sufficient cash or other liquid assets to sustain both day-to-day operations and vigorous growth? Working capital is calculated by subtracting current liabilities by current assets.

- *Net profit margin.* Usually expressed as a percentage of sales, net profit margin is the amount left over after operating costs, interest on debt, and taxes have been paid. Analysts say a company's profit margin is being *squeezed* when operating costs are rising faster than earnings. Smart investors go for companies whose sales and profit margins are both expanding.

Timing—both market timing and corporate or industry timing—is the third key to making money in stocks, after quality and value. It is also the trickiest, often involving a great deal of intuition and guesswork. For example, relatively few investors foresaw the October 1987 market crash, or even the much milder 1989 downturn. To be even moderately successful at timing requires sophisticated research, an acute awareness of market trends, and knowledge of fluctuations in the domestic economy as well as the economies of foreign nations. One general rule to keep in mind, however, is this: when interest rates rise, stock prices fall, and when rates fall, stock prices usually go up. The goal of the market timer is to buy when the market is at or near a cyclical low and sell at or near a cyclical high.

Industry timing takes advantage of the fact that the stock prices of certain industry groups rise and fall with the overall economy. In a booming economy, construction and home building, automobiles and trucks, clothing, textiles, airlines, agricultural equipment, heavy machinery, rubber, and leisure time generally flourish. In a recessionary or slow-growth economy, they often falter. For investors who buy only quality stocks, market timing is less important than it is for those who buy more speculative issues. Quality players can simply ride out recessionary periods in the secure if not certain knowledge that, over time, the market will recover and rise beyond its previous peaks. Meanwhile, they own dividend-paying shares in companies that are financially strong and will continue to grow even through recessionary economic cycles. For a guide to the indicators to buying and selling stock, see Chart 26.

BUYING OPPORTUNITIES AHEAD

What will the stock market do in the 1990s? No one knows for sure, but PaineWebber has forecast a 5,000 Dow Jones Industrial Average by 1995. Mary C. Farrell, a member of the firm's investment strategy team, says the early years of the decade could "provide the good buying opportunities to position yourself for what we think will be a continuation of the bull market which began in 1982." Global developments lend support to the thesis of a roaring stock market, Farrell argues.

"Glasnost is a big factor. The Russians are having to make real inroads to improve their economy, which is a disaster. To the extent that they reduce their defense spending, we can too, and that helps us bring our deficit down. Europe 1992 should really unleash some good growth in Europe, which will likely have a reasonably strong impact on us. And the Pacific Basin continues to grow very well."

While acknowledging the existence of severe economic and social problems in some parts of the world, Farrell believes that world-wide political and economic environments "have never looked better." At the same time, the savings rate in the United States has started to move up because the baby boomers are headed into early middle age.

"Traditionally," she says, "people save more in the 40s. They have already formed households, bought all the stuff for the kids, bought their durable goods, and now it's just savings. As the baby boomers become savers rather than borrowers, it should help bring U.S. interest rates down." Moreover, she adds, the huge mountain of baby boomer savings will flow into financial assets, helping to boost stock prices.

"The 1990s could very well be a period like the 1950s—very moderate economic growth, inflation under control, moderate earnings growth, but a fabulous period for the Dow."

GET PROFESSIONAL INVESTMENT ADVICE

As we have said before, and will say again, investing your money without professional advice by someone you know and trust is a dangerous game.

CHART 26
Guide to Technical and Other Timing
Indicators to Buy or Sell Stocks

Even if you're skeptical of the value of technical indicators, don't ignore them—they can be self-fulfilling.

Transactions of investors who do follow them can affect securities prices up or down. Also, you might use indicators to corroborate or question your intended moves based upon fundamental analysis.

Capsulized in this report are the major indicators used by media—print to electronic—in coverage and discussion of the financial markets.

Indicators to the Stock Market

- **ADVANCE/DECLINE (market breadth)**
Indexes showing number of stocks up (bullish) vs. number down (bearish).
- **BUYING POWER (potential demand)**
Changes in cash and cash equivalents (such as Treasury securities), available to buy stocks—in customers' accounts, accounts at brokerage firms and in equity mutual funds.
- **CONFIDENCE INDEX**
Confident outlook for the stock market when lower-grade bonds are up. Lack of confidence when investors stick to high-grade bonds.
- **DIVERGENCE**
Change in market direction or movement of types of stocks when "secondary" stocks (smaller companies and more speculative stocks) move *opposite* of continuous new highs or lows of dominant blue-chip stocks.
- **DOW THEORIES**
Market direction is indicated when the Dow Jones averages terminate *above or below* where they have penetrated prior highs or lows.
- **HIGH/LOW DIFFERENTIAL**
Increasing or decreasing spread in number of stocks hitting new highs vs. number setting new lows.
- **PRICE/EARNINGS RATIO (stock price divided by earnings per share).**
Bullish when p/e for stock averages or indexes is well below the long-term p/e average.
Bearish when well above.
- **RESISTANCE AND SUPPORT LEVELS**
It's bullish for stock averages or indexes trading within a narrow price range for a long time to "pierce" (rise above) the "resistance" level (top of this range).
It's bearish to "violate" (drop below) the "support" level (bottom price of this range).
- **YIELDS**
High or low on stock averages or indexes compared to previous may signal changes in stock and bond prices.
(Or yield spread or gap between stock dividend yields and bond interest yields.)

Source: SPARN 2/90.

This is particularly true when investing in common stocks, which are buffeted by so many different, often poorly understood, economic forces.

Consider the unfortunate case of Tom T. Forced into early retirement by a corporate reorganization, Tom suddenly found himself out in the cold with only $200,000 in savings and future Social Security benefits to last the rest of his life. He knew that, given the lifestyle he enjoyed, he would run out of money in five years, ten if he pinched pennies and sponged off his children. Tom thought about his situation for some time and finally came up with a bright and shining idea. "I'm as smart as anybody," he said to himself. "I'll take my $200,000 and run it into a million or two by trading stocks and options in the market." Within six weeks Tom had to borrow bus fare from his son. He was flat broke, a victim of what the Greeks call *hubris*— arrogant pride—and what some other folks call plain stupidity.

MISTAKES TO AVOID

Investors, including professionals, make a great many mistakes buying and selling stocks. Mistakes go with being a player. "When you think you made every mistake," says one portfolio manager, "a new one proves you wrong again." But there are other, worse mistakes you can make. Professor Leimberg, a crusader for personal financial management, has compiled a list of ten that you would do well to consider:

Mistake 1. You don't know where to begin investing—so you don't.

Solution: Just *do it*, realizing that if you don't you may never attain financial security.

Mistake 2. You have a dream rather than a goal.

Solution: You must write down definite monetary objectives using specific and reasonable assumptions. The key is to start now! Starting early cuts down the annual amount you need to invest in order to meet your goal and gives you more time to correct any mistakes.

Mistake 3. You are afraid to take risks—so you risk it all!

Solution: No risk, no reward. Doing nothing is the greatest risk of all. What else threatens your success—inflation, high interest rates, economic downturn? The solution is diversification—divide your assets among a variety of investments.

Mistake 4. You want it all—at no cost—in ten minutes.
Solution: Invest for the long haul. Says Professor Leimberg: "You can lose money fast in the stock market but it's hard to make it fast."

Mistake 5. You haven't protected your assets.
Solution: Never move on to the next plateau of risk until you've adequately protected the assets and income you already have. Make sure you have adequate amounts of life and health insurance, disability protection, car and home insurance, business interruption and an "umbrella policy" to cover the catastrophic level of loss. Make sure you have the proper balance of liquidity.

Mistake 6. You're not willing to stay on a financial diet.
Solution: Put a fixed amount or a fixed percentage of your income aside for savings and investing before you pay other bills. Capitalize on the miracle of the "forgotten" automatic investment. Increasing the rate of investment is as important as increasing the rate of return on an investment.

Mistake 7. You lose sight of the bottom line.
Solution: Only the money you get to keep—after both investment expenses and taxes—is there to invest or to provide you with current financial security. How much does this investment cost compared with other investments you could be making? Are you paying too much in income taxes on your investments? When you die, will your family pay too much in death taxes and other settlement costs before getting the use of your financial assets?

Mistake 8. You're willing to repeat the mistakes of the past.
Solution: Get rid of credit cards you don't use—especially if you have to pay an annual fee. Break the "plastic addiction." Cut down on your consumer interest expenses.

Mistake 9. You throw up your hands when you see what it takes.
Solution: People "play" the market. They haven't figured out

that investing takes work and careful thought. Work your investments with the same thought and care you'd give to building a
lifeboat—because nobody (but you) will be there to rescue you
financially when your ship hits a reef. Investing takes patience,
conviction and courage.

Mistake 10. You want someone else to make you rich.

Solution: Mental laziness is a major reason most people don't
become wealthy. They buy stocks, bonds, real estate and other
investments on a tip from their golf partner or hair dresser. In
other words, they buy blindly without knowing why they are buying the investment or what it is supposed to do for them. The best
investment, bar none, is self-education. With the help of competent
financial planning professionals, you should annually measure
your needs, establish a priority of needs, give first preference to
those goals most important to you, and develop a work plan to
make certain that you're on target to meet your financial independence objectives. And remember that the finest plan is worthless until it is put into place.

DO YOUR HOMEWORK

We've said much about doing your homework on the companies whose
stocks you may want to buy, and about keeping abreast of developments in
the marketplace and the economy. Whether you're a novice or a seasoned
investor, however, you will make more money and fewer mistakes in the
long run if you have a depth of knowledge about investing that you can
gain only by reading some of the classic books in the field. Following is a
recommended reading list that some of the country's smartest investors
swear by:

Security Analysis (McGraw-Hill, 4th edition, 1962), by Benjamin
Graham and David L. Dodd. This book has remained in print for
more than 50 years and many professional investors regard it as
the bible of security analysis. Graham, who died several years ago,
taught finance at Columbia University. Investors Warren Buffett,
Walter Schloss and William Ruane were among Graham's students
who became legends in their own time.

The Intelligent Investor (Harper & Row, revised, 1965), also by Graham. For the average investor, this is a more accessible distillation of the master's wisdom. The message of both books: smart investors pay 50 cents to buy corporate assets worth a dollar.

The Battle for Investment Survival (Simon & Schuster, revised, 1965), by Gerald M. Loeb. Loeb's book offers a lucid discussion of investment timing, financial reports, and selling—and the pitfalls that investors encounter at every turn.

How to Buy Stocks (Bantam, sixth edition, 1977), by Louis Engle, a former executive of Merrill Lynch. Among many other matters, Engle offers suggestions for judging investment advisors.

Common Stocks and Uncommon Profits (Harper & Row, revised, 1959), by Philip A. Fisher. A classic text by one of the prophets of patient, long-term investing.

Conservative Investors Sleep Well (Harper & Row, 1975), also by Philip A. Fisher, who spent years managing money for wealthy clients.

Super Stocks (Dow Jones-Irwin, 1984), by Ken Fisher, son of Philip. This book explains the benefits of exploring out-of-favor stocks on the basis of their price-sales ratios.

The Money Masters (Harper & Row, 1980), by John Train. Profiles of Philip Fisher, Warren Buffett, T. Rowe Price, John Templeton, Benjamin Graham and other wizards of investment.

Street Smart Investing (Random House, 1983), by George B. Clairmont and Kiril Sokoloff. A readable introduction to basic analytical tools, including book value, working capital, price/earnings ratios, return on equity, and cash flow.

Heads You Win, Tails You Win (Stein & Day, 1979), by Ray Dirks. An excellent beginner's book on conservative stock investing, *Heads You Win* can help almost any investor find bargains in down markets.

9

Mutual Funds

BUILT-IN SAFETY

A mutual fund is an investment company—a company that makes investments on behalf of individuals and institutions who share common financial goals. The first funds were created for investors of moderate means, and they have prospered as one of the small investor's best options. Because of their built-in safety feature—diversification—mutual funds are widely recommended for nearly all investors, and certainly for those who are building a retirement nest egg or who depend in part on their investments for retirement income. The kind of mutual fund you select for your retirement savings will depend on your age, financial resources and tolerance for risk.

Particularly in today's volatile financial marketplace, mutual funds offer investors a generally safer, simpler, more convenient, less expensive and less time-consuming method of investing in a portfolio of securities such as stocks and bonds than trading them individually. (See Chart 27 for types of mutual funds.)

HOW MUTUAL FUNDS WORK

The funds pool your money with that of other shareholders who have similar investment objectives. Professional money managers then use the pool to buy a wide range of stocks, bonds, or money market instruments that, in the manager's judgment, will help you achieve your objectives. There are funds designed for income, aggressive growth, capital appreciation, and tax advantages. The securities owned by the mutual fund comprise its underlying portfolio. The fund earns money on those securities and distributes the earnings to its shareholders as dividends or, if the securities are sold for a profit, as capital gains. Typically, investors may elect to have their

CHART 27
Types of Mutual Funds*

Money Market	Bonds	Bonds and Stocks	Diversified Common Stocks	Specialty
• General • Prime rate • Foreign currency • General tax-exempt • State tax-exempt	• U.S. government securities • Ginnie Mae • Various types of mortgage-backed securities • Various types of other asset-backed securities • Municipals (some funds specialize by quality or by term) • Corporate (some funds specialize by quality or term)	• Balanced (commons, preferreds, bonds) • Convertible bonds and preferreds	• Primarily higher income • Primarily income plus some growth • More for growth plus medium income • Primarily growth • Aggressive appreciation	• All-purpose ("all-weather" asset managing) • Market timing • Sectors (single industry or related industries) • Geographical (U.S. sectors, U.S. and foreign securities ["global"], foreign only ["international"], individual foreign countries)

- Small companies
- Over-the-counter (OTC)
- Low-priced
- Option (income or growth)
- Exchange
- Social conscience
- Index
- Hedge

- Zero coupon (government and/or corporate)
- Convertibles (and bond-warrant units)

Classifications include both open-end and closed-end mutual funds. *Objectives, investment strategies and tactics, and risks* will vary among individual funds within the types.

In addition to bonds, some *bond funds* also invest in bills, notes, debentures and other debt securities. Many *common stock funds* also include small holdings of bonds, preferred stocks and "units" (which may comprise warrants attached to bonds). Portfolios of *diversified common stock funds* also may include small holdings of bonds, preferred stocks and units. Holdings of *specialty funds* are primarily in common stocks (or issues related to stocks, as in the case of option funds).

Source: SPYF p. 170.

dividends and capital gains automatically reinvested in the purchase of additional shares.

As a mutual fund investor, you buy shares of the mutual fund itself, but each fund share represents ownership in all its underlying securities. Dividends and capital gains produced by these securities are paid out in proportion to the number of fund shares you own. Even if you invest only a few hundred dollars, you get the same investment return per dollar as those who invest tens of thousands.

Your investment in a mutual fund is liquid. You can cash in all or a portion of your shares at any time and receive their current market value, which may be more or less than the price you paid. You do not need to find a buyer yourself. The fund stands ready at all times to redeem its own shares. Current per-share values are calculated daily based on the market worth of a fund's underlying portfolio of securities. These values change not only as the values of the underlying securities move up or down, but also as the fund alters its portfolio by buying new securities or selling those it already owns. You will find the per-share calculations (known as net asset values or NAVs) published daily in the financial sections of most major newspapers (see Chart 28).

The diversification common to mutual funds reduces the risk associated with investments in stocks and bonds that can turn sour and fall in value, sometimes swiftly and dramatically. By distributing the pool of shareholder dollars across dozens of securities, a mutual fund also increases your chance of picking up winners. Most individual investors would find it difficult to amass a portfolio as diversified as that of even a small mutual fund. Through pooling of your money in a money market mutual fund (more about these later), you can also take advantage of the current market interest rates paid on money market securities. These short-term instruments, issued by government agencies, large banks, and leading corporations, are among the safest of investments. But many are offered in amounts far too large or in forms too inconvenient for individuals to buy. By owning them indirectly through money market mutual funds, individual investors and small businesses can reap the same high yields that institutional investors realize on these securities.

Mutual fund management companies often sponsor so-called fund families—different funds that invest in different securities and pursue varied investment objectives. Usually, you can switch your money from one of these funds to another with a toll-free telephone call.

CHART 28
Mutual Funds Listings in Your Daily Newspapers

Fund Name	NAV	Offer Price	NAV Chg.
Fund X	16.11	N.L.	+.16
Fund Z	17.89	18.44	1.27

- NAV is the net asset value per share. That is, net value of all holdings divided by the number of shares owned by the fund's stockholders.

- Offer Price is what you would pay to buy each share.
  Certain offer prices are at NAV. These are known as "no(sales)load" funds, abbreviated to N.L.
  Others are higher in price because of an added sales charge. These are "load" funds which generally charge 5% to 8½% commission.

- NAV Chg. is the change in asset value per share between the market's close yesterday and today.

- An "r" following some funds listed denotes that fund charges a fee (usually ½% to 1%) to redeem shares.

A PROFESSIONAL IN YOUR CORNER

Professional management of your money is another important reason to consider investing in mutual funds. Fund managers, backed by large research departments, make their decisions based on extensive, ongoing economic analysis of the financial performance of individual companies and specific security issues, taking into account general economic and market trends. The fund manager or specialist in his or her research department stays in nearly constant contact with the management of companies whose stocks they own. Most large companies have one or more senior executives whose sole job is to communicate with security analysts and portfolio managers. Analysts also visit company plants and other facilities from time to time. After analyzing all the data and other information available, fund managers choose investments that best match the fund's objectives. The mix of these investments is adjusted frequently as changes take place in the markets, the economy or in a company's performance. While professional money management has long been available to large institutions and wealthy investors, mutual funds bring this expertise to even the smallest investor.

LEGAL PROTECTIONS

Mutual funds are regulated by the U.S. Securities and Exchange Commission (SEC) and are required to provide shareholders with periodic reports on what each fund is doing and what is happening to its investments. In addition, the investor receives a yearly statement detailing the federal tax status of his or her earnings from the fund. For tax purposes, a mutual fund acts merely as a conduit. Dividends and capital gains are treated substantially as if investors had bought and sold the underlying securities themselves.

Four federal laws and myriad state laws are on the books to protect investors who assume the risks inherent in investing in securities, including those of mutual funds. The Investment Company Act of 1940 requires all funds to register with the SEC and to meet certain operating standards. The Securities Act of 1933 mandates specific disclosures. The Securities Exchange Act of 1934 sets out antifraud rules covering the purchase and sale of fund shares, and the Investment Advisers Act of 1940 regulates the advisors to the funds.

THE SAFEST FUNDS

Some funds are considered safer than others, largely because of the types of securities they buy and thus the risks inherent in their portfolios. Funds which invest only in U.S. treasury securities are perhaps the safest. But you should not consider any mutual fund investment until you have enough facts on which to base an informed decision. Your "due diligence" research should always include a thorough reading of the fund's most recent prospectus, which will spell out the following:

- The fund's investment objective—what financial goals it is aiming for.

- The investment methods it uses in trying to achieve these goals.

- The name and address of its investment advisor and a brief description of the advisor's experience.

- The level of investment risk the fund is willing to assume in pursuit of its investment objective. This will typically range from maximum to minimum risk, depending on the type of fund.

- Any investments the fund will *not* make (for example, real estate or commodities).

- Tax consequences of the investment for the shareholder.

- How to purchase shares of the fund, including the cost of investing.

- How to redeem shares.

- Services provided, such as Individual Retirement Accounts, automatic reinvestment of dividends and capital gains distributions, check writing, withdrawal plans, and any other features. The prospectus also explains how these services work.

- A condensed financial statement (in tabular form, covering the last ten years, or the period the fund has been in existence if less than ten years) called "Per Share Income and Capital Changes." The fund's performance may be calculated from the information given in this table.

- A tabular statement of any fees charged by the fund and their effect on earnings over time.

Among the items you should check first in the fund prospectus are these:

- *Minimum.* If the minimum dollar amount required to open or add to an account is too high for you, read no further. Most funds require an initial minimum investment of anywhere from $500 to several thousand dollars, and minimum additional investments of $100 or more.

- *Objective.* Be sure the fund's objective matches your own. For example, if you need a steady source of supplemental income, a fund whose objective is long-term capital appreciation may not be suitable.

- *Performance.* Pay special attention to long-term performance in both rising and falling markets. If the numbers from the per-share table don't please you, move on to the next prospectus. But even if they do please you, don't fill out the account application just yet.

- *Risk.* Different investors can tolerate different levels of risk. A stellar performance in the past won't mean much if you are too worried about your investment to sleep at night.

- *Features.* If any particular feature is essential to you, such as check writing, telephone exchange, automatic investing, etc., check to be sure it's there.

If you feel you need more information about the fund before you invest, ask for the *"Statement of Additional Information"* (SAI), also known as Part B of the prospectus. Mutual funds must provide this document free of charge to anyone who requests it. Among other items, the SAI includes a list of the securities in the fund's portfolio at the time the SAI was written, a list of all the directors and officers of the fund, including their occupations and compensation, the name of anyone who owns a "controlling" proportion of fund shares (25 percent or more), and the fund's audited financial statements.

While you're at it, you might also ask for the fund's latest report. This document usually includes a description of how the fund fared during the period covered, its financial statements for the period, and a list of the securities the fund held in its portfolio at the time the report was written.

Finally, you should check on the intentions of the fund manager. If you find a fund you like, but its manager is about to resign, you'd be wise to reconsider. The fund manager is key to a strong performance.

AUTOMATIC PAYMENTS

Most mutual funds have programs allowing shareholders to receive regular automatic payments from invested principal and/or dividends and capital gains distributions. Such programs can be particularly helpful to supplement your other retirement income. Chart 29 indicates how long your accumulated investment will last during retirement if the percentage rate of withdrawal each year exceeds the mutual fund's percentage of average annual rate of return. (The average annual rate of return is equal to the per-share increase in net asset value, plus reinvested dividends and capital gains distributions.)

If your mutual fund's rate of return exceeds your withdrawal rate, your capital will never be depleted. For purposes of interpreting the chart, assume that your investment is worth $150,000. The fund's average rate of return is 10 percent. If you systematically withdraw 11 percent each year, your principal will last twenty-five years—the number of years found at the intersection of the 10 percent return and the 11 percent withdrawal.

A HISTORY OF RAPID GROWTH

The first American mutual funds were organized during the 1920s. They are now the nation's fourth largest financial institution—behind commercial

CHART 29
A Withdrawal Plan for Mutual Funds

Most mutual funds have programs allowing shareholders to receive regular automatic payments from invested principal and/or dividends and capital gains distributions. Such programs can be particularly helpful to supplement your other retirement income.

This guide indicates how long your accumulated investment will last during retirement if the percentage rate of withdrawal each year exceeds the mutual fund's percentage of average annual rate of return. (The average annual rate of return is equal to the per-share increase in net asset value, plus reinvested dividends and capital gains distributions.)

If your mutual fund's rate of return exceeds your withdrawal rate, your capital will never be depleted.

Your investment is worth $150,000. The fund's average rate of return is 10%. If you systematically withdraw 11% each year, your principal will last 25 years—the number of years found at the intersection on the chart of the 10% return and the 11% withdrawal.

Rate of Annual With-drawal	Average Annual Rate of Return on Your Mutual Fund Investment													
	1%	2%	3%	4%	5%	6%	7%	8%	9%	10%	11%	12%	13%	14%
	Number of Years Your Money Will Last													
15%	6	7	7	7	8	8	9	9	10	11	12	13	16	21
14%	7	7	8	8	8	9	10	10	11	12	14	17	22	
13%	8	8	8	9	9	10	11	12	13	15	17	23		
12%	8	9	9	10	10	11	12	14	15	18	24			
11%	9	10	10	11	12	13	14	16	19	25				
10%	10	11	12	13	14	15	17	20	26					
9%	11	12	13	14	16	18	22	28						
8%	13	14	15	17	20	23	30							
7%	15	16	18	21	25	33								
6%	18	20	23	28	36									
5%	22	25	30	41										
4%	28	35	46											
3%	40	55												
2%	69													

banks, savings and loans, and insurance companies. One reason for this growth is their performance record relative to what the individual might expect investing on his or her own, without the benefits of diversification and professional management. Individual fund performance varies, of course, but on average over the long run, the growth of stock funds (those which invest in the common stocks of corporations) has paralleled the growth of the U.S. economy. Similarly, the performance of other types of funds reflects the long-term movements of more specialized, professional markets—money market funds reflect activity in the short-term money market; bond funds, the bond market; tax-exempt funds, the municipal bond market, etc.

Growth in the number of mutual funds available, and the value of their assets, has been extraordinary. Since 1965, the industry has grown from about 170 funds to more than 3,100. Only two decades ago, total mutual fund investment amounted to some $48 billion. But fund sales in each of the past four years have exceeded that total by a considerable margin, and total assets today exceed $1 trillion. According to Barbara Levin of the Investment Company Institute, a trade group, most investors held on to their fund shares, including their stock fund shares, after the October 1987 crash. And on average, many investors who own stock funds have done well even during a period which includes the 1987 unheaval.

"It turns out, for example, that if you had purchased an 'average' stock fund at the end of 1986, you would have gained over 18 percent on your investment by the end of 1988," says Levin, "even though you would have experienced a sharp loss just ten months after your purchase."

In addition, if you had purchased an average-performance fund ten years ago, you would have achieved an annual total return of 15.4 percent for that period (January 1, 1980 through December 31, 1989). Some funds don't always achieve the average, of course, and some funds consistently do better. That's why you must select carefully. After the 1987 market break, an Investment Company Institute survey of fund investors showed that safety of principal was more important to them than total return as a consideration for selecting funds.

OPEN-END AND CLOSED-END FUNDS

There are two broad categories of mutual funds, open-end and closed-end, although most are the former type. An open-end fund places no limit on the number of shares it will sell. It simply creates new shares when new buyers come forward, or existing owners want to add to their holdings, and buys back (redeems) shares for investors who want to get out. In contrast, a closed-end fund limits the number of shares outstanding, like any corporation.

After a closed-end fund's startup or initial public offering, fund shares are traded on one of the major stock exchanges or in the over-the-counter market, like regular stocks. That's why they are sometimes called publicly traded funds. When you buy or sell shares in a closed-end fund, usually through a broker, you pay a commission, just as you do when buying or selling most other securities. Moreover, the share prices of closed-end funds are based on supply and demand in the market. When the share price of a closed-end fund is higher than its net asset value (NAV is the value of fund assets, minus liabilities, divided by the number of shares outstanding), the fund's shares are said to be selling at a premium. Conversely, those shares priced lower than net asset value per share are said to be selling at a discount. For example, if a fund has a net asset value per share of $15, based on the current value of its portfolio, but is priced at $12, it is selling at a 20 percent discount.

Over the past several years, the share prices of most newly issued closed-end funds investing in equity securities (stocks) have dropped to a discount from net asset value. Viewed from one perspective, when a share of a closed-end fund is selling at a 20 percent discount, every $12 invested in a share puts $15 to work for you. You don't realize that value, however, until the share rises in value to the $15 level, or the fund is liquidated or converted to an open-end fund. In either of these events, the investor gets a windfall, since liquidation or conversion is at net asset value. You should also be aware that closed-end fund shares sometimes fall in value immediately following their initial public offering. Experts say the reason for this decline may be due to heavy selling by big institutions immediately following the offering. Except for initial public offerings, investors obtain shares from current holders through a broker. Shareholders wishing to sell must find a buyer in the marketplace. Price, therefore, is a function of the market forces of supply and demand.

Closed-end fund managers oversee a fixed pool of assets. Cash available for investment does not fluctuate due to redemptions or purchases of new shares by investors. Thus, fund managers can concentrate on long-term investment objectives without need for liquidity to meet shareholder redemptions. Closed-end funds fall into several general and, in some cases, overlapping categories. Regardless of category, however, each fund has an investment objective—such as long-term capital appreciation, current income with capital preservation, or income with the potential for capital appreciation—and a carefully designed investment policy to help the fund reach its goal. Following is a brief description of the most common types of closed-end funds.

- Balanced funds invest in common and preferred stocks and bonds. Because these funds diversify not only within each security class but also across types of securities, they are usually a more conservative investment vehicle than common-stock funds.

- Bond funds invest in a range of bonds, including high-quality corporates, low-rated (junk) or unrated bonds, U.S. government bonds, municipal bonds, and bonds of foreign governments. Foreign bond funds enable investors to take advantage of currency fluctuations. As with any fixed-income investment, the prices of closed-end bond funds move in opposite directions from interest rates.

- Convertible bond funds invest in bonds that can be exchanged for another type of security, normally the common stock of the company issuing the convertible. Some convertible bond funds also have a high percentage of convertible preferred stock in their portfolios. Convertibles often provide relatively high fixed-income yields in comparison to some other investments and also have a potential for capital gains.

- Diversified equity funds invest primarily in a diversified portfolio of common stocks, although they may hold cash, bonds, or other defensive securities under certain market conditions.

- Dual-purpose funds aim to meet two distinct and different investor goals with their securities. This approach requires two classes of shares, such as income shares to receive all the fund's net investment income, and capital shares, which reflect changes in the value of the fund's portfolio.

As with open-end funds, there are three basic kinds of return for investors in closed-end funds:

1. *Dividend income.* Funds receive interest and dividend income from the securities in their portfolios. This income, minus fund operating costs, is distributed to shareholders as dividends.

2. *Capital gains distributions.* Most funds buy and sell portfolio securities throughout the year. If a net gain is realized from these transactions, most funds pay all or most of the money to shareholders as a capital gains distribution.

3. *Capital gains.* If you sell shares in the fund for more than you paid for them, you have made a capital gain through your transaction.

Similar to closed-end funds, open-end mutual funds are classified by one of several primary investment objectives: income, growth, aggressive growth, or tax benefits. Income funds focus on stable returns by investing in stocks that consistently pay top dividends, and/or interest-bearing debt instruments such as government or corporate bonds. Growth funds invest in stock or other securities that are expected to show above average price advances over the long-term. An aggressive growth fund puts its share-holders' money into securities its manager thinks will experience shorter-term price gains. Generally, appreciation funds are somewhat riskier than those focused on income or growth over time. Tax exempt funds help investors avoid taxes on their investment income, often by investing in tax-exempt municipal bonds.

MONEY MARKET MUTUAL FUNDS

Money market funds come in two varieties—money market mutual funds and tax-exempt money market mutual funds. Investors use these funds for one or more of four different purposes: first, as a parking place for cash between financial transactions; second, as a cash management account where you can earn market rates on the money you use for ordinary bill-paying; third, as a high-yield savings vehicle when, because of economic conditions or financial circumstances, other options look too risky; fourth, as a source of tax-free income, when you invest in tax-exempt money market funds, also known as short-term municipal bond funds.

Many people use their money market fund as a permanent savings or cash-management tool and add to it periodically for other purposes, such as a major purchase, or the retention of emergency funds in case of a job loss or serious injury. Nearly half of all money market fund investors plan to use the money to supplement their retirement income. A third use the funds for general savings.

Money market funds get their name from the types of securities in their portfolios—money market securities. Many financial and industrial companies borrow large sums of money for a short period of time—no more than a year—by issuing money market securities in exchange for cash. Most money market funds limit the average maturity of their portfolios to 120 days or less. Average maturity at year-end may be only 30 or 31 days. In other words, the average fund was exposed for only a month to the risk that interest rates would change markedly or that the loans it had purchased would not be repaid.

The institutions that borrow in the short-term money market use several different kinds of instruments. The federal government borrows by way of treasury bills (T-bills) and federal agency notes, major corporations by way of IOUs called commercial paper, and banks issue large certificates of deposit (CDs) and make agreements to repurchase government securities. Tax-exempt money market funds invest in bonds with short maturities issued by states and municipalities to finance public projects. A typical money market fund will be about 50 percent invested in commercial paper, 15 percent invested in repurchase agreements, 10 percent invested in T-bills and other government securities, 11 percent in commercial bank and domestic CDs, with the remainder in Eurodollar CDs and bankers' acceptances. These borrowers—banks, large corporations, and federal, state and local governments—are among the most creditworthy institutions in the country. They agree to pay the lender back quickly, with interest.

Most money market funds manage their portfolios with the aim of holding their net asset value (the price at which you buy and sell shares) constant at $1 per share with no load (sales charge). In contrast, the net asset value in other types of mutual funds rises and falls as the values of the underlying portfolio securities change. Although all investments entail some risk, their constant net asset value makes money market mutual funds one of the safest investments available. While they are not insured, chances are remote that you would lose any of the principal you invested in a money market fund. By law, the funds must stand ready to redeem your shares on any business day. If you need to cash in all or a part of your money-fund investment, the fund will issue a check to you or, in many cases, wire the money to your bank account. In addition, most money market funds offer check writing privileges.

A money market fund receives interest payments on its loans to government agencies and private companies. These payments are passed through to you as dividends. Most funds credit dividends to your account every business day and pay them on a monthly basis. The yield on a money fund is the rate of return on your investment, expressed as a percentage. Because all money funds calculate their yields in the same way, as prescribed by the Securities and Exchange Commission, you can compare yields among funds. Although yields can change from day to day, you can usually follow the changes in your daily newspaper. Money fund yields are tied to market interest rates. When interest rates go up, so do yields. When the rates go down, yields follow. Chart 30 illustrates how the money market mutual funds are listed in the daily newspaper.

TAX-EXEMPT MONEY MARKET FUNDS

Tax-exempt money market funds offer all the advantages of their taxable counterparts, plus earnings that are exempt from federal taxation. Their yields are lower, however, to take into account the extra benefit provided by tax exemption.

Municipal bonds offer one of the few sources of tax-free income allowed by the Tax Reform Act of 1986, and single-state bond mutual funds provide an extra tax benefit. Since they invest only in short-term bonds and other short-term securities issued by state municipalities, all income earned on these bonds is usually exempt from state as well as federal income tax. The investor, however, must be a resident of the state issuing the bonds to harvest the tax advantage of single-state funds. (Multistate bond funds also have a double-exemption feature for residents of the handful of states with reciprocal exemptions for other states' obligations.)

Tax exemption is a major attraction for many investors, particularly those who reside in areas with high state and local income taxes. Although the 1986 tax law lowered the top tax rate for individuals to 28 percent, a surcharge at the highest income levels lifted the effective rate to 33 percent. In 1990, of course, Congress increased the top rate to 31 percent and made other changes that hit high income taxpayers. In addition, in high-tax states that conform to the federal tax system, many investors pay proportionately higher state income taxes because of the elimination of most deductions and traditional tax-advantaged investments. Not surprisingly, single-state funds are especially big hits in such high-tax states as New York, California and Massachusetts. New Yorkers, who have a top tax rate of 13.5 percent, have access to over 73 tax-exempt bond mutual funds. Californians, with an 11 percent top rate, can choose among 104 bond funds, the biggest block of all among single-state funds. Massachusetts taxpayers, with a rate of 10

		Average	Average	Effective
CHART 30 **Money Market Mutual Funds Listings** **In Your Daily Newspaper**				
Fund Name	Assets ($ million)	Maturity (Days)	Yield .(%)	Yield (%)
Fund X	9.69.5	43	7.45	8.10

- Average Maturity refers to the money market investments held by the fund.
- Average Yield is average over the 7 days to the weekly listings in media.
- Effective yield is compounding—that is, with dividends (from interest) reinvested (you will see the same thing with banks showing effective yield on accounts with interest compounded).

percent on dividends and capital gains, plus a surtax of 3.75 percent, are offered 24 funds.

To cite one example, a California resident with a combined state tax of 11 percent and federal tax of 28 percent, and earning a 7.2 percent yield on a California single-state bond fund, would reap a gain equivalent to a *taxable* investment yielding 11.5 percent. That's significant in today's market.

Demand for state specialized funds is currently at its highest level, with little evidence of slowing, according to the Investment Company Institute. The assets of these funds have also grown at an astonishing pace. At the end of 1985, the single-state funds had assets of $13.2 billion. Their assets today exceed $69.8 billion. Single-state funds are not a new wrinkle on the mutual fund scene. They have been a standard option for investors in California and Pennsylvania since 1977. All fifty states now have single-state bond mutual funds.

HELP WITH UNAVOIDABLE TAXES

While mutual funds offer investors many advantages, including a measure of tax avoidance, fund owners must keep abreast of tax obligations they cannot avoid. These obligations include dividend distributions and profits from sales of shares. In addition, mutual fund shareholders pay taxes on long-term capital gain distributions passed through by the fund to its shareholders as a result of the sale of stocks or bonds in the fund's portfolio. Capital gains flow through as dividends taxable as ordinary income. Dividend income is taxed as ordinary income like dividends on any other kind of investment. Interest from money market and bond funds is also considered dividend income and taxed accordingly. Reinvested dividends are taxed as ordinary income just like cash dividends.

If all this sounds like a lot of bookkeeping, don't panic. The fund keeps track of it for you. Recordkeeping is one of the most valuable services provided by a mutual fund. Once a year, the fund sends a form (Form 1099-DIV) to each shareholder. (The form is sometimes found at the bottom of your annual statement.) The 1099-DIV lists your total distributions for the year. They are then broken down and identified as:

- Dividend income.

- Net capital gains, if any.

- Any distributions that represent a return of capital.

The key points are these:

- You report dividend income along with your other dividend income for the year.

- You include all capital gain dividends along with your other long-term capital gains.

- Distributions that represent a return of capital are not taxable but require that an adjustment be made reducing your basis in your fund shares.

It's very important that you keep track of the purchase prices and dates of all your fund shares, including reinvested distributions. Then, if and when you decide to liquidate or exchange some of your shares, you will be able to identify those shares with the highest purchase price and request that the fund sell them first, allowing you to realize a smaller capital gain.

If you use this method, you should request some form of written confirmation from your fund. The strategy could save you a lot of taxes, especially if capital gains continue to be generally taxed as ordinary income.

Don't forget that exchanges between funds in a family of funds also are taxable transactions. They represent redemptions or sales of shares. Nor should you forget that while most or all interest income on municipal bond funds is tax free, capital gains distributions are not. They represent your part of any profit realized when fund managers sell bonds from the portfolio at a gain. You may occasionally see these gains reported on your 1099-DIV.

MUTUAL FUND INVESTMENT FORMULAS

Some mutual fund shareholders use formulas to guide their investing. Among these formulas are dollar-cost averaging, fixed ratios, variable ratios and market indicators. The most popular and easiest is dollar-cost averaging, which takes the ups and downs in the market and turns them to your advantage.

Dollar-Cost Averaging. The principal of dollar-cost averaging is this: You invest equal amounts of money at regular intervals, usually every month or every quarter, no matter how high or how low the share cost. The beauty of the technique is that it minimizes market judgment except at one vital juncture—when you are selecting a fund at the start of the program. Averaging will not protect you from a poor fund manager. After that, it's essential that you stick with your game plan through good markets and bad. The more you tinker with it, the more you rob the technique of its essence— blind objectivity. The system's secret is that it assures you of buying more shares of a fund when the price is low than when it is high.

Let's say, for example, that you buy $100 worth of fund shares every three months, and that the fund you have chosen is selling at $10 per share. You invest $100 and receive ten shares. You again invest $100 the following quarter. The fund is now selling at $5 a share and you receive twenty shares. Three months later the price is back up to $10 and you receive only ten additional shares. You now own forty shares after a total investment of $300. However, with an ending market price of $10 per share, your shares are actually worth more than you paid for them. The average price per share over the three quarters represented here ($25 divided by 3) was $8.33. But the average cost to you ($300 divided by 40 shares) was $7.50.

Dollar-Cost Averaging (fluctuating market)

Regular Investment	Share Price	Shares Acquired
$100	$10	10
100	5	20
100	10	10
Total $300	$25	40

Average share cost: $7.50 ($300 divided by 40)

Average share price: $8.33 ($25 divided by 3)

Let's look at another example showing what can happen as the market rises. First, let's increase our quarterly investment to $300. When everyone else is paying high prices for a great many up-market shares, you'll continue to invest the same $300 each quarter and buy fewer shares.

Dollar-Cost Averaging (rising market)

Regular Investment	Share Price	Shares Acquired
$300	$ 5	60
300	15	20
300	10	30
300	15	20
300	25	12
Total $1,500	$70	142

Average share cost: $10.57 ($1,500 divided by 142)

Average share price: $14.00 ($70 divided by 5)

The average price then is $14, but the average cost is only $10.57 per share. When you compare the $10.57 figure with the $14 figure, you can appreciate the savings you get with the dollar-cost averaging method. Over the short-term, dollar-cost averaging doesn't guarantee you a profit. You've got to have the emotional and financial resources to stay in the game for the long haul.

Fixed Ratios. Using this technique, you invest fixed percentages of your overall mutual fund holdings in some combination of income, growth, appreciation and tax-advantaged funds, buying and selling shares to maintain these percentages.

Variable Ratios. You modify the investment percentages assigned to funds with different objectives, based on your analysis of the market and certain technical indicators.

Market Indicators. These are technical benchmarks which show variations from prior trading patterns. They signal possible turning points that trigger decisions to buy or sell.

CHART 31
Guide to Income-Oriented Mutual Funds

Virtually all mutual funds pay some dividends—from their net income (interest and dividends they earn from their portfolio holdings, less the funds' expenses and management fees). But dividend yield is slight for equity (stock) funds whose primary objective is long-term growth or shorter-term maximum capital appreciation.

The other types of mutual funds, below, vary in their income orientation. Those whose yield is the highest also are the riskiest—investing mostly in "junk (low-quality) bonds."

You may need income from your mutual funds to supplement your other income because of your lifestyle or because you're retired. However, if possible, you also should try to invest for some potential long-term growth (as well as necessary current income) to offset the eroding effects of inflation. But not to such an extent as to risk preservation of your capital, which is paying you needed dividend income.

When applicable, you also should determine which will yield more net income to you: higher-paying but taxable dividends vs. lower-paying but tax-advantaged dividends.

MONEY MARKET MUTUAL FUNDS

(Unlike the other types of income-oriented mutual funds below, the prices of money market funds do not fluctuate.)
- GENERAL MONEY MARKET FUNDS (they generally invest in money market instruments of domestic and foreign issuers, including: CD's, bankers' acceptances, and time deposits of financial institutions; short-term commercial paper, notes and bonds of corporations; and bills, discount notes, and other short-term obligations of government agencies and other issuers).
- U.S. GOVERNMENT SECURITIES MONEY MARKET FUNDS (debt obligations issued or guaranteed by the U.S. government or its agencies).
- TAX-EXEMPT MONEY MARKET FUNDS (short-term debt obligations of municipalities).

BOND FUNDS

(In addition to the categories below, some bond mutual funds are classified by the lengths of maturities of bonds they specialize in: "short-term"—generally less than 3 years; "intermediate-term"—generally 3 to 10 years; "long-term"—generally 10 years or longer. Some diversified bond funds may invest in debt issues of foreign governments and corporations. Some specialize in foreign issues.)

U.S. Government (safest of all investments):
- U.S. TREASURY SECURITIES FUNDS (bills, notes, and bonds).
- U.S. GOVERNMENT SECURITIES FUNDS (Treasuries plus debt issues of other U.S. government agencies).

Municipals (bonds and other debt issues of state and local municipalities or their specific projects; interest is exempt from federal tax, and also state and local taxes if investor lives there):
- BETTER-QUALITY MUNICIPAL BOND FUNDS (quality as graded by independent rating services, such as Standard & Poor's and Moody's).
- LOWER-QUALITY MUNICIPAL BOND FUNDS (as graded or unrated; lowest-quality known as "junk bonds").

CHART 31 *(continued)*

● INSURED MUNICIPAL BOND FUNDS (slightly lower yield, because of the cost of the insurance, for the extra safety).

Mortgage (and Other Asset) Backed (securities collateralized by pools of mortgages):
● GINNIE MAE FUNDS (mortgage pools via Government National Mortgage Association [GNMA], known as Ginnie Mae).
● MORTGAGE SECURITIES FUNDS (Ginnie Mae and other government and commercial mortgage-backed securities).

Corporates (bond and other debt obligations issued by corporations):
● BETTER-QUALITY CORPORATE BOND FUNDS (quality as graded by independent rating services, such as Standard & Poor's and Moody's).
● LOWER-QUALITY CORPORATE BOND FUNDS (as graded or unrated; lowest-quality known as "junk bonds").

Zero coupon (government and corporate bonds issued at a deep discount from face value, with interest accumulated to maturity; you could stagger redemptions to produce accumulated interest by investing in zero coupon funds with various targeted maturity dates).

BOND AND STOCK FUNDS

● CONVERTIBLE FUNDS (preferred stocks and bonds convertible into shares of common stocks).
● BALANCED FUNDS (common stocks, convertibles, preferred stocks, bonds, money market instruments).

EQUITY INCOME FUNDS

● EQUITY INCOME FUNDS (higher-yield dividend-paying stocks).
● DUAL-PURPOSE FUNDS' INCOME SHARES (the other shares in dual-purpose funds get the appreciation).
● INCOME AND GROWTH FUNDS (more income plus some growth).
● GROWTH AND INCOME FUNDS (more growth plus medium income).
● INCOME-ORIENTED SECTOR FUNDS (such as sector funds specializing in utilities or real estate or other fields usually higher-yield).
● OPTION INCOME FUNDS (options for income rather than appreciation).
● MIXED INCOME FUNDS (high-yield stocks, options for income).

Source: SPYF p. 168–9.

In Chart 31 we have prepared a guide to income-oriented mutual funds. For a list of more than 3,100 mutual funds, their addresses, phone numbers, and investment objectives, send $5 to the *Guide*, Investment Company Institute, 1600 M Street NW, Suite 600, Washington, DC 20036. The Institute is the national association of the investment company industry. Its members represent more than 90 percent of the industry's assets and have over 30 million shareholders.

10

Real Estate

It's an oft-repeated tale and true—half the great fortunes in America were built on real estate. It's also true that most of the small fortunes were built on real estate, including, most likely, your own. If you are like the majority, you bought into the American Dream at an early age by making a down payment on a home, paid off your mortgage slowly over the years, traded up to a bigger and better place when able, watched the value of your holding escalate, sometimes dramatically—and bingo, you eventually became the proud father of a personal fortune. That's the way it was done in the past, and that's the way it will be done in the foreseeable future. Real estate values fluctuate, to be sure. Sometimes, in some parts of the country, they remain depressed for years. But if you use your common sense when buying, and hold on, you almost never miss by buying a home. It's not a question of whether you are going to make a profit, but of how much.

Over the past decade, indeed, steep runups in real estate values have left many homeowners with huge profits when they sell. But if you buy another house within two years that costs as much as or more than the one you sold, the tax on your profit is postponed. If you are age fifty-five or older and the house was your principal residence for three of the last five years, you are entitled to a once-in-a-lifetime capital gains exclusion of $125,000. Eventually the IRS will want to hear from you, but careful planning can lessen the tax bill when it finally arrives.

Keep thorough records for as long as you own the house. Maintain a separate folder with your financial records for receipts and cancelled checks documenting capital improvements over the years, plus any deductible casualty losses or depreciation. If you live in a cooperative, keep records of your assessments.

A capital improvement is any installation or renovation that adds to the value of the property—replacing a roof, building driveways, garages, fences, gates, installing central air conditioning and burglar alarm systems. Even some cosmetic changes and repairs can be deducted as capital expenses if they are part of a major renovation.

The reason for safeguarding records showing the costs of capital improvements is something called *basis*. Basis is normally calculated as the price paid for the property plus closing costs and capital improvements. When a property is sold at a profit, the taxable portion is the difference between the owner's basis and the price he or she obtained. Increasing your tax basis to its legal limit in each property you sell is your most important means of holding on to your profits. And don't overlook the fact that you can also deduct the costs of selling, including real estate commissions and legal fees.

SELL CREATIVELY FOR TOP DOLLAR

When you sell a home these days you must work harder and more creatively to obtain full value. First and foremost, don't let your emotions get in the way. Treat the sale as you would any other business deal. Don't try and sell the house yourself. Give it to a licensed broker who is a member of the local multiple listing service. The broker will screen out unqualified buyers and the MLS will almost certainly bring your property to the attention of many more potential buyers. This is especially important in a depressed market. It's estimated that only 11 percent of all home owners sell their houses themselves, and the reasons are obvious. To act as your own agent, you must remain available to potential buyers, escort strangers through, and perhaps be forced to listen to their criticisms of a home you may have cherished. Some of the would-be buyers may be sightseers. Some may not even be able to afford your house. Some may be given to stealing your nice things as they wander through. And if you fail to mention any major defects in the house (a basement that floods during winter, for example), you may be sued later on.

CONSIDER HOLDING THE BUYER'S MORTGAGE YOURSELF

● If done correctly, owner financing is one of the best deals around for both buyer and seller. Many buyers are more concerned about the down payment and the monthly payments than they are with the sale price. If you are in a comfortable cash position, consider offering the buyer a slightly better mortgage rate as a means of swinging the sale at your price. Your money will be secured by real estate whose value you know intimately. The worst that can happen if the buyer defaults is that you get your property back. To avoid potential problems, however, make sure the buyer can afford your property, and have an experienced lawyer draw up the mortgage contract.

CURB APPEAL HELPS SELL

Buyers yearn for physical and economic security. Make your house look as safe and secure as possible. Test its *curb appeal* by approaching it from up and down the street. Consider a paint job and minor repairs if the house looks a bit too dowdy. Make sure the inside of the house conveys a strongly positive sensory impression. Open curtains and blinds, let in as much sun as possible. Air out the rooms and turn on the brightest lights before a potential buyer arrives. Place bowls of flowers and potpourri in every room. Tune your stereo to pleasant background music. All such small touches will enhance the appeal of your house.

SELLING IN A DOWN MARKET

If a downturn in the real estate market looms just at the time you are ready to sell—a time when every owner seems to be rushing to market but all the buyers have vanished—you must be especially careful about pricing your property and selecting a sales agent. Home owners are notorious for letting their affection for their homes cloud their judgment of a proper sale price. The experts say that, bad market or good, you should set the price of your house at fair market value when you first offer it for sale. Failing to price sensibly may do you out of a quick sale. To arrive at this theoretical value, call three or four of the best real estate firms in your area. Tell each you are considering listing with them, but you first want to know what they think your property is worth in today's market. Another way of putting this question: "How much can I realistically expect to get if I want to make a sale within 90 to 120 days?" When the agents' estimates are in, ask each to explain how they arrived at their number. Usually, the agents will cite the sale prices of comparable houses, or the asking prices of similar properties currently on the market. They may also call your attention to properties which have not sold because their price tags are considered too high.

In addition to pricing your home realistically, you must also choose the right real estate firm and the right agent. Generally, you should select a firm that specializes in selling properties in the same price range as your own. Check newspaper ads and For Sale signs on properties in your area, or ask your banker or a local title company officer to recommend a company with a top sales record. To find a suitable agent, ask the manager of the firm you select to recommend someone who is experienced but not a star producer. Star producers usually concentrate on listings they can turn over quickly. You want an agent who will focus on your property.

Always remember, whether selling or buying, that a real estate agent is legally bound to work for the seller. To avoid potential lawsuits, the National Association of Realtors has urged the states to require that agents inform buyers of this by means of disclosure forms, and some states have done so. Homeowners have successfully sued their brokers or agents for:

- Failing to pass on every offer for the seller's consideration.

- Telling buyers the seller would accept less than the asking price.

- Not telling sellers that buyers would pay more than they were offering.

- Not identifying buyers adequately. For example, an agent who failed to reveal that the buyer was a relative might be laying the groundwork for a lawsuit.

SOME IMPROVEMENTS PAY, SOME DON'T

If you are planning to sell your home within one or two years, don't remodel. Large-scale improvements pay for themselves only through overall appreciation over a number of years. Few major improvements, if any, will pay back more when you sell than you invested. Some may even make the house less attractive to buyers, particularly those that reflect idiosyncratic taste and those that are inappropriate to your neighborhood or even the climate in your area.

You will probably be able to recoup all or most of your investment if you:

- *Update your kitchen.* The kitchen is the focal point of modern family life, the place where today's family congregates and socializes. But don't go overboard. It would be folly to spend $50,000 renovating the kitchen of a house worth only $125,000. Keep your spending in proportion, say 5 percent of your home's fair market value.

- *Modernize a bathroom.* A renovated bathroom with vanity, neutral-colored tiles and a new tub/shower combination enclosed by glass is a sound investment. You can expect to recoup dollar for dollar.

- *Install a fireplace.* In a temperate climate, nearly every homeowner seems to want a fireplace, even if it is seldom used. You will nearly always get your money back when you sell.

- *Add a room.* If it's a third bedroom or a family room, you are not likely to lose money on this improvement. Don't go for a fourth or fifth bedroom, however, because families today are generally smaller than they were twenty or thirty years ago. Most potential buyers will not pay for that much unneeded space.

- *Add a deck or screen porch.* Like a fireplace, these improvements are relatively inexpensive and will pay you back handsomely if they are at least 15 feet by 20 feet and are built with pressure-treated lumber.

- *Install a skylight.* Another inexpensive item, a skylight will probably return 100 percent of your investment.

Think carefully before making any of the following improvements.

- While finished basements with big wet bars were the rage in 1950, people today prefer a family room on the living level near the kitchen. You probably won't recover more than 25 percent of your investment in a finished basement.

- Install a pool only if you live in a warm climate and if many of your neighbors have them. You are unlikely to get your money back, however, if you live in an area where pools are the exception rather than the rule and there's a short season for outdoor swimming. In these circumstances, the effort required to maintain a pool and the cost involved may even make your property less attractive to potential buyers.

- Hot tubs, tennis courts and greenhouses are luxury items that generally will not return more than 25 percent of your investment when you sell.

HOME OPTIONS FOR EMPTY NESTERS

When Joe and Sheila packed their youngest daughter off to college, they suddenly felt lost and lonely in their big eight-room house (not counting the butler's pantry or the screened porch). Their two older sons were already married and living in their own homes. On a Saturday morning a few weeks later, Sheila was sipping coffee on the porch, deep in thought, as Joe scanned the morning paper.

"Put the paper down, Joe, and listen to me a bit," she said. "I just want you to know I'm not going to dust and vacuum those three empty bedrooms."

"I thought the cleaning lady did that."

"She does. What I mean is, why should we pay to have it done, either."

Joe had been expecting just such a reaction from his wife, and he was prepared.

"What you mean is, this place is too big for us, with all the kids gone."

"Yes, it's too damn big and it's too much damn trouble."

Sheila was on the verge of tears now, thinking about herself and Joe knocking around alone in the huge, silent house.

"Well, take it easy, babe. I'm with you. If I never paint another window trim, it'll be too soon."

"Can't we buy something different, smaller, but very, very nice?"

"C'mon, let's take our walk. We'll talk about it."

"You're going to fight me on this, aren't you?"

"Nope. It's exactly what I've been thinking. We need a change, new space, live the way we want to live." And waving a hand toward the house, he added, "Now that the nest is empty."

Joe and Sheila usually walked a brisk three miles every morning, weather and other things permitting. This morning, however, they were more focused on plans for the future than the pace they should be keeping.

"We could just rent a beautiful apartment somewhere on the water," Sheila suggested.

"That's a thought," said Joe. "Let somebody else worry about the upkeep."

"Or we could buy a condo or a townhouse," she added.

"I like that better. I like owning the place I live in," said her husband. "Would you consider a smaller single-family house or a two-family house that would provide us with additional income?"

"No. Not if I have a choice. We've done the house bit, and I don't want the bother anymore. I think what I want is a beautiful condo apartment overlooking the city and the harbor."

"If that's what you want, who am I to say no?"

"Why is this so easy?" Sheila asks, eyeing her husband.

"We agree, that's all. Don't be so suspicious. I'm ready for a change as much as you are."

THE MANUFACTURED HOME OPTION

For less affluent empty nesters, such decisions may not be so easy. If retired or about to retire, they may have to consider other, less expensive options. Manufactured homes, once known as mobile homes, have long been popular among retired couples as an alternative to a house or condominium. During the past two years alone, more than two million manufactured homes have been built, representing over 14 percent of all new U.S. housing construction and a quarter to a third of all new single-family homes sold.

Cost is the driving force in the manufactured housing market, although many retired persons also prefer the ease of a mobile home lifestyle. In 1987, the latest year for which figures are available, the average cost of a multisection, 1,450 square foot mobile home was only $32,400, plus roughly 15 percent for locally mandated installation requirements. That compares with an average $135,900 for new site-built homes and $112,100 for used site-built homes. Owning a manufactured home is actually less expensive than renting a house or apartment, according to the Manufactured Housing Institute. The median monthly housing costs for manufactured-home owners are $294, compared to $332 for house and apartment renters, and $463 for site-built home owners. However, a mobile home has to be put on a site—a mobile home park, trailer park, or on land that is appropriately zoned—and in states such as Florida the monthly charges for the use of the site and facilities (utilities, parking space, boat docking and recreational activities) can add considerably to monthly expenses.

Since 1976, mobile home construction has been governed by a strict national building code administered by the U.S. Department of Housing and Urban Development. The code regulates design and construction, strength and durability, fire resistance and energy efficiency, installation, and performance of heating, plumbing, air conditioning, thermal and electrical systems. All manufactured-home buyers are protected, even after they move in, by a formal, uniform national consumer complaint process managed by HUD, which has the authority to require repair of an imminent safety hazard or major defect for the life of the home. Buyers are also protected by state and local consumer protection laws.

A notable advantage of these homes is that you have instant housing with instant furnishings. Nearly all models come equipped with new appliances, tables, chairs, beds, sofas, carpets, draperies and other basic furnishings. The homes are compact and relatively easy to maintain.

Financing terms for mobile homes are gradually improving, experts say, as more financial institutions enter the lending market. Both the FHA and VA have insurance and loan-guarantee programs for the homes, with reasonable down-payment requirements, interest rates, and adequate ceilings for today's market. Buying a mobile home is at least as important and complicated a transaction as buying any other home. And remember this is not a camping trailer. You cannot hitch it to your car and tour. Manufactured homes can only be moved by professionals using special equipment, and the cost is hefty.

The choice of a manufactured home over an apartment or a house built on-site is often a matter of economics, but can also be a lifestyle decision. For many Americans, the advantages of such a home far outweigh the disadvantages. Unfortunately, consumers often make costly errors in acquiring and locating their homes. Over 50 percent of these homes are placed on individually owned property in suburban areas or in rural or small-town locations. What buyers often forget is that many municipalities have zoning regulations limiting the placement of manufactured housing. Check local zoning restrictions long before you decide to buy.

The basic purchase price of a manufactured home nearly always includes transporting the structure to the site of your choice within a prescribed area and setting it up for initial operation. It is always wise, however, to ask whether this is included in the price, and to have it written into the sales contract. In addition to the price of the home, the cost of several extras must also be considered. Steps with handrails are required for every outside door. Skirting to protect the foundation and provide ventilation and access is often required, and certainly desirable. Many states require that homes be anchored to the ground for protection against high winds. All these items should be decided upon at the time of purchase, and can be included in the financing. When buying skirting, however, get estimates from more than one company. And make sure your anchoring conforms to local building codes.

When you go to buy a manufactured home, shop thoroughly. Look at many different models. Interrogate every dealer about pricing details, financing arrangements, locating, transporting, installing, anchoring, warranties on appliances, and repair and maintenance. This is one of the more important purchases you are likely to make, so don't rush it.

Most young families and some older ones make a downpayment on a manufactured home and finance the balance. Roughly 90 percent are personal property loans of up to fifteen years, not mortgages. Be sure and check all financing arrangements available. Do not sign any contract until you fully understand exactly what you will get and what it will cost. Don't sign any contract with blank spaces. Don't rely on verbal agreements. Get everything in writing and save a completed copy for your records. Also be sure you distinguish between the manufacturers's and the retailer's responsibilities in setting up and servicing your home. You could be headed for trouble unless these are defined at the time of the sale and put in writing.

When choosing a manufactured home community, look beyond such obvious factors as appearance, lot size and landscaping. Find out about garbage and trash removal. Ask also about use of laundry facilities, swimming pool, tennis courts and clubhouse. Never accept a park owner's oral promises of future facilities. Find out exactly what is included in your rent and what isn't. Above all, demand a written lease. Don't be in a hurry to select a community. Visit several, at different times of the day, in good weather and bad. Talk with residents and with the park manager. Ask yourself if you are prepared to live up to the rules, and whether current tenants are doing so. Some manufactured-home-park owners may try and charge you an exit fee when you decide to sell your home. Such fees are illegal in many states, but still occur in others. Find out before you move into a park if you will be charged an exit fee. If the answer is yes, you might want to find another park.

INVESTING IN REAL ESTATE

In spite of everything—tax reform, the birth dearth, a low rate of national growth, overbuilding during the 1980s, and the savings and loan crisis—there's money to be made in real estate. But you can't do it with your eyes closed anymore. You have to look harder, work harder and be more selective. Real estate is not the stock market. It is now and always has been a *local* market. Prices vary widely across the country. You must look at it on a city-by-city basis, even a neighborhood-by-neighborhood basis. Cities and towns in the oil patch, particularly Texas and Oklahoma, have experienced a real estate depression in recent years, while buyers and renters in cities like Washington DC, San Francisco, Seattle and Portland, Oregon, are scrambling for housing and driving up prices to sometimes alarming heights. Even at the height of the housing recession in Houston, the vacancy rate for the best apartments was low.

Follow these guidelines and keep thorough records, using Chart 32 as a record of investments, and you have a chance of making good money in rental real estate:

- *Buy only bargains.* Your first profit should be the one going in. Look for neglected properties you can improve cosmetically and raise rents without losing tenants, or properties with excessive expenses you can trim to improve your return. When inspecting a property, check for additional rental unit possibilities in basements, attics or vacant garages.

- *Stay close to home.* As a rule, you're better off buying in your own area, where you know the market. It's also an advantage to be able to hire tradesmen in your community for improvements and upkeep, and to make your deals through familiar brokers and lawyers. Taxwise, it's easier to prove you're an active rather than a passive investor when the property is nearby. This is important because an active investor can use some losses, perhaps due to initially upgrading the property, to offset salary or portfolio income.

- *Don't neglect, don't overimprove.* While neglecting the upkeep on a rental property can lead to big expenses down the road, you can also lose money by overdoing upkeep. Don't install new carpeting if the old is in good condition. Don't install new appliances unless they are really needed, or unless it will allow you to raise rents. Don't repaint simply because the tenant wants a different color.

- *Houses versus apartments.* There are advantages to both rental houses and apartments. Houses appreciate faster on the average. But the rental market for houses is weaker overall than the market for apartments. More affluent families usually prefer to own rather than rent in order to take advantage of tax breaks. Apartments attract a larger pool of middle-income tenants, and an occasional vacancy won't destroy your bottom line. A vacant house, on the other hand, is 100 percent vacant.

- *Concentrate on basics.* Look for moderately priced houses with strong curb appeal in safe neighborhoods, good public transportation and easy access to shopping. The rental market for big houses is small. Low-cost, low-maintenance property such as a condominium or duplex is usually ideal. Your objective is to collect rents from tenants who don't call to complain about a problem every other week.

- *Anticipate problems.* Before you buy, make sure you can rent the property. Is the area zoned for rentals? How many tenants are allowed in the building? Does it meet all the local criteria for a certificate of occupancy? Have the building inspected by a professional, and look for hidden problems on your own—rotted flooring under carpets, toilets that leak when flushed, fuse boxes that are too small, a faulty furnace, termites or carpenter ants in beams and timbers. Even professionals sometimes overlook critical defects.

BUYING FORECLOSED PROPERTIES

Real estate experts say foreclosed properties are often excellent deals for investors seeking rental income, equity accumulation and capital appreciation. The key, of course, is careful selection of the property. Your emphasis should be on location, condition, price, and the rental market in the area. If you are new to the game, begin with a moderately priced house that requires only a general cleanup and fixup, not one that needs structural work. Reconstruction costs can quickly get out of hand, and the lower the price the more people there are who can afford to buy or rent it. You can obtain information on both FHA and VA foreclosure lists from the real estate owned departments of banks, weekly foreclosure lists published by the federal agencies, classified sections of your newspaper, and from VA and FHA-approved real estate brokers. Other sources of foreclosed properties include tax sales at the county courthouse, Internal Revenue Service sales and Marshall sales. Another way to find excellent buys is to approach the owner of a property prior to his or her foreclosure date. Make an offer that will give you the house at a bargain and save the current owner's credit rating.

Tax sale bidding usually begins at the level of the tax judgment against the property, and you must come up with all the money that day. The law requires that lenders or loan guarantors offer the properties at fair market value. You may find a bargain, however, where a bank-foreclosed house has been on the market over a year and has been reappraised downward. FHA-foreclosed properties usually require a downpayment of only 5 percent and no closing costs. VA foreclosures may require only 2 percent down and no closing costs. If you're buying as an investor and don't intend to live there, however, your downpayment in both cases will probably be 20 percent. Anyone who buys a VA-foreclosed property can get a VA-guaranteed loan, except in cases where a competing buyer is a veteran, and you are not. Unless you're a foreclosure expert and have a lot of time to devote to your searches for deals, consider working with a foreclosure specialist. You'll find them among independent real estate operators. Ask your bank for names. Check each candidate's track record and reputation for honesty. Fort Lauderdale real estate broker Allen Gelman points out that if you have the ready money and a keen eye for housing, you can often purchase property at half its fair market value.

Using the formula in Chart 33, you can calculate the rate of return on a cash investment in real estate property.

WHAT TO PAY FOR RENTAL PROPERTY

Buying rental property must be approached with a hard eye for numbers. The only factor to be considered is this: Will it turn a profit? Here are several formulas for determining how much you can afford to pay for rental properties:

- Gross rent multiplier (asking price divided by the gross annual rent you expect to receive). The GRM helps you determine whether or not the asking price is fair in relation to the rent the building can generate. If the asking price of a rental house, say, is $100,000, and it brings in rent of $9,600 a year, the GRM equals 10.4. The higher the multiplier, the less desirable the property, and most experienced investors won't consider a GRM of more than 8. If you multiply the annual rent of $9,600 by 8, you will see that the asking price for the property should be $76,800, rather than $100,000. Unless you can get the owner to lower the sale price to that vicinity, you should consider walking away from the deal.

- Gross income multiplier (monthly rent times 100). This formula also gives you a rough idea of what the asking price of a rental property should be. The monthly rent in the previous example was $800. If you multiply that by 100, you arrive at a value of $80,000 for the property. GRM and GIM should not be relied upon solely for determining the value of a rental property, but they can save you from wasting time on properties that are overpriced.

- Capitalization rate (net operating income divided by asking price). Net operating income (NOI) is the yield on your investment. It is the money left in your bank account after you have paid all the costs of owning except your mortgage. These costs normally include taxes, repairs, maintenance and insurance, among other items. Example: You're considering a property with an asking price of $100,000. The owner reports that his net operating income is $8,000. You divide $8,000 by $100,000 and find a yield of 8 percent. That's about the minimum return most investors today would consider, and many insist on yields of 10 or 12 percent. The capitalization rate formula is probably the single best mathematical tool for determining whether buying a rental property makes economic sense. You must be certain, however, that all the expenses of owning have been plugged in. Ask for a copy of the owner's tax return related to the property. It may show expenses you won't discover any other way. Also check with property management firms and local real estate agents who specialize in commercial properties about vacancy rates in the area. A vacancy rate of 5 percent is considered acceptable. Be wary of any higher number.

REAL ESTATE INVESTMENT TRUSTS

You need not own property directly to make money in real estate. Publicly-owned real estate investment trusts (REITs) are somewhat akin to mutual funds—with diversified holdings, professional management, and accessibility to small investors. But REITs are less like open-end mutual funds, which constantly sell more of their own shares and are obligated to redeem shares, than like closed-end funds, which have a fixed number of shares you may buy and sell through your broker as you would any stock traded on an exchange. REITs come in three varieties:

CHART 32
Form to Copy to Record
Your Investments in Real Estate

☐ Own Residence

☐ Rented Out

Type of Property _____

Address _____

City _____ State _____ Zip _____

Purchase Date _____

Total Cost of Purchase _____

Name(s) of Owner(s) _____

Percentage of Ownership _____

Location of Owner(s) Records _____

Original Amount of Mortgage(s) (and Any Other Relevant Loans)	Interest Rate	Amount and Period of Each Payment	Dates of First and Last Payments	Name, Address, Phone Number of Mortgagor(s) and any Other Lenders	

- Equity REITs invest in ownership of properties.

- Mortgage REITs lend money, including funds for construction and development.

- Hybrid REITs do both.

Some real estate investment trusts specialize in investments in a certain geographical area. Others focus on particular kinds of real estate, such as healthcare facilities, shopping centers, hotels and motels, office buildings, apartment complexes, or industrial or mini-warehouses. Many REITs, however, invest nationwide in a variety of areas.

Infinite-life REITs continue indefinitely, while finite-life REITs (known as FREITs) are organized with a predetermined date of liquidation, when

CHART 33
Calculating Mortgage Payments to Achieve a Desired Rate of Return on a Cash Investment in a Real Estate Property

1. First calculate the amount of debt you can handle while still realizing the desired rate of return on your investment:
    A. Cost of rental-income building $280,000
    B. Cash that you're considering investing 80,000
    C. Mortgage that would be required $200,000
    D. *Desired percent return on cash investment of $80,000* 12%
    E. Present gross rental income from this building $54,000
    F. Less: Present operating expenses* and allowances
            for rental delinquencies and vacancies 16,000
    G. Present net operating income .... $ 38,000
    H. Less: 12% return desired on cash investment of $80,000 9,600
    I. Net amount that you would have available for debt service
        (paying mortgage and interest) .... $ 28,400
    J. Divide the net amount that you would have available for debt service ($28,400) by the mortgage required ($200,000):

$$\frac{\$\ 28,400}{\$200,000} = .142(14.2\%)$$

   K. The result in this example, 14.2%, is known as the *annual constant*. It is the maximum percentage of the loan that you could pay each year and still receive the desired percentage on your cash investment.

*Operating expenses are cash charges such as property taxes, wages of management and maintenance personnel, insurance premiums, maintenance operations, etc.
  Operating expenses do not include non-cash charges, such as depreciation and investment tax credits.

2. Now calculate your monthly and annual mortgage payments.
    A. Select mortgage term .... 30 years
    B. Select mortgage interest rate 13%
    C. Consult interest table below. Find intersection of year and
        % 11.07
    D. Divide your intended mortgage amount   ($200,000 ÷ $1,000)
        by $1,000 200
    E. Multiply C by D. This is the total   (11.07 × 200)
        monthly payment covering principal and interest $2,214
    F. Multiply E by 12 for total annual payment covering   ($2,214 × 12)
        principal and interest $26,568
    G. You calculated that you had $28,400 available for debt service on your $200,000 mortgage. Your mortgage calculation shows that you have to pay only $26,568 each year to cover principal and interest. This means that you could realize a greater return than the 12% you desired. The difference provides you with a cushion for possible increases in operating expenses and rental delinquencies and vacancies.

CHART 33 (*continued*)				
	Mortgage Term			
Interest Rate	*15 Years*	*20 Years*	*25 Years*	*30 Years*
10%	10.75	9.66	9.09	8.77
11%	11.36	10.32	9.81	9.52
12%	12.00	11.02	10.54	10.29
13%	12.65	11.72	11.28	11.07
14%	13.32	12.44	12.04	11.85
15%	14.00	13.18	12.81	12.65
16%	14.69	13.91	13.58	13.45
17%	15.39	14.67	14.39	14.26
18%	16.10	15.43	15.17	15.08

Source: SPYF p. 208–9.

they must sell all their assets and distribute net proceeds to stockholders. REITs distribute most of their net income as dividends, and capital gains may be distributed as properties are sold. Many have high yields. Generally, REITs do not afford tax benefits. When earnings are sheltered by depreciation, however, some of their payouts may be classified as a nontaxable return of capital. REITs are subject to the fluctuations of both the real estate and stock markets. Before investing, check their reports for objectives, holdings and performance over various time periods.

REAL ESTATE SECURITIES

If REITs aren't for you, and if you don't care to invest in properties you have to manage, you may want to consider investing in publicly traded real estate securities:

- Stocks and bonds of companies involved directly or indirectly in real estate. Those involved directly include developers, builders, building

CHART 34
Figuring Monthly Mortgage Payments

Use the table below to calculate monthly mortgage payments.
A. Select mortgage term　　　　　　　　　　　_____
B. Select mortgage interest rate　　　　　　　　_____
C. Consult table. Find intersection of year and %　_____
D. Divide your intended mortgage amount by $1,000　_____
E. Multiply C by D
   This is the total monthly payment covering principal and
   interest　　　　　　　　　　　　　　　　　_____

Interest Rate	Mortgage Term			
	15 Years	20 Years	25 Years	30 Years
10%	10.75	9.66	9.09	8.77
11%	11.36	10.32	9.81	9.52
12%	12.00	11.02	10.54	10.29
13%	12.65	11.72	11.28	11.07
14%	13.32	12.44	12.04	11.85
15%	14.00	13.18	12.81	12.65
16%	14.69	13.91	13.58	13.45
17%	15.39	14.67	14.39	14.26
18%	16.10	15.43	15.17	15.08

Source: SPYF p. 192

supply manufacturers, and mortgage insurers and sponsors. Those initially involved engage extensively in real estate activities even though it's not their only business.

● Stocks and bonds of companies with large real estate holdings. These companies own large tracts of land but are not perceived as being in the real estate business. They include railroads and some companies engaged in oil and gas production, agriculture, forest products manufacturing and mining.

● Government and commercial mortgage-backed securities. These securities, issued by various government agencies and by publicly and privately owned companies, are backed by pools of mortgages.

- Securities of companies investing in real estate within a group framework. These include mutual funds, unit trusts, and limited partnerships that specialize in investing in real estate holdings. They also include real estate investment trusts.

Above all, you will need to have a long, clear picture of what your monthly mortgage payments will be. Chart 34 gives the spread.

Part III

Lifestyles in Retirement

11

Retire to the Future

DEFINED BY THE JOB

It's hardly surprising that many people approach their retirement with a freightcar-load of mixed emotions. For men in particular, but also for an increasing number of women, the job has defined a large part of their existence. One of the first questions you are asked by people you meet at parties and in other social arenas is, "What do you do?"—meaning of course, "What is your job?" Socially it is an easy way of breaking the ice, a topic you can finesse in a hundred different ways until you and your new acquaintance can discover some common interests. But it also places you in an immediately defining societal context, however superficial that context may be in measuring who you are as a human being and what you might be like as a friend.

Take one example. Historically, writers of film scripts and popular novels have often (and falsely) depicted accountants as outright nerds, seldom permitting the poor sadsacks even a few eccentricities. They are seen instead as faceless men with no imagination, no spark—boring by definition. Is it any wonder that in certain social situations today you don't often hear an accountant actually admit, "I'm an accountant." You hear, rather, "I'm a CPA," or "I have my own accounting firm," or "I'm at Arthur Andersen & Company." That takes the curse off. That adds status to an oral resume and makes the speaker somebody to reckon with. The real attention-getters, though, are hot comebacks like "I'm in advertising," or "the entertainment business," or simply "Wall Street." Both men and women are instantly intrigued by almost any person involved in one of these glamorous business and professional activities, with their overtones of money, power and sex. If you can mention one of them your listener will ease in closer, alert and eager to hear all about the juicy shenanigans you must be up to. And while the reality of the speaker's day-to-day work in his or her field actually may be mundane, it is the listener's perception that counts.

The job not only defines your social standing in varying degrees, it also provides powerful ego support. Through the 1950s at least a man's ego rested on the foundation of his job, which made him the family breadwinner and ultimate ruler. And even with the lifestyle revolutions that have since swept the social landscape, this is still largely true for American men. A man without some sort of a job may feel hard put in our society to keep up the pretense that he is a man at all. If you can't work, a little devil in your mind nags, "What good are you?" As a retiree who has already worked forty years or more, you have no objective reason to feel any guilt and many people are able to ignore it, but only to a degree. You may never be able to rid yourself of the work ethic entirely, buried as it is in your deepest subconscious.

IS THERE LIFE WITHOUT A JOB?

You may also worry simply about getting bored. As a working man or woman, you had somewhere to go and something to do nearly every weekday of your life. Vacations and holidays may have been sweet, but real life meant going back to work on Monday morning. That made you feel right with the world. It gave form and discipline to your existence and a sense of purpose. In retirement these work-connected lifelines will be severed and you may feel cast adrift on an ocean with no horizon, a sort of limbo or, worse yet, a purgatory on earth. How many flowers can I cultivate, you may ask yourself? How many times a week can I play golf? How many newspapers, magazines and books can I read before it all becomes a blur? And how much television can I watch before my mind runs down and turns to catfood?

Add these doubts to your concerns about money, and you may find the prospect of retirement less than welcome. We have talked with a number of people sixty-five and over who are still on the job. Most say they like to work, want to stay mentally sharp and to maintain the sense of usefulness and fulfillment that goes with working. Some even like the feeling they are continuing to contribute to the gross national product, even when it means paying more taxes. Boston University researchers have found that most workers take some form of bridge employment between their principal career jobs and full retirement. This interim occupation often turns into a second career running ten years or more. One in five retirees returns to work in their original career occupation within three years of their initial date of retirement. Does this suggest most American workers can't live on what they thought were adequate retirement nest eggs? Or that some people never think of themselves as nonworkers? Or is it a way of postponing retirement? Perhaps it is some of all three. In any case, most Americans between the ages of sixty and seventy are now too lively to be considered aged, and income-producing activity is one natural outlet for their energies.

On the other side of the equation, seven of ten retirees surveyed by RAI Division, Hearst Business Corporation, said they do not want to return to work. Less than 2 percent of those surveyed said they wanted to work full time. The mean age of retirement in the Hearst study was 62.1 years, and the age range was from twenty-nine to eighty-nine. It is difficult at best to compare the two studies directly, since the former is a study of numbers and the latter a study of attitudes. One encouraging clue for pre-retirees in the Hearst study, however, suggests that retirement may have a lot more going for it than you might think. If 70 percent of retirees in fact don't want to go back to work, and less than 2 percent want to go back to work full time, it's entirely possible most people really *like* being retired. We suspect that is really the truth of the matter. And one of the secrets to overcoming your anxieties about retirement is to determine that you are retiring not *from* your job and your past, but *to* the future, to an active and exciting new life.

PICK YOUR RETIREMENT DAY CAREFULLY

The exact date you select for retirement can sometimes make a substantial difference in your finances, according to Associate Professor Robert J. Doyle, Jr., of the American College in Philadelphia. "As an example," says Professor Doyle, "your pension computation formula may produce a higher benefit because an additional year of service is counted if you work only one or two additional months. Or a slight delay in retirement may enable you to receive a matching employer contribution to a savings or thrift plan, gain rights to additional shares of company stock, or be credited with another month of paid vacation time." For reasons such as these, Professor Doyle points out, it usually pays to look at each and every employer fringe benefit and ask when it is most advantageous to retire: When planned? Earlier than planned? Later than planned?

A specific retirement date can then be selected that is most beneficial to you. Doyle notes that some business organizations offer special early-retirement packages designed to encourage employees to retire if they are above a certain age. The package may include a Social Security supplement to tide the retiree over until he or she becomes eligible for Social Security benefits. But Professor Doyle, who is also a Chartered Life Underwriter, a Chartered Financial Consultant and author of the book *Tax-Sheltered Investments: A Guide for Professionals,* cautions: "These offers can be very attractive. Nevertheless, the package needs to be examined carefully on a benefit-by-benefit basis to determine whether accepting the offer is in your best interest." He notes that most people retire at about age sixty-two, corresponding to the start of actuarially reduced Social Security benefits. But if you find after taking stock of your financial situation, that your expected income in retirement won't be adequate to maintain the lifestyle you want, you may choose to work longer simple to add to your retirement nest egg.

DECIDING WHERE TO LIVE

One of the first issues you must consider when contemplating retirement is where you are going to live. Many experts say the best place to retire is in the same community, or at least the same area, in which you lived during your working years. The reasons are fairly obvious. First, it's familiar territory. It's home and it feels like home. Second, a majority of your children probably live nearby, although some may be scattered across the country or around the world. You can easily visit back and forth, sharing in the family's love and watching your grandchildren grow and develop. Your family will also be quickly available whenever you need help. Many of your old friends may remain close by as well, adding to your sense of belonging and of a complete and fulfilled existence. (In cases where your only children live far away, however, you may justifiably feel compelled to go to them.) Need more help in your decision to stay or go? Take the quiz in Chart 35.

If you seek change, adventure, better weather or more economical living, then you must go for a new location, but look carefully before you leap. Begin the process of evaluation many months or even several years before your retirement, for the choice is a critical one and factors have to be weighed that bear on your lifestyle, your tax situation, even your estate.

First, consider what you are looking for in making a move. Is it a different way of life altogether—the country not the city? The shore not the mountains? Is it to be closer to your family or friends? Or perhaps it's a matter of personal finances—of being able to get along on less money—or having more money to follow an avocation such as sailing? Whatever the reason, you should consider the following criteria in making your choice:

- Climate and environment.

- Cost and availability of housing.

- Other costs of living.

- Quality of medical services.

- Recreational and cultural activities.

- Special services for retirees.

One way to test a potential retirement community is to vacation there. But don't make your decision on the basis of only one visit. Go several times during different seasons of the year. Ask other retirees about the advantages and drawbacks of the area. Get a feel for the location by subscribing to a local newspaper. Talk with a local accountant about the state and city taxes you'll be paying in the new location. Florida and some other states, for example, have an intangible tax—an annual levy on the fair market values of stocks and bonds. Many states give retirees various kinds of breaks on property taxes, but some do not. Some states don't levy an income tax on Social Security payments, or on federal pensions. Some even exempt private pension payments. Others offer income tax credits. To obtain a free pamphlet, "State Tax Information for Relocation Decisions," write AARP Fulfillment, 1909 K Street NW, Washington, DC 20049.

RESORT PROPERTY CHECKLIST

Those who can afford it often seek resort properties when they think of retiring. Living a life of leisure in a beautiful, sunny resort area sounds romantic and it often is, but first-time buyers of this type of property should proceed with particular caution. When you are ready to begin looking for your special place in the sun, follow this checklist:

- Check the track record of the builder if you are buying into a newly built resort complex. Is he likely to deliver on promises? Will he be agreeable to adding or subtracting in response to your personal requests and requirements? Read the builder's prospectus carefully.

CHART 35
QUIZ: Should you stay or should you go?

Some people will have no problem at all making such a decision. Others might agonize themselves into making a wrong one. There probably is no right answer but as an assist we've set out some basic requirements for a good life—and a little gracious living.

Using 5 as high mark, rate the listings below on a 0–5 basis. Add up your total score and see how your tally translates at the foot of the illustration.

Location

Age demographics .... _____
Availability of apartments, other rental residences .... _____
Availability of houses, condos, co-ops for sale .... _____
Banks, stockbrokers, lawyers, financial planners, insurance agents,
tax preparers .... _____
Bowling, golf, tennis .... _____
Camping, hiking, boating, fishing .... _____
Cemeteries, funeral homes .... _____
Concerts, fine arts.. _____
Continuing adult education .... _____
Cost of housing .... _____
Cost of living .... _____
Crime rates, person (murder, assault, rape, robbery) .... _____
Crime rates, property (burglary, vandalism, auto theft) .... _____
Cultural activities.. _____
Driver-license tests .... _____
Economic outlook for the area.. _____
Full- and part-time job opportunities...................................... _____
Gardening soil, pests... _____
Gyms, swimming .... _____
Health-care costs .... _____
Health-care practitioners .... _____
Hospitals, other health-care facilities .... _____
How cold the winters .... _____
How hot the summers .... _____
Libraries .... _____
Local household income and net worth ranges.............................. _____
Local taxes on retirement income .... _____
Manufactured-home communities... _____
Movie theatres.. _____
Museums .... _____
Own-business opportunities.. _____
Parks, coastline, lakes, rivers, zoos, wildlife refuges .... _____
Performing arts .... _____
Police, firefighting, sanitation .... _____
Political .... _____
Post office.. _____
Property insurance rates.. _____

CHART 35 (*continued*)	
Property taxes	————
Public transportation	————
Restaurants	————
Retail shopping and services	————
Retirement communities	————
Sales taxes	————
Sports events	————
State and local income taxes.	————
Utility costs	————
Weather variations and hazards.	————
<u>TOTAL SCORE</u>	————

Over 200—definitely, a top retirement location for you. 180-199—Very likely. 160-179—Somewhat, consider further. 140-159—Marginal, be very careful. Under 140—Forget it.

Source: SPARN 11/89.

- Property on the waterfront in a development is, generally, a better investment and has greater rental potential even though it is usually more expensive. Before buying, check on water pollution controls and possible soil or beach erosion.

- Check the entire property map—not only the sections already constructed, but those planned for the future. That splendid view of the ocean from your unit's terrace may be irresistible when you buy, but if there's an empty lot in front of you the developer's long-term plan may call for another building. Then you may find yourself looking at a wall, not an ocean. Get protection in your contract, written down, not as a verbal assurance.

- Study the property carefully. Is routine maintenance up to standard? Are the grounds, roads and facilities well kept? Check built-in fire warning and escape mechanisms at the complex.

- Security is important in a resort complex. Is the area well protected? If you plan to be away for considerable periods of time, is there a watch system, and is this part of the service or is there a fee? How about protection against natural hazards—floods, hurricanes, avalanches? What would a natural catastrophe do to your investment? What kind of insurance is necessary?

- Look at the available recreational facilities. Are there enough swimming pools for the number of residents and guests in the complex? Are golf, tennis and other sports available? Is there an extra charge? Are the sports facilities owned by the complex? If they are leased, can fees be boosted without the owners' approval? If you plan to rent out your property, could your renters use the facilities without charge or at a modest fee? The more recreational possibilities available, the greater the rental potential.

- Consider the accessibility of the complex. How distant is the closest major airport? Are there bus routes or taxis nearby? How about proximity to hospitals and healthcare centers.

- Investigate the region carefully. You might have been dreaming of this area all your working life, but will it suit you in retirement? Are there activities, amusements and amenities geared toward an older population? Is the area on the way up or down?

- Check on the current cost of living. Compare prices for groceries, restaurants, shops. Will the area be too expensive for your retirement income?

DON'T RULE OUT RETIRING ABROAD

If you've been fantasizing about retiring abroad, don't dismiss the idea as an aberration. Millions of Americans before you had a similar dream of living in a foreign land and acted upon it. Some to work, some to study, some to retire. In 1988, there were more than 2.5 million U.S. citizens living in other countries. Most of them were in Europe, Canada or the Caribbean. Several hundred thousand were in the Middle East, Asia or Africa. Twelve years ago, Jack, an association executive, bought a modest house in the Pyrenees. Four years ago he retired to his "castle in Spain" and is living there happily. Over sixty-five, Mary B. was tired of working but had too little income to live in Los Angeles. She is thriving today on her Social Security and a small pension on a remote Greek island—not so remote that her friends don't flock to Greece and seek her out. Neither has a French chateau nor an English manor house, but life is good, the experiences fresh, the challenges invigorating.

Before you start packing, think it through. Do some research and make your decision knowing as many facts as possible—the delights and the drawbacks.

- Will you be welcome?

- Can you obtain a residence permit?

- What other documents and papers might be required? For example, some countries may demand a financial statement to show you will not become a liability on their social services.

- Will you have a language problem?

- Do you understand the culture and can you be comfortable with it?

- What is the dollar exchange rate?

- Does your spouse really share your enthusiasm?

- Will you pay dual taxes?

- Would it be possible, should you desire it, to obtain a part-time job?

- What kind of medical insurance will cover you in another country?

- How easy or difficult will it be to keep an eye on your personal and financial affairs?

- Are you escaping a personal problem such as the death of a spouse or estrangement from children? Psychologists say you can't run away, no matter how much mileage you put between yourself and the source of your trouble. Leave on an upbeat note with a positive outlook.

But don't let the stay-at-homes talk you out of retiring abroad either. It makes sense if you want to rejoin family members or friends, or return to your cultural roots—and it doesn't have to be forever. Perhaps you just want to experience living in a different culture for a lengthier time than a two-week vacation has allowed, or you want a slower pace of living, or to become familiar with different values. And just perhaps your life-long image of Shangri-La has always been a cottage in Devon, or a bungalow on Bali.

Before selling your home and pulling up stakes take a long vacation in the host country. Make some tentative connections with a local banker, lawyer, physician or with American expatriates already living there. When you do move begin by registering with the U.S. Embassy. In return, the U.S. Department of State will extend its protective arm and an embassy or local consulate could even become a source of your first social contacts. Making the proper arrangements before you leave will ensure that you have no difficulty receiving your Social Security or pension check. If you do have trouble, a U.S Consular official can help you. The State Department, through its Overseas Citizens Services, is ready to help before you go and after you arrive. For a recorded message or to ask specific questions of a State Department Advisor, you may call (202)647-3444.

WHO WILL BE FRIEND AND NEIGHBOR?

Another important issue to be considered in deciding where to retire is this: Should you live in an area dominated by other people your own age? Or should you settle or stay in a mixed-age neighborhood? If you remain in your old neighborhood there is no relocation shock and no need to build a new social life or support system. Some people also say that family and young friends help keep them young, and they opt to stay away from the "old fogies." But Dr. James Mold, assistant professor of family medicine at the University of Oklahoma Health Sciences Center, and Dr. Jacques Cook, a certified social worker and associate professor of psychiatry at Oklahoma, argue that for some retirees a support system is more attractive if it is made up of persons their own age.

Mold and Cook list these advantages of moving into an area dominated by older persons:

- Being with people who have similar interests.

- Being with people with whom you can share lifetime experiences.

- Being with people with leisure time so activities can be coordinated.

- Having a close-knit circle of understanding friends.

On the other hand, say Professors Mold and Cook, there also are advantages to living in a mixed-age community:

- Having someone younger and stronger nearby to help in an emergency.

- Having the opportunity to become a mentor to a younger person.

- Having transportation assistance available, especially for those living alone.

No matter what social support system you prefer, you would be wise to take major lifestyle changes into account as well. These could include a spouse becoming ill or handicapped. They might also include remarriage or a new career launch.

THE SEAWANE CROWD MOVES TOGETHER

Your finances, health, age at retirement and marital status will probably play the dominant roles in your decision about where to retire. Beginning in the 1970s, a large number of couples from the Long Island, New York, community of Hewlett Harbor retired within a few years of one another and moved virtually *en masse* to the Woodlands golf-course community near Fort Lauderdale. All were reasonably close in age and close enough in terms of income. Nearly all had belonged to the Seawane country club and were generally long-term friends or acquaintances. Although no one planned the move to Florida in any comprehensive way, the so-called Seawane crowd wound up retired or semiretired within a short walk or a few minutes drive of one another. They simply joined the Woodlands Golf Club and more or less resumed their community life in the new location. During the hot South Florida summers, they migrated back to apartments in Hewlett Harbor or fanned out to Spain and other parts of the world. Some of the couples had worried about becoming bored in Florida, but the nearness of many old friends, continuing business interests, the ability to travel and frequent visits by children and grandchildren ultimately convinced most that boredom was not to be a problem. Overall, retirement for the Seawane group has seemed a largely happy experience.

JACK'S EXPERIENCE

Across the country, in a West Coast city, retirement has been an entirely different sort of experience for a man we have known for a long time and will call Jack M. A steelworker, Jack retired at sixty-five with a comfortable nest egg of savings, a liberal pension plan and medical insurance program as well as Social Security benefits. He also owned a nearby rental house and a vacant lot on the outskirts of the city. Jack could have afforded to retire in another state or another country, but his wife had passed away several years earlier, he had already lived and worked in three diverse parts of the country, and that sort of change was not his cup of tea. In addition, three of his four sons and a dozen grandchildren lived within a half-hour drive of his home. Jack was not about to move anywhere—except, as it happened, to a nursing home. He developed Parkinson's disease shortly after leaving his job and within a few years needed full-time care. The upside to Jack's otherwise sad story is that his children and grandchildren visit him often, he is picked up and taken to one of their homes on holidays for family get-togethers, he likes the food and even some of his companions in the nursing facility, and he seems reasonably content. He isn't wintering in Florida and summering in Europe, but he isn't alone and destitute. A Southerner by birth, and a child of the Great Depression, Jack's greatest fear in life was that he would end his days "in the county poorhouse." Life dealt him a bad gene, to be sure, but he hasn't been taken down by poverty or lack of his family's love and attention. His family has made all the difference.

THE LOVE OF CHILDREN

Family made the difference too when another acquaintance of ours decided to retire. We will call him Elliott, and his wife Jean. Jean had been a homemaker since the couple married when she was nineteen after World War II. Elliott and Jean raised four bright children. The two older offspring were girls, the two younger were boys. All four had grown into responsible, educated, productive adults with children of their own, and they adored their parents. The family always seemed to have plenty of money, and Jean in particular never gave a serious thought to the possibility that someday she might not have so much of it. What Jean wanted, and Jean wanted a lot over the years, she got. Elliott went along with the spending to please his wife, and because he enjoyed the luxuries as much as she and felt proud that he could provide them.

The family lived in a large Colonial-style home, beautifully decorated by Jean, which Elliott built in an expensive suburb of Chicago a few years following the couple's marriage. Every winter they went on long vacation cruises or rented expensive chalets in the Caribbean. When they were in their mid-teens and early twenties the four children all travelled to Europe on several occasions. All things considered, the family enjoyed an idyllic lifestyle, and flourished.

As the owner of a small steel-fabricating company which he inherited from his father, Elliott made it all possible. But while he also invested some money in stocks for his retirement, his business ultimately failed because of foreign competition and his assets fell somewhat short of being able to provide the lifestyle he and Jean had long enjoyed. They stretched a little too far to buy a new retirement home with a swimming pool in Arizona, and stretched again in furnishing the place. In half a dozen years, even with trimming back on their expenses, Elliott and Jean needed some financial help. Luckily for them, their four children came to the rescue. The oldest daughter and her husband took over the cost of providing her parents an automobile. The other three chipped in toward monthly living expenses and also provided cash in emergencies. They felt such sharing was the least they could do for having been given the opportunity to prosper and live happily themselves.

We repeat these stories to illustrate some of the fears and problems you may encounter in retirement, even if you have been moderately prudent throughout your working life. Things happen. No one is perfect and no one can foresee the future. But you will find in reality that most of your concerns are misplaced. After some initial job-separation shock, you will probably find in fact that you are having a ball, that perhaps for the first time in your life the future is really yours to enjoy.

12

Don't Let Them
Push You Around

YOUR POLITICAL CLOUT

Remember that you and others in your age group have enormous financial and political clout. Studies show that Americans over the age of fifty control fully one-half of the nation's disposable income, placing you at ground zero for the legions of bombardiers in advertising and marketing. After decades of discounting you, major advertising agencies now study you from head to toe, divining how to get your attention, cater to your needs and arouse your desires, all the better to separate you from a pot of your cash. What they are finding in their studies is that you like quality products and don't mind paying for them, that you are lively, sexy, innovative, more willing to try new things than anyone suspected, certainly more than many self-obsessed baby boomers. They also find that you hate being categorized and lumped together by euphemistic nametags like mature consumer, senior citizen, or golden harvest gang.

In their book *Age Wave* (Tarcher, 1989), Ken Dychtwald and Joe Flower point out that for the first time in America's history people over sixty-five now outnumber teenagers, a consequence of the fact that during the past century the older-American population has multiplied three times as fast as the population at large. Because of this demographic revolution, Dychtwald and Flower predict that the concerns of middle-aged and older Americans will dominate U.S. political priorities for some time to come. They also argue that even the physical design and environment of the country will change to accommodate a middle-aged and older population. Doorknobs may be replaced by levers, and traffic lights may change more slowly, allowing time for the less agile to get across intersections. Be that as it may, demography is destiny, and demography is now on the side of retirees and others over the age of fifty. The sheer weight of your political and economic power is brought to bear in the voting booth and through a number of potent organizations such as the American Association of Retired Persons (AARP) and the National Council on the Aging (NCOA), both headquartered virtually within hailing distance of Capitol Hill. Perhaps the lesser known of the two groups, NCOA, was established some forty years ago to serve as a national source of information, training, technical assistance, advocacy and research on every aspect of aging. NCOA's membership includes individuals, voluntary agencies, associations, business organizations, labor unions and others united by commitment to the principle that the nation's older persons are entitled to lives of dignity, physical and mental well-being, and to full participation in society. The membership of the powerful AARP, which anyone fifty or over can join, now exceeds 30 million.

GRANNY-BASHING

What is granny-bashing, really? Could it be a game perhaps? Or a bit of black humor aimed at older people? No, not quite either of those. Granny-bashing is in fact as real and as common as child abuse in this country—and as cruel. Defined precisely, granny-bashing refers to the physical violence that all too many adult children administer to their aging, defenseless parents. It springs often from the misguided anger and frustration that wells up in offspring because mom and dad have become for them an almost unbearable burden. The parents have emotional and sometimes overwhelming physical and financial needs, but few resources. So the kids get revenge on the old folks for being helpless and dependent by beating them up. Granny-bashing is a dirty little family secret that makes life a living hell for some parents who should be loved and venerated. To overstate the case, however, would be misleading. Dr. Daniel Thursz, president of the National Council on the Aging, has pointed out that the vast majority of American families—85 percent, in fact—contribute financially to the care of their older or younger members. "We don't give enough credit to the family in this country for its sense of responsibility and generosity toward the family unit," Dr. Thursz argues. "Children take care of parents and grandparents, and grandparents take on their grandchildren. This selfless sharing of financial resources adds immeasurably to the quality of family life."

Granny-bashing is nevertheless one of the shames of our society. Defined more broadly, the term can be applied to a wide range of insults, indignities, slights and abuses that individuals and institutions may attempt to visit upon older people. The good news is that you don't have to take it. You can stand up for your rights, make sure you get all the retirement benefits you have coming, and completely redraw your life, if necessary, for long-term active, independent living.

A BATTLE OF GENERATIONS

Observers have been saying for years that a battle between age groups was inevitable in the United States. Their theory is that as baby boomers pass retirement age, beginning in about twenty-odd years, the number of people creating wealth will be far fewer than the number consuming it. The youngsters of the year 2015 or thereabouts may then become fed up with the economic load they are carrying, the argument goes, and will indulge themselves in a national frenzy of granny-bashing.

The prospect of such a rebellion is one of the reasons advanced for segregating the Social Security Trust Funds and dedicating them to Social Security benefits in the next century. By the year 2000, experts say, the combined surpluses of the Old Age and Survivors Trust, and the Disability Insurance Trust, will probably reach $1.4 trillion. By 2013, they predict, the surpluses will approach $1.7 trillion. At that point, however, demographics turn the system around. Writing in *Newsweek*, Paul Craig Roberts, who holds the William E. Simon Chair of Political Economy at the Center for Strategic & International Studies in Washington, says the annual Social Security surplus turns into an annual deficit. Eight years later, Roberts adds, the accumulated cash surplus will have been used up, leaving the system facing trillion-dollar deficits. Accumulated interest on the surplus can carry the system a while longer, but to overcome the deficits would require an annual payroll tax of 24 percent.

Social Security payroll taxes were substantially boosted by legislation enacted in 1983, at a time when the system seemed threatened with bankruptcy. The law decreed a further increase in 1990. It also directed that trust fund surpluses be invested in special government bonds. The proceeds from the bond sales could be used (and are being used) by the government to pay its bills. And while Social Security is legally not a part of the federal budget, it is nevertheless included in the total "unified" budget for purposes of meeting the deficit-reduction requirements of the Gramm-Rudman-Hollings law. Critics of the 1983 Social Security legislation, including one of its architects, Senator Daniel Patrick Moynihan of New York, say the use of trust fund surpluses to pay current government bills is poor fiscal policy. "I don't think we should mask the deficit by pretending that trust fund surpluses are general revenues," says Moynihan. "The funds hold IOUs for every penny, and the money will have to be paid back." A more important concern is whether the money will be there when it is needed to pay benefits to baby-boom retirees. Not only is the money being spent to pay the government's current bills, but as the surpluses in the funds have mounted so has political pressure to use them for a variety of new or expanded social programs—roads, housing projects, education, health care, even a proposal that the government give parents $2,000 a year for every child they have under age sixteen, to promote fertility.

The issue of who will pay and when they will pay for the healthcare of older citizens was central to the 1989 debate over the Medicare catastrophic coverage legislation. It is now manifest in the drive by industry to reduce or abandon benefits for retirees. A more ominous threat is *triage*, or the rationing of healthcare. Some analysts observe that triage already takes place, when doctors limit tests and medical procedures, and hospitals discharge patients early under government pressure to reduce healthcare costs.

It is startling even to think that medical treatments may someday be denied to individuals when they become eighty, although such a proposal was advanced in a 1988 book, *Setting Limits*, by Daniel Callahan, director of the Hastings Center, an influential think tank in Briarcliff Manor, New York. Similar proposals have also been offered in Europe, and must be taken seriously. Other ideas hatched at the Hastings Center have been adopted by the American Medical Association, according to Gerard Bradley, a law professor at the University of Illinois. Should you be concerned? Yes. Should you be alarmed? No. Should you be prepared to stand up and fight for alternative schemes that are more in harmony with the requirements of constitutional law, the goals of nondiscrimination and the basic concepts of fundamental morality? Absolutely!

WATCH OVER YOUR BENEFITS

If you are retired or eligible to retire with liberal healthcare benefits, you should keep a close watch on your benefits package. Cutbacks in Medicare coverage, a growing pool of retirees, anemic company earnings and skyrocketing healthcare costs are causing thousands of employers to take a dyspeptic second look at the retiree medical benefits they have been offering. Attitudes toward these benefits will unquestionably harden further during the next few years. In 1991, companies must begin phasing in a new accounting rule requiring them to show retiree health liabilities on their balance sheets. Experts say the new accounting requirement could reduce the net income of many firms and affect their credit rating. Quite understandably, the new corporate battlecry is "contain costs and trim benefits." Thomas A. Jorgensen, a partner in Calfee, Halter & Griswold, a Cleveland law firm, points out that ERISA, the federal Employees Retirement Security Act of 1974, requires employers to set aside reserves to cover pension costs. (ERISA also set up the Pension Benefits Guarantee Corporation.) But retiree medical coverage isn't secured by federal statute. Companies have the right to change or deep-six these benefits, and health consultants say more and more companies may feel compelled to do just that.

Your ability to influence company decisions in the healthcare area is limited, particularly if you're a number of years away from retirement. But if you are already retired or eligible to retire, you may have more influence than you think. To defend your benefits, consider the following steps:

- Ask your company for a statement of benefits offered under its federally approved retirement plan.

- Request a separate statement spelling out healthcare benefits. Save all the documentation you can get your hands on, including employee benefit handbooks, written summaries, letters and statements indicating the nature of the benefits the company has promised.

In a legal dispute between you and your employer, these materials will become extremely important. Jorgensen says courts generally are deciding retiree healthcare issues on the basis of what was promised the employee. When a company has not reserved the right to modify or cut off benefits, courts often decide such benefits are protected contractually. Any action you take to protect your benefits must be timely, however. The first time you discover your medical coverage is being reduced, contact the company at once for an explanation. Don't wait for the second round of cuts. If you fail to question changes immediately, the company may argue in court that it has the right to reduce benefits because previous changes were not challenged.

In all likelihood, there will be times when you will need a lawyer to help you protect your rights as an older person. A new field of specialization in law is emerging in response to the increasing numbers of Americans past middle age—and the particular problems they encounter. Called *elderlaw* by some practitioners, the new discipline has little connection with legal matters traditionally associated with older people, such as drafting wills and trusts or assisting in estate planning. The new elderlaw specialists focus instead on these problem areas:

- Fighting age discrimination. An elderlaw attorney might file suit, for example, to recover loss of income due to age discrimination by an employer.

- Establishing eligibility for Social Security or Supplemental Security income. If you feel you are being denied these benefits unfairly, consider consulting an elderlaw attorney.

- Obtaining state or federal medical assistance for one spouse, while preserving the healthy spouse's home and other assets.

- Arranging a conservatorship for someone able to live at home, but no longer competent to manage his or her financial affairs.

- Setting up a durable power of attorney for payment of healthcare expenses.

- Winning rights for grandparents to visit the children of their divorced offspring.

- Protecting older persons from physical abuse by close relatives (granny-bashing)—a form of family violence thought to be as prevalent as child abuse.

The American Bar Association has set up a Washington-based Commission on Legal Problems of the Elderly. The group conducts training programs for ABA members throughout the United States. Its seminars concentrate on the complex regulations that control benefit programs and on a lawyer's duty to represent the older client rather than the inheriting offspring, among other concerns. Some thirty states also have organized bar committees to assist lawyers with Social Security eligibility requirements and living wills (i.e., written statements to withhold or withdraw life-sustaining treatment when death appears inevitable). Don't be overly concerned about having the money to pay for an elderlaw specialist. California attorneys Michael and Myra-Gerson Gilfix have won a ruling that the Older Americans Act, which provides federal funding for legal services for the elderly, applies to all older citizens regardless of income.

Living a longer and livelier life, as most of us plan to do, means staying on top of many simple legal rights that help protect our personal financial security. A recent book, *Your Legal Rights in Later Life*, (Little, Brown and Company, $13.95) considerably eases the task. Written by John J. Regan in conjunction with the Legal Counsel for the Elderly, the book was published by the American Association of Retired Persons and is a real gold mine of legal-rights information. The author argues persuasively that due to the complexity of the system, rights to retirement income, health care and related assistance are not always evident. And yet as individuals we are often the most effective defenders of our rights. In particular, Regan's book offers strong chapters on consumer rights—and warnings on the kinds of dangerous contractual clauses known to have been imposed, often illegally, by creditors. Following is a sampling of the comments Regan offers in his chapter on consumer rights:

- *Balloon payments.* (This is a final payment that is much larger than other installments). While creditors generally can offer contracts containing balloon payments, they must disclose the fact in advance. The danger is that you won't be able to afford the balloon payment and will be forced either to refinance the debt at a much higher rate of interest, or lose your purchase.

- *Security interests.* Many states prohibit this type of floating security interest. If you buy a car on credit, the creditor may use it as collateral for your debt. Regan advises walking away from any deal where the creditor insists on a security interest in goods that are not part of the immediate sale. For example, if you buy a washing machine, the creditor should not use your previously purchased television as collateral for the washing machine.

- *Wage assignments.* This is a contract provision that gives the creditor the right to collect a debt from the consumer's wages in case of default. Many states either prohibit assignments or exempt a certain amount of wages from the assignment, the author points out.

- *Obligations of co-signers.* If another person becomes responsible for your debts, many states require that the person be notified as to the nature of his or her responsibility prior to the contract going into effect.

- *Acceleration clauses.* Under an acceleration clause, the creditor has the right to demand immediate payment of the entire balance. Since these clauses are legal, you must protect yourself by reading the fine print in a sales contract and then deciding whether you want to sign such an agreement.

A willingness to defend your rights is one way to making sure that you remain the master of your own retirement rather than a potential victim.

THE GROWING SOCIAL DILEMMA

Thirty years ago we reported that nearly 75 percent of all Americans over sixty-five had no income whatsoever or incomes of less than $1,000 a year. We were recently reminded of that fact by a reader with a long memory, Vera A. Fossali, a certified financial planner and an agent of Monarch Life. The income figures have changed, she observed, but the problem continues.

"How difficult it is," she said, "to encourage clients to start early, to protect themselves from becoming a financial burden to their families and government."

By mid-1985, only 1.9 percent of men and 4 percent of women over sixty-five had incomes of less than $2,000, and only 12.4 percent of all those over sixty-five were below the poverty level. The fact remains that aging in America, although it is no new phenomenon, presents one of the growing social dilemmas for young people and for the government. At all but the highest income levels, building retirement income can be difficult and fraught with uncertainties. This despite changed conditions which help older Americans. Social Security provides a floor. There are tax incentives for savers. Pensions, largely an executive perk in 1985, today protect 111 million covered workers and their dependents.

A NATIONAL RETIREMENT POLICY

While as a society we are struggling for answers, there is a growing movement to rationalize the problems of aging through a national retirement policy. At the core of this discussion is the question of pension portability. It is not clear what portability means as a term or in its impact on business and individuals. Nevertheless, legislation mandating portability is at least on the minds of many lawmakers and social thinkers.

The concept of pension portability has long existed in Europe, where state-run clearing houses ensure that an employee's pension remains intact for his or her working life, regardless of job moves. President George Bush is on record as favoring pension portability and former Secretary of Labor Elizabeth Dole has come out four-square for the idea. In a speech to the AFL-CIO executive council, she solicited the advice of that group on "how to enable the worker to take pension benefits from job to job to job." An expert in the field, James A. Curtis, chairman and CEO of the employee benefits firm of Milliman & Robertson, believes that pension portability is inevitable because of the increased mobility of our society and the trend toward a service-oriented economy, conditions which require the retraining and relocation of millions of workers. "Some sort of central clearing house will be established for portable pensions," says Curtis, "and this will be greatly facilitated by the availability of less expensive computers with advanced technology."

The National Association of Manufacturers is among the organizations that support pension portability. The American Academy of Actuaries, a professional association of more than 8,000 actuaries, 85 percent of whom are involved in pension 158sign, argues that portability requires a retirement income policy yet to be formalized. The group has called for a moratorium on legislated changes in pension systems until previous changes have been implemented and studied. In their view, a national retirement policy is a critical first step. The academy's testimony to Congress has suggested that the pension debate is fueled by the government's need to increase revenue, rather than, as it should be, the need to resolve a major social issue.

"We cannot overemphasize the need for a more stable pension environment," the actuaries told a congressional subcommittee. "For the better part of two decades, the voluntary private pension system has been subject to continuous rule changes. The sum total of these almost annual changes has been unnecessary complexity, increased administrative expense, and the loss of focus on what the law and policy should be: (1) to encourage employers to offer pension plans to their employees, and (2) to protect the retirement income provided by those plans."

The actuaries' statement added: "Any legislative response to portability is without teeth if it does not address inflation protection. And any action on inflation protection is partial and flawed if it does not consider post-retirement as well as pre-retirement inflation."

Another group, the American Society of Pension Actuaries, is even less circumspect. "Decisions are made ad hoc on Social Security, on private pension plans and on taxing contributions and benefits, without any established idea of what it all adds up to," the society charges. "There is now no policy that assures adequate retirement income to all Americans. The need is urgent for an integrated and cohesive policy and for the means to achieve it. The future stability of the American economy is at stake, not only the welfare of its senior citizens."

The ASPA sees the need for a four-legged pension system, comprising Society Security, private pension plans, personal savings and optional continued work after first retirement. It calls for a new Commission for a National Retirement Income Policy, including members of Congress, representatives of the Social Security Administration, professional experts, and representatives of the public.

In the view of Milliman & Robertson's CEO James Curtis, a stable, acceptable employee benefits structure would be good social policy, relieve the government of the large cost of providing for great numbers of people who come to retirement without income beyond Social Security, and take employee benefits out of the arena of political whim and budget desires. Curtin says Congress has to be shown that a sound program shouldn't be thought of in terms of lost dollars. Rather, he argues, it will pay off for all taxpayers through greater productivity and job satisfaction, along with self-sufficiency during retirement.

All these ideas are heartening, but what has really happened? Not much. The most serious discussion still is confined largely to pension actuaries and benefits consultants. Both provide expert testimony. Neither can lobby. Meantime, there is no group of citizens or even of employers that we have been able to identify seeking early congressional action. Perhaps it's time for a coalition to form. As in so many instances, your elected representatives need to know what you think.

But even with a national retirement policy the only real financial security you are likely to have will come from your own efforts. Social Security and pension plans provide a base, but rarely will they let you maintain your lifestyle. Whatever your age, begin now to plan your financial future through insurance and annuities, securities, real estate and other wealth builders. If, along the way, you get some breaks from Congress, consider it a bonus.

13

Working After Retirement

Several fundamental changes in the nation's business climate and work force have recently combined to create vast new employment opportunities for older Americans. The first is a shrinking pool of younger workers. Second is the availability of many older individuals who want to work full time or part time. Third is the intensifying pressure on U.S. corporations to cut costs in the face of tougher foreign and domestic competition. Finally, it has perhaps belatedly dawned on many business executives that older workers have a great deal to offer. They are valued in particular for their strong work ethic, knowledge and experience and low absenteeism, all factors that contribute to cost effectiveness. They also have a strong positive influence on a company's younger workers, increasing their reliability, productivity and morale, and even reducing the rate of job hopping. Some companies use retirees to train their new young workers. Hiring older workers also makes sense for other business reasons. Average part-timers earn less than comparable full-time employees, and many part-time jobs don't provide expensive fringe benefits.

The U.S. Bureau of Labor Statistics says that during the past six years the number of part-timers increased 7 percent, to nearly 20 million. Those fifty-five years of age and older jumped to 334,000 and now comprise more than 18 percent of the total part-time work force. Nor is the trend likely to end anytime soon.

Studies show that the number of Americans twenty to twenty-nine years of age will drop from approximately 41 million in 1990 to 34.5 million by the year 2000. Most of the part-time jobs currently are in sales, particularly telemarketing, and service industries—messengers, receptionists and fast-food counter workers. But there also are a growing number of job opportunities for retired professionals and the highly skilled. Aerospace Corporation of Southern California has developed a program it calls casual employment. Retired employees are allowed to work up to one thousand hours a year (about half-time) without losing pension benefits.

During the decade of the 1990s the Bureau of Labor Statistics foresees an explosion of jobs in the computer and data processing industry and in the fields of healthcare, electronics repair and maintenance and personal services. These occupations offer full-time or part-time employment opportunities for tens of thousands of older workers.

This is especially good news for U.S. working men and women, former Labor Secretary Elizabeth Dole believes, because it means that issues once defined as social problems will be dealt with more out of economic necessity. Dole observes: "In tighter labor markets, employers can't afford to discriminate. They cannot afford to put workers at health and safety risk. In tighter labor markets, they cannot afford to ignore workers' obligations to family. Employers who do so will simply lose out to employers who don't. Some employers will falter and fail—and they deserve to. We have within our reach the fulfillment of a long-awaited dream—that every American who wants a job can have a job."

So there you have it. In the foreseeable future, older people who want jobs or need jobs will probably have little trouble finding them. For some, the work will mean being able to make ends meet, to remain financially independent. For others, it may mean the pride and comfort of their pre-retirement standard of living. For still others, extra income may translate to a few added luxuries. For all, work is a measure of insurance.

There are many different comforts in knowing you have options. If you have lived well most of your life, it will prove to be embarrassing and degrading if you are forced to live below the financial level of close old friends in retirement. And after a lifetime of work, of rearing and educating your family, paying your taxes, contributing what you could to society, you are entitled at the very least to your human dignity.

TO BE AN ENTREPRENEUR

Have you yearned forever to be an entrepreneur? Have your own business? Be your own boss? The impulse is powerful, virtually a force of nature, and retirement may provide the perfect opportunity for you to realize the Great American Dream. You are finally free from the time constraints of a breadwinner's job. You have time on your hands and business ideas on your mind. You have income from your savings and investments, your company pension and Social Security (unless you retired before age sixty-two or elected to delay benefits until the normal retirement age of sixty-five). Now you can become a true-blue, feet-on-the-desk, cigar-chomping capitalist! And if you begin your enterprise on a modest scale and set moderate goals you may escape many of the agonies that beset and frequently defeat younger entrepreneurs—the need to raise substantial capital, the loneliness of going it alone, the frantic race to succeed before you run out of money, the pressures on your family life—and all the rest. As an entrepreneur you will be joining a teeming army of other dreamers like yourself.

Since 1970 the number of retirees and wage-and-salary workers who started their own businesses soared more than 500 percent, outpacing the growth of the regularly employed by more than 50 percent each year. In 1988 alone, more than 700,000 corporations, 500,000 sole proprietorships and 100,000 partnerships were launched. Several factors underlie the surge. One is the compelling personal urge to have it all, to be both financially and professionally independent, to build wealth and work where you live, not be forced to live where you work. Among budding entrepreneurs still working at a regular job, the financial support of a working spouse also has been a liberating factor. Retirees of course have their pension and other income. Further impetus has been added by the loss of hundreds of thousands of middle and upper-level management jobs due to the restructuring of corporate America. Automation of the workplace continues to be a factor, along with the increasing tendency of companies to farm out more work, including even staff functions.

The most phenomenal growth in the ranks of entrepreneurs appears to be among regularly employed part-timers who launch moonlighting enterprises largely to supplement their salaries. Joining them are older Americans, driven by the need to supplement pension and Social Security benefits, who are using the skills they acquired over a lifetime to start their own small businesses.

CONSULTING

Consulting is a favorite retirement career among professionals and highly skilled persons, and there has never been a better time to move into a consulting career. It is a business you can easily conduct out of a home office with a telephone, fax machine, word processor and a few supplies. From a company's point of view, the use of consultants can cut payroll and the burden of benefit packages. Many companies retain their own retired executives as consultants.

Unless you can go back to work for your former employer, however, think it through before hanging out your shingle as a consultant. Here are three more or less typical case histories which illustrate how to enter the field—and how not to:

> Jack, forty-eight, was a nuclear physicist, working for a major defense contractor. After long analysis and discussion, he and two friends concluded they could realize more income and have more control of their work if they were independent. Four years later they have all the government contracts they can handle. The patented medical technology devices they developed are being tested in hospitals.

> Marvin, sixty-seven, who had been a senior partner in a well-known management consulting firm, followed another path. He retired at sixty-five. Five years earlier he had headed the team that reorganized a large insurance company. When the company recently changed direction, the chairman called him out of retirement to do additional studies. He's working full time on a retainer.

> Charles, sixty, was the vice-president for corporate communications of a New England manufacturing company. Caught in a merger, he decided to become a consultant. His first move was to sell stock to a couple of dozen friends and family members. He had no business plan and failed to develop enough clients to build the business before his capital ran out. Now he's in the job market.

If you are contemplating a move into consulting, consider the following suggestions:

- Don't bother with it unless you believe you have the skills and knowledge that others will want to buy.

- Ask yourself whether you are well enough known in your field to attract clients. Have you been networking? Are you active in your professional and trade groups?

- Getting your first contracts may take months. Do you have adequate resources to meet your financial needs in retirement, plus those of your business, until you can turn a profit?

- Do you know where the business will be coming from?

- Keep your overhead low. Plan out the entire enterprise before you announce it. Create a business plan. Make lists of potential clients. Work out your sales pitch. Decide what you will charge and how you will bill your clients. Draw up sample contracts. Design stationery and forms.

- Be as visible as possible before you launch. Book speaking dates or publish articles in the journals your prospects read.

- Think and act positively. You may spend the first few weeks talking to prospects. Let them catch your enthusiasm and confidence, your deep belief in what you're offering.

- Check with your professional or trade groups. They may have guidance material tailored to your field.

- Invest in a no-nonsense book on the subject. We recommend *Consulting, The Complete Guide to a Profitable Career,* by Robert E. Riley. The Publisher is Charles Scribner's Sons, New York. The price is $19.95.

BUYING A FRANCHISE

Franchise outlets account for a third of all retail sales in the United States, exceeding $600 billion a year. There are more than half a million franchise outlets, and the number is growing. Increasingly, industry sources say, franchises are attracting retired persons who want to continue working. They also are winning over individuals who want a second career in preparation for retirement. Franchisers welcome the trend. Spring Crest Company, Inc., which manufactures draperies and window treatments, retails exclusively through franchisees and has attracted recently retired couples. The company's president likes retirees because they are experienced, mature, enthusiastic and, best of all, often well financed.

The franchise contract calls for owner-management. That means you'll work long hours. Inactive investors are seldom welcomed, unless they are part of a management syndicate. Be warned, too, that not all franchise offers are of the same quality. Enough fraud exists in franchising to warrant caution. In an uncertain economy, your most important consideration may be to choose recession resistant products or services. The primary source of information on franchises is the International Franchise Association (IFA), 1350 New York Avenue NW, Washington, DC 20005.

The IFA says you need professional help when you become serious about investing in a franchise. That means you should consult your lawyer and your accountant. The IFA also warns that you need to evaluate the nature and characteristics of the operation that interests you, the costs of the franchise, the availability of financing, the prospective returns, the training and experience and work involved. A good starting point in your investigation is "What You Need to Know When You Buy a Franchise." It contains basic information you need and describes more than 600 franchising companies. The directory is available from IFA for $6.95 to cover postage and handling. Write to IFA's Washington address. IFA also publishes a magazine, *Franchising World*. The cost is $13.95 for a year's issues. You might also ask for "Franchise Publications," a flyer describing other books, videotapes and audiotapes. To obtain a copy of "Facts on Selecting a Franchise," write to the Council of Better Business Bureaus, Inc., 4200 Wilson Blvd., Arlington, VA 22203. Other sources of information are your local library, the regional offices of the Federal Trade Commission and the Small Business Administration, and your local Better Business Bureau. IFA-sponsored trade shows can also be helpful. Marty Monroe, a retired U.S. Army major, found his answer at such a show. There he met George Louser, president of Wash On Wheels, a business he could run from his home. "Everything that has happened since I've been a franchisee is super," says Monroe. "At retirement age, I am in business for myself, but not by myself."

PLAYING THE MARKET

Many retirees have discovered "day trading" in stocks as another entrepreneurial approach to supplementing their income and having a bit of fun at the same time. A day trader is an investor who buys and sells a stock on the same day, basing his or her decision on the anticipation that the share price will rise in increments as low as an eighth or a quarter of a point within a 24-hour period. York Securities, a small discount brokerage with what it says is a "very low" commission schedule, has more than 200 retired clients who have become day traders for their own accounts.

"Day trading on small upticks is only possible if the commissions are low," says David J. Corcoran, York Securities president. "For example, an investor buying 1,000 shares at 20 and selling them at 20-and-a-quarter through York would pay $150 in commission. The profit to the investor after commission is $100." On a similar trade, he adds, the investor would lose money at most traditional discount brokers. Many of York's day-trader clients work from their homes, where they have access to stock prices through personal computers. They usually do their own charting of stocks or have access to professional technical analyses. Some traders do as many as ten transactions a day.

"It's not what you trade but how you trade that counts," says Corcoran. "It doesn't matter if you buy blue chips or penny stocks as long as you perceive them as showing a consistent price improvement that warrants buying and selling the same day after a modest profit gain." Corcoran points out that an investor interested in day trading can learn charting in a college-level course or from available books on technical analysis. "My retired clients believe charting is more fun than fishing or playing golf," he adds. Be warned, however, that day trading is not for rank amateurs. Make sure you know what you're doing before you try it.

RETAILING

Many retirees cap their working careers by acquiring and running a small retail establishment. A distant relative of ours sold his large automotive repair business to retire, soon became bored, then bought and returned to work as manager of a modest bagel delicatessen in southern Florida. The owner-operator of a country store in upstate New York spent most of his working life as an agent for a large insurance company. During the summer and early fall months he and his wife stocked the store with delicious vine-ripened tomatoes and organically grown vegetables, which attracted customers from miles around. Another agent of our acquaintance became a distinguished historian and writer after thirty years with New York Life. He was recently inducted into the South Dakota Hall of Fame for works which include *The Carving of Mount Rushmore* and *The Night of Popping Trees*, a vivid account of the Indian wars of the 1870s, including the battle of Wounded Knee.

If retailing, consulting, buying a franchise business or day trading aren't of interest, but you'd still like to put your creative money-making ideas to work, or if you're counting down to retirement and wondering if you can put your avocation to dollar-making use, you might try *Moonlighting* by Carl Hausman and the Philip Lief Group (Avon Books, $7.95). This cheery paperback lists "148 Ways to Make Money on the Side." Most of the businesses discussed can be worked out of the home, and most can function with a staff of one. The book provides startup costs, estimated hours per week, and number of staff required, if any. It has headings that describe "What You Will Be Doing," "Getting Started," "Markets," "How to Find Clients," as well as "Resources" and "Networking." Hausman's business roster runs the gamut from addressing service to word processor. Even if your particular interest isn't included, you will find enough good, practical information to set you up. For anyone who even daydreams of a little business on the side, this book is a solid first step.

RESEARCH AND DEVELOPMENT BEFORE YOU GO INTO BUSINESS

Paving the way for a successful entrepreneurial business startup is a mental and emotional process that won't cost you a dime. All you need is a willingness to spend a little time on R&D—research and development. Your first move is to examine your motives. By themselves, wishing you could make more money, or dissatisfaction with an existing job, aren't reason enough. Owning and operating a business takes profound commitment, conviction and motivation. If you encounter periods of frustration and disappointment, as you almost certainly will somewhere along the way, it may test your character and demand all your strength to stay in the fight. Before jumping in, you must even consider how you might survive a worst-case scenario—the possibility that you will lose your entire investment in the business and even lose face among family and friends.

Studies show that most people plunge into business blindly, not knowing why, although most *say* it's for personal satisfaction or financial independence. This may partially explain why 50 percent of all new businesses fail within five years and why others become stagnant, earning barely a living wage for their owners. Yet if you aren't conscious of your true goals in creating a business, you can't devise a strategy for realizing its full potential. Putting it another way, if you don't know where you are going, any road will take you there. To avoid falling into the trap, you should first list your personal goals and what the business must do to meet them. Then describe how and when those business goals might be reached. Finally, take the list to someone whose business judgment you trust and ask for an evaluation. Generally, you will have to make revisions. But when your goals finally do become realistic, you are ready to move on to the next step in your analysis.

That may well be an examination of your entrepreneurial qualities. No definitive personality type is required to be successful as an entrepreneur, but certain personal attributes are highly advantageous. Among them are the ability to change with the times, to accept a certain degree of risk with confidence, a talent for organizing your time and workload, and a relentless drive to follow through on projects. Without follow-through, you are almost surely doomed to failure.

After careful analysis of your motives, goals and business aptitude, you are ready to pick the type of business you will enter. Common sense suggests that you select a field in which you have extensive knowledge, experience and existing contacts, and one that offers you enjoyable, satisfying work. It's also essential that your retirement lifestyle allows you the time to successfully operate the business. If you aren't shooting for the moon, you may also need to determine whether your income from the work is likely to measure up to your needs and expectations, and whether it carries the social status you want.

Your next major task is to select a product or service that people want and will pay an adequate price to buy. Get a good handle on market potential by reading trade publications and talking with industry experts. Test your idea on others, allowing them to respond openly. Frame your inquiries so there is no pressure to please you with the answers. Then ask yourself the most searching questions that come to mind. Will people actually buy my product or service? How often? What need does it satisfy? How much will the market be willing to pay? How will I overcome my potential customers or clients' natural resistance to a new product or service? (If all else fails, consider a free sample.)

Finally, you should make a diligent effort to learn about your proposed business from others who are active in the field already. Telephone first, but arrange face-to-face meetings if you can. Be sure you make two points on every call: (1) You are not asking for confidential information, and (2) you do not represent any sort of future competition. Not everyone will be willing to spend time with you, even on the telephone, but others may feel flattered that you think their experience and opinions are worth taking into account. Among the questions you should explore with the established entrepreneurs are these:

- What are the major challenges to be confronted by anyone entering the business?

- What kind of business experience is needed for successful management of the enterprise?

- Are there particular personal qualities that contribute to long-term success in the field?

- How much time will I have to spend selling? Dealing with suppliers? Doing bookkeeping?

- How many employees will I need on startup and how much time will I have to spend training them? Can I use part-timers or temporaries? Can I use older people?

- Are there any tricks of the trade that will be helpful to a new operator?

- How much money can I expect to make in this business and how long will it take?

- What level of sales and financial results should I expect in my first year of operation? Second year? Third year?

- How much money do I need to enter the business? What are the principal costs? Are employee benefits a major expense? Can I lease or rent the equipment I will need? How much reserve capital should I have to give myself a real shot at success? Most small businesses fail either because of poor management or lack of adequate capital.

- Is this the type of business that can be sold at a profit when I am ready to get out?

As we said before, the research and development phase of your new business won't cost you anything. It's all head-and-leg work that will give you reassurance you have chosen your field correctly, or possibly save you from making a terrible mistake. Remember that if your first business idea is no good, you can always go on to another. And if you're not cut out for entrepreneuring, it's far better to find out before you have committed your hard-earned money.

FINANCING A BUSINESS

The simplest and safest type of business to start is one you can finance out of your own pocket and operate out of your home or a small office. (If you intend to work out of your home, make sure you won't run afoul of any zoning regulations in your area.) Even if you fund the business yourself, however, by all means write a business plan. A business plan serves a number of vital purposes. First, it forces you to research and develop your business idea. Only by careful analysis of all the details yourself can you arrive at a complete understanding of the risks, costs, feasibility and ultimate promise of the idea. Second, a written business plan is essential for raising outside capital. Most investors won't give you a penny on the basis of an oral presentation, no matter how eloquent. It can also be used to help convince sellers, suppliers, franchisers or others to extend you working capital in the form of credit. Third, after your firm is set up and operating, a business plan is an invaluable reference document. It contains budgets, sales forecasts, revenue targets and other data against which to measure your progress. A business plan is a road map which clearly shows your final destination, your method and route of travel, and where you are at any given moment. When you feel you are ready to write the plan, ask your lawyer, accountant, stockbroker and business friends to loan you samples of business plans that others have written, particularly those in your own or related fields. The nearest field office of the Small Business Administration may also be able to provide sample plans. If you need help with the composition, check the classifieds for freelance writers in your daily newspaper and in magazines aimed at entrepreneurs. Business plans differ widely, depending on the type of business involved and the planned scale of the operation, but typical plans include the following categories of information:

- A summary description of the business you propose to create.

- A discussion of the industry that shows where and how your business will fit in—your niche—and why it should prosper in the face of any existing or future competition. Demonstrating that you have a monopoly on a product or service, or that you can effectively preempt competition, will make almost any potential investor sit up and take notice.

- An analysis of your current and future markets. Describe your customers or clients and their buying needs.

- Your marketing strategy—how you are going to get customers or clients to buy your product or service. In some situations you may be able to get future clients to write "letters of intent" stating their intention to buy your product or utilize your service once you are up and operating.

- Management. Smart investors know that management is one of the keys to the success of a business. Present your experience and qualifications, and those of any other principals in the company, in the most concise and forceful language possible, but don't overdo it. Hyperbole and horn-blowing invite skepticism on the part of investors and lenders. Describe the company's management structure and ownership. Specify the number and compensation of any employees. Don't suggest that you plan to increase your own salary anytime soon. Investors want to get their money back before your standard of living rises. List your company directors and consultants, if any, providing brief resumes for each.

- Risks. A thorough statement of all the general and special risks that go with buying a share of your business, including the possibility that investors will lose their entire investment, is a desirable and usually required part of any business plan.

- Financials. Make detailed financial projections of anticipated expenses and revenues for at least three years, preferably five. Declare the amount of money you and other principals are investing, how much additional you are seeking to raise and in what form—through equity participation, loans or a combination. Be specific about how you plan to use investors' money to produce and deliver your product or service.

While it may not be written into your business plan, you should also be prepared to discuss with potential investors how you believe they will be able to get their money out of the company in three-to-five years, and how much their investment might be worth at that time. To illustrate, we recently reviewed a preliminary offering memorandum and business plan for a niche-market video production company. The principals were investing $400,000 of their own money and seeking an additional $1.6 million through sale of limited partnerships at $50,000 each. When the issue of return on capital was raised by a potential investor, they explained that they believed the company could achieve revenues of $20 to $25 million in five years, at which time it might go public or sell out to a major media company. If its profits on, say, $20 million in annual sales were $3 million, and the company sold at a multiple of seven times earnings, it would be worth $21 million dollars. The original $2 million investment would therefore have increased on the order of slightly over ten times. It is this type of potential return on investment that sometimes entices investors to take the high risks involved in startup companies with no operating history.

When you have completed a draft of your business plan, it is advisable to have both your lawyer and accountant examine it for conformity to federal and state laws and regulations, and to accepted accounting practices. If you are seeking a substantial amount of money and can afford the cost, ask your accountant to help you make your financial projections and your lawyer to do the final draft of the plan. If it isn't credible, you won't get far with investors.

If you need outside capital to help launch your new business, you will probably find that raising this capital is extremely difficult even at times when investors are feeling generally confident. If you can go it alone financially, without endangering your future retirement income, do so. Then you are responsible only to yourself. When you take on outside investors you take on a burden of obligation. Even the generous old uncle who hands you a check for $50,000 and tells you with a smile not to worry about paying it back may turn on you if things go badly. You may have stresses enough just running a new business. You don't need outside investors harassing you with their pointed questions about why you aren't making more rapid progress. If you have no choice in the matter, if you have done your homework and are convinced in your own mind that you won't fail, then here are some suggestions for raising the necessary capital while minimizing your need for it.

- Hire your lawyer and accountant on the basis of a modest advance retainer, with the understanding that if the business is funded they will receive full compensation for any work which they have performed. Many lawyers and accountants are willing to work on this basis if they believe in you and your idea, so don't hesitate to ask.

- Use and expand your network of contacts in the business and financial communities to help you find a packager, underwriter or individual investors. Your broker, banker, friends, relatives and former business associates may know a number of venture capitalists who might be interested in the deal you are offering. Or they might help you develop a list of individual investor prospects. You may even find several small investment firms that specialize in the field you want to enter.

- Contact the International Venture Capital Institute, P.O. Box 1333, Stamford, CT 06904 (Telephone: 1-203-323-3143) for a list of venture capital clubs and leads on packagers and private investors who are looking for new investment opportunities.

- You may also want to obtain a copy of *Pratt's Guide to Venture Capital Sources*, published by Venture Economics, P.O. Box 348, 16 Laurel Avenue, Wellesley Hills, MA 02181. The cost is $95, plus $5 for shipping.

- *The Encyclopedia of Small Business Resources*, by David E. Gumpert and Jeffry A. Timmons, is a first-rate overview of organizations that offer financial and other types of assistance to small entrepreneurs. Their book is published in paperback by Harper & Row.

- Talk with local "business incubators" and other state, county and city development agencies that offer loans, low-cost office space, tax breaks and other forms of assistance to small business enterprises. Regional competition for new businesses and the jobs and tax revenues they create has led to a proliferation of public agencies offering aid to entrepreneurs.

- A list of hundreds of small business investment companies can be obtained from the National Association of SBICs, 1156 15th Street NW, Suite 1101, Washington, DC 20005. SBICs are private venture capital firms licensed and partly financed by the U.S. Small Business Administration and have provided financial help to thousands of small companies.

Investors and particularly venture capital firms will show more interest in your enterprise if they know you are investing a good deal of your own money. They want to know that you have enough confidence in the business to put your own money on the line. In addition, most prefer to invest in companies with an operating history, a stream of revenue, the potential to achieve millions of dollars in sales in a few years, and a willingness to go public. Many have very firm policies against putting money into startup situations. Even if a venture capitalist thinks you have a great business idea, and a corner on your market, he or she may say "go out and prove it and call me when you need money to expand." On the other hand, you may get lucky and find a venture capitalist who becomes so excited about your proposed business that he or she will actually help you write, revise or restructure your business plan. You won't know until you try.

Depending on the type of work involved, one sound strategy for getting a business started with little or no capital is to use "sweat equity." Get your first contracts, do the work yourself, and use your profits to expand. Several friends of ours pooled enough of their money to invest in just one rental apartment in Florida. Then they used their profits from that initial investment to buy a second rental. Now they have ten apartments and a growing bank account.

One of the keys to financial success in running a service-related company is to hold your overhead costs in check. Keep your staff to a minimum. Hire part-timers and freelancers to reduce payroll taxes and avoid costly medical benefits and insurance plans. You can always hire extra workers when needed during your busy season. Find new employees by word of mouth to save on advertising and agency fees. If your office is located in a building with other service firms, and you have more space than you need, rent it out. Cut costs by sharing the more expensive overhead items, including computer time, duplicating and a receptionist. Buy used office furniture from a dealer, or ask the building manager to let you know when other tenants are moving out. You may be able to buy what you need directly from them. Keep a tight rein on travel and entertainment expenses. Save time and money by meeting clients in your office. Rather than going to a restaurant, bring in salads, sandwiches, coffee and soft drinks. Take advantage of sales and order your supplies in bulk from companies that specialize in supplying small businesses. Most accept phone orders, give discounts to regular customers and deliver free of charge. Look for opportunities to barter your services for those of other professionals, such as your dentist or accountant.

Your ability to become a successful entrepreneur when you retire, and the type of business you chose to start, will probably be dictated by the skills, experience and financial resources you have accumulated during a lifetime of work. It may be a very simple, unglamorous service requiring a few hours of your time each day. Or it may have the potential to make millions of dollars for you and other investors willing to cast their lot with you. The Great American Dream comes in many sizes and styles. Whatever your personal dream, keep it in perspective. Don't risk money you can't afford to risk. The legendary entrepreneurs, the Fords, Edisons and Disneys who created mass-produced Model T's, electric light bulbs and Magic Kingdoms, were driven more by ideas and innovation than by pursuit of the conventional entrepreneurial goals of wealth and independence. They believed that if you had a good idea and a good strategy for making it work, the money would follow.

14

Too Good to Be True

THREE BIG LIES

If merchandisers have begun to pay special attention to older Americans because of their growing numbers, affluence and desire for quality products and services, no less may be said of the world's flim-flam specialists. There is no "typical" fraud victim. But for reasons probably having to do with their perception of older people as mentally less competent—a misperception in most cases—and worried about the adequacy of their retirement nest egg, swindlers have a particular affinity for preying on retired and other older persons. They are thought to be the easy marks on every con man's hit list. The Federal Trade Commission estimates that American consumers, including retirees, lose $40 billion a year (that's about $1 million an hour) investing in deals that turn out to be fraudulent.

To protect yourself, be on the lookout for the con artist's three big lies:

1. You can make a lot of money.
2. You can make it quickly.
3. It's a sure thing.

You certainly do not have to be dumb, greedy or older to get taken. You can have an IQ in the genius range and still lose your shirt. A former economist for the Federal Trade Commission was swindled. So was a federal appeals court judge, a National Football League coach, and the lieutenant governor of a state. The pitches of professional flim-flammers are so polished they can induce temporary stupidity in judges, lawyers, economists and politicians with about the same ease they empty the bank accounts of the allegedly less sophisticated investors.

And once you've been bamboozled by a con man's honeyed lies, the chances of getting your money back are virtually nil. Even in cases where money is recovered through legal actions by federal, state or local law enforcement agencies, consumers often get back less than 10 cents on every dollar invested. The reason is that companies engaged in fraud often operate a particular scam for a short time, quickly spend the money they take in, and close down before they can be detected. The operators then open another phony business under a new name.

BURNED OVER AND OVER

Ordinary horse sense would suggest that a person who got burned once in an investment scam would shy away from the bait the second time around, but often that's not the way it works. It's not uncommon, in fact, for people to invest in phony schemes again and again—like a fool in a casino who keeps playing because he thinks there's a chance of winning back his money.

Some repeat victims can't seem to resist the hypnotic pitches of a particular salesperson. Some continue to pour good money after bad as a way of denying to themselves that they are being hoodwinked. Others are lured back by a salesperson's promise of recovering past losses.

This odd, fatal tendency of many defrauded investors to gamble again and again makes con artists eager to keep in touch with their victims. Hustlers and promoters are known to pack lists of their best customers from one boiler room to another. With a new scheme to peddle, and sporting a new name and a new accent, they repeatedly solicit their strangely loyal victims.

THEY GET YOU BY PHONE

Investment frauds are sold in a variety of ways—print and television advertising, for example—but three out of every four of the scams investigated by the Federal Trade Commission are sold by telephone. In the hands of a skilled swindler, the telephone is clearly a powerful and versatile capitalist tool. Everyone with a listed phone number is vulnerable to the siren song of the charlatan. The popularity of the telephone, and the ease of setting up and dismantling fraudulent telephone operations, recently has led to a dramatic increase in telemarketing investment fraud, according to law enforcement authorities.

CON MEN TRADE ON NEWS EVENT

Fraudulent telemarketers are supremely clever and resourceful at generating plausible investment ideas. Among current favorites are works of art, gemstones, rare coins, oil and gas leases, interests in oil wells, applications for cellular telephone licenses, precious metals such as gold and silver, and strategic metals such as chromium. Con artists often choose to peddle investments that most consumers know little about. They also tailor their offerings to capitalize on current news events. For example, fraudulent sellers may offer you an investment based on the scarcity of a foreign metal after news of a trade embargo. At another time, they might offer you an investment in a new, widely publicized high-tech product. Keeping up with world news and playing on it to flim-flam investors is a con man's stock in trade.

Swindlers obviously weave their web by creating an illusion of legitimacy, by feeding you a set of facts that may be 95 percent true and only 5 percent fabrication. Notoriously glib, their years of selling experience and natural sales talent make them masters at the games they play. At times, one can only marvel at their ability to deceive the most sophisticated and skeptical of investors. Frequently, they will "confide" in you that they have high-level financial connections and inside information. To close a sale quickly, they may even offer you phony statistics or price quotations. They often misrepresent the significance of a current event, or stress the uniqueness of their offerings to try and dissuade you from verifying their story. Many will offer to buy back your investment after a certain period—anything to get you to make a quick decision without checking.

CALLS FROM THE BOILER ROOM

The heart of a telemarketing operation is usually centered in a "boiler room," a setting filled with desks, telephones, and salespeople who spend their days calling hundreds of prospects all over the country. You may be contacted by one of these boiler room operators if you respond to a newspaper ad or fill out a card asking for more information about an investment. More likely, you will receive a cold call based on nothing more than the fact you are listed in a telephone directory.

Because it is so difficult to recover money paid to fraudulent sellers, the best defense you have is to refuse to give them your money in the first place.

If you are approached by anyone selling an investment opportunity, re-member the following cautions. They may help you avoid investing with a bogus firm.

Here are some suggestions to help you avoid the "royal fleece":

- If a deal sounds too good to be true, it's probably a scam. No legitimate salesperson will ever claim to offer a risk-free investment. If it's really a sure thing, the person on the phone wouldn't be calling people about it. Big returns usually mean big risks. Any claim that there is little or no risk involved in an investment should act as a red flag.

- Don't be pressured into buying. High-pressure sales tactics that urge you to buy now or forever lose your opportunity to profit are clear signals that the caller may be crooked. When you are being pressured or annoyed, simply hang up the telephone.

- Invest in business opportunities you know something about. It is un-likely you will make money in a business deal that you cannot under-stand or verify. You especially should be wary of any investment where you need to rely exclusively on the seller's representations of the in-vestment's value.

- Be skeptical of any unsolicited phone calls about investments. Think twice before you buy investments from out-of-state salespeople you don't know. You may find it impossible to get your money back if a deal sours.

- Get all the information you can about the company and verify the data. Before you invest with any company, check the seller's prospec-tus with someone whose financial advice you trust. Also check the company's reputation with appropriate local, state and federal con-sumer protection agencies. We will provide you with a partial list of such agencies at the end of this chapter.

- Any resistance you encounter from a seller when you ask for additional investment information or references should make you suspect. Even if you do receive additional references, keep in mind that they may not provide reliable information about the investment or the com-pany. For example, a bank may tell you that an investment company has an account, but this does not mean the company is legitimate.

- Beware of testimonials. Fraudulent companies sometimes hire references to claim that the firm's investments brought them sudden wealth. A Ponzi scheme, where promoters use the money from new investors to pay high returns to early investors, may explain why the company is praised.

- Beware of salespersons who ask a string of questions that require "yes" for an answer. For example: "Would you like to make a lot of money on a small investment with little risk?" Later your answers will be twisted to make you feel foolish if you don't go along with the scam.

- If in doubt, do not invest. Before you invest, insist that the entire proposal be mailed to you, using the U.S. Postal Service. This is a big turn-off for con artists, who do not want to run afoul of the postal inspector. You should also ask questions and seek information from a variety of sources. If you cannot get solid information about the company and the investment, do not risk your money.

- Remember that con artists count on your gullibility and laziness—they bet that you won't really go to the trouble of checking out their organization or scheme. Generally, it is a good idea never to invest on the basis of an unsolicited telephone call from someone you don't know.

BE WARY OF "PINK SHEET" STOCKS

It also is wise to be extremely wary of the market for some 11,000 fitfully traded stocks listed in the Pink Sheets, published daily by the National Quotation Bureau. Although pink sheet stocks include thousands of legitimate securities, experts say this market is rife with scams. Regulators simply lack the manpower and monitoring systems to keep track of the market, and it offers strong temptations to con artists out to bilk the public. A favorite among unsavory stock promoters is the "pump and dump" scam. Acting in league with rogue brokers, the promoters pump up the share price of shell or otherwise worthless companies with sales pitches that are pure hype and hot air, then dump the stocks on unsuspecting investors for huge profits, which the brokers and promoters split. Investors, meanwhile, are left stranded with worthless paper.

BUYING INTO A DIRT PILE

A precious metals swindle called the "dirt pile" scam has been growing in popularity because it sounds foolproof to many investors. It works like this: you receive an unsolicited telephone call offering you an opportunity to invest in a certain amount of "unrefined" gold ore. The ore is guaranteed to contain a specified amount of gold, and you purchase it well below the per-ounce market price of the yellow metal. Then you wait, *always in vain*, for your riches to come pouring in. The hitch is that your gold is spread through the ore in quantities too small to recover. True, the pile of dirt you purchased does contain gold, but there's no economical way to extract it. Your dirt, usually tailings from mines, is worthless.

TRAVEL PACKAGE MISADVENTURES

Of course scams are not limited to mere "investment opportunities." Many amazing and colorful varieties grow in the swindler's garden of fakery. Ever been tempted to buy one of those bargain-priced travel packages sold over the telephone? Be careful. Your dream adventure will become a costly misadventure if you fall victim to a travel scam. While some of the travel offerings are legitimate, many have the sole aim of defrauding consumers of millions of dollars each month. The schemes take a number of nefarious forms.

Increasingly common is one that involves phony travel clubs. You pay a membership fee of $50 to $400 to receive a travel package that includes round-trip air transportation for one person and lodging for two persons for a week in Hawaii, London, Paris or another destination. The catch? You must purchase a high-priced, roundtrip ticket for your companion from the fraudulent travel operator. The usual result is that you end up paying two to three times the cost of buying your own tickets in advance or through an airline or reputable travel agency.

A second type of travel scam begins when you receive a postcard saying that you have been "specially selected" to receive a free trip. The postcard instructs you to call a phone number, usually toll-free, for details. Once you call, you are told you must join their travel club to be eligible for the free trip. Sometimes, a credit card number is requested so your account can be billed for the membership fee. Only after you join are you sent the vacation package with instructions on requesting reservations for your "pre-paid" trip. As a rule, your request for reservation must be accompanied by another fee. The catch here? New charges are being added at every step along the way. In the end, you never get your "free" trip because your reservations aren't confirmed or you must comply with hard-to-meet hidden or expensive conditions.

The sales pitches for phony travel packages usually have the following in common:

- *Oral misrepresentations.* Whatever the particular scheme may be, telephone salespeople are likely to promise you a deal they cannot deliver. Unfortunately, you often don't realize this until after you have paid your money.

- *High pressure or time pressure tactics.* Scam travel operators are likely to tell you that they need your commitment to buy right away or that this "special offer" won't be available tomorrow.

- *"Affordable" offers.* Unlike investment fraud operators who try and persuade you to spend thousands of dollars, travel scam artists usually pitch their offers in the $50 to $400 range. Since this sum is often in the price range of those planning vacations, the package may appear to be reasonably priced.

- *Contradictory follow-up material.* Some firms may agree to send you written confirmation of the deal. You usually will find, however, that the literature bears little resemblance to the offer you accepted. Often, the written materials will disclose additional terms, conditions and costs.

SELF PRESERVATION

It is sometimes difficult to tell a legitimate sales pitch from a fraudulent one, but there are some things you can do to protect yourself:

- As always, be wary of "great deals." One tip-off to a travel scam is a very low-priced offer. Few legitimate businesses can afford to give away things of real value or to undercut substantially everyone else's price.

- Don't let yourself be pressured into buying immediately. Generally, a good offer today will remain a good offer tomorrow. Legitimate businesses do not expect you to make an instant decision.

- Ask questions. Find out exactly what the price covers—and does not cover. Ask if there are any additional charges later. Get the names of specific hotels, airports, airlines and restaurants that your package includes. Contact these places yourself to double-check arrangements. Find out exact dates and times of arrivals and departures. Ask about cancellation policies and refunds. If the salesperson on the phone cannot give you specific answers to your questions, this is not the deal for you.

- Do not give your credit card number over the phone. One easy way for a scam operator to close a deal is to get your credit card number and then charge your account. A common ploy is to ask for your credit card number for purposes of "verification." Say no. Never give your credit or charge card numbers, bank account numbers, or any other personal information, to unsolicited telephone salespeople.

ART SWINDLES ON INCREASE

Over the past several years you have no doubt read numerous press accounts of great works of art selling at auction for millions of dollars. Con artists use such familiar facts in their efforts to convince you they have possession of an undiscovered masterwork, or have a source of quality artworks priced far below their true value. Popular art scams recently have included fake lithographs, etchings and prints of works by Salvadore Dali, Pablo Picasso, Marc Chagall and Joan Miro. Other recent news stories about the rising value of rare coins have led to scams involving misgraded or inferior coins.

If taken in by a pitch for a fake work of art, you will receive only a tiny fraction of the value promised. After paying from perhaps $500 to $5,000, you may get a counterfeit worth no more than a poster you might buy in a museum. Many bogus pieces are simply copies of lithographs produced in the styles of well-known artists. To put it bluntly but honestly, the art "dealer" you trusted has turned you into a sucker.

Art scams are old. Only the twist is new. A common tactic is to send you a letter describing a contest or drawing giving away a free original lithograph by a famous artist. You are asked to return the postcard with your name, address, and phone number. Once your postcard is received, you are quickly telephoned for additional information—usually your credit card number. At some point, your caller will initiate a broader discussion about buying art, using glowing terms—"fabulous opportunity," "one-time offer," "limited edition," "excellent investment." You may be told that a famous artist is near death and that you should buy now, since the value of his or her works will increase after death. You also may be told that, if this happens, the company will gladly buy back the print or painting at two to three times what you paid for it, or that you can always resell the work elsewhere at a huge profit. You are assured of getting a "certificate of authenticity" for the work. And, often, you are promised a trial examination period with a 30-day money-back guarantee.

Some swindlers will send you slick promotional brochures and news clippings touting the credibility of their firm and the authenticity of their art works. Some have been known to fake Dun and Bradstreet reports to impress you with the financial stability of their company. Others may offer you "limited editions" which are actually printed for all takers. Still other operators have opened art galleries—displaying fake art alongside authentic works.

CONSULT AN AUTHORITY

Although there may be no foolproof way to protect yourself when you decide to invest in art, the following suggestions may be helpful.

- Consult a reputable art authority, appraiser or museum curator before purchasing any valuable work of art. The technology for reproducing and imitating art today is so sophisticated that even experts may have trouble detecting fraudulent work without careful study. Most people cannot tell the real thing from a fake. In addition, ask the seller for specific information about the work, including edition size and type of print (lithograph, etching, silk screen, woodcut, etc.). This information will help an expert in his or her evaluation.

- Avoid buying art over the telephone. Even a trial examination period or a money-back guarantee may not protect you. Many consumers have found that once they agree to examine a piece of art and give out their credit card number, it is nearly impossible to return the art and get their money back.

- Be skeptical of authenticity claims. Fraudulent companies typically distribute "certificates of authenticity" and other documentations that are as fake as their works of art. Authenticating materials are only as good as the firm that issues and backs them. Stay away from "art appraisers" recommended by the seller. They are usually on the seller's payroll.

If you get stuck with a fraudulent work of art, first try and resolve your dispute with the company that sold you the piece. If that doesn't work, contact your local consumer protection agency, Better Business Bureau, county district attorney and state attorney general to report the company. You should also write the Federal Trade Commission in Washington, DC. Although the FTC does not generally intervene in individual disputes, the information you provide may indicate a pattern of possible law violations by one company requiring action by the commission.

Due to the growing interest in all types of American folk art—ranging from weathervanes to old furniture to handmade quilts—flimflammers have recently been attracted to this field. At Christie's, a major New York gallery, sales of American folk art have recently doubled. And because the supply of really fine examples of folk art is limited, prices have gone through the ceiling. It is not unusual, for example, to find paintings from this period that sell today for $100,000, while a few years ago they might have gone for a few thousand. Still, the fact that you can purchase small, inexpensive folk art pieces for under a hundred dollars makes this type of art affordable for many consumers.

The fakery in American folk art comes in three forms. First, downright phony objects that were made with the purpose of defrauding consumers. Second, items that were refinished, repainted or otherwise "improved" to make them seem more valuable than they really are. Third, craft or folk objects that were made recently, but resold many times and therefore have become confused with real antiques.

In buying folk art, experts say you should take the following precautions:

- Insist on a sales slip that includes a description of the piece, who made it, when it was made, any restoration performed, and the price you are paying.

- Do business only with established dealers who have good reputations.

- Call an expert for help. You may be able to commission a regular dealer to buy a specific object at auction. For perhaps an additional 10 percent of the purchase price, you get not only the dealer's guarantee, but sound advice as to whether the object is a worthwhile buy.

- Learn the basics. Be suspicious of excessively dirty, stained or corroded objects, especially art on paper. Usually, family records and portraits were preserved with great care.

MAGAZINE SUBSCRIPTIONS

Surely one of the most common types of telemarketing frauds is that offering you a "free," "pre-paid," or "special deal" on magazine subscriptions. If you receive such a call, and you will probably receive hundreds in your lifetime, listen carefully before you answer. A hurried "yes" to the salesperson may obligate you to years of monthly payments for magazines you may not really want or could buy elsewhere for less money. In some states, once you orally agree to receive these magazines, you may be legally obligated to pay for them. When buying magazines over the phone, you do not have the advantage or protection of first seeing the written terms of the sales agreement.

Thousands of consumers buy magazine subscriptions from legitimate salespeople over the telephone every year. Yet, according to the Federal Trade Commission, some consumers are tricked by unscrupulous salespeople into paying hundreds of dollars for multiyear subscriptions. The fraudulent sellers make presentations so slick that many consumers are unaware they have purchased magazines until they receive the written agreement.

Phony magazine sales techniques vary. Instead of an initial phone call, you may receive a postcard that mentions nothing about magazine subscriptions. The card may ask you to call a telephone number about a contest, prize, or sweepstakes entry. If you call, you may be told about contest prizes or drawing dates. The conversation, however, soon turns into a sales talk about buying magazine subscriptions. Be on your guard against callers who:

- Imply that they represent major credit card companies or magazine publishers or that their purpose in calling is something other than selling magazine subscriptions.

- Encourage you to make purchases without giving you total costs. For example, you may be offered magazines for just a "few dollars a week." That may sound like a bargain until you realize that you could be paying hundreds of dollars for subscriptions that regularly sell for less.

- Say they are approved or regulated by federal, state or local government. In fact, no governmental body actually approves magazine-selling operations.

If you are actually interested in buying magazine subscriptions over the phone, at least insist on (1) knowing the total cost of each subscription and the total cost of the package you are being offered, and (2) receiving a written copy of the sales terms offered over the telephone *before* you agree to buy.

There is no federal law governing cancellation of telephone agreements, but certain local and state laws require sellers to provide a cancellation period for telephone sales. Keep in mind, however, that once you agree to buy magazine subscriptions over the phone, you cannot simply call the company to cancel your order if you change your mind. Magazine subscription companies do not honor oral cancellations. They must be in writing and occur within a limited time period.

Even so, in most states you *can* cancel telephone subscriptions by acting quickly. Watch for your sales agreement to arrive in the mail. It may come in a plain or junk mail type envelope. Look for the provision in the agreement that allows you to cancel. Generally you have three days in which to act. The notice may be difficult to find, but often it is attached to an inside page of multiple copies of the sales agreement. Sign and return the notice to the proper address—which also may be hard to find—by certified or registered mail. You may need proof of your mailing date. If you can't send the cancellation by certified mail, photocopy the signed and dated notice and keep it for your records. You should also immediately contact your bank or credit card company to stop any unauthorized payments.

Listed below are government agencies and business organizations that register, regulate, investigate, or monitor companies and individuals who offer goods and services and investment opportunities to the public. If you have questions about a company or an individual, or you wish to make a complaint, contact one or more of these offices. When you seek information, be aware that the absence of complaints filed with governmental and private agencies does not mean that a company or an investment is necessarily sound.

- The Federal Trade Commission is a law enforcement agency that investigates and prosecutes a variety of investment frauds. If you have questions or complaints about claims made in advertising or in telephone promotions for investment services, write the Federal Trade Commission, Investment Fraud Project, Bureau of Consumer Protection, Washington, DC 20580.

  Your state attorney general's office and your local district attorney's office investigate and prosecute fraud cases. You will find their telephone numbers by checking your local directory in the state and local government section.

- Your state securities commission, securities department, or department of corporations regulates the public offer and sale of securities by companies in your state. You can get the name and telephone number by calling the operator in your state capital.

- The Chief United States Postal Inspector, United States Postal Service, Washington, DC 20260, handles complaints about bogus mail-order investment services. The postal service has jurisdiction over fraudulent business operations that use, advertise, or sell through the mail. The Federal Bureau of Investigation also has jurisdiction when investment offerings constitute mail or wire fraud, or other violations of criminal law.

- The Commodity Futures Trading Commission regulates most firms that deal in commodity futures markets. Futures trading markets include petroleum products, U.S. government securities, foreign currencies, options on futures contracts, and dealer options. Write the Commodity Futures Trading Commission, 2033 K Street NW, Washington, DC 20581.

- The Securities and Exchange Commission is a federal agency that regulates the public offer and sale of securities. Contact the Securities and Exchange Commission, 450 Fifth Street NW, Washington, DC 20549, or call (202) 272-7440.

- The Better Business Bureau mediates disputes between consumers and businesses and may be able to inform you about complaints lodged against local investment firms. Contact the Better Business Bureau in the city in which the firm is located for information or to report a problem. For the phone number of an out-of-state bureau, write to the Council of Better Business Bureaus, 1515 Wilson Boulevard, Arlington, VA 22209.

- The National Association of Securities Dealers is a self-regulatory organization that governs stock brokers. Check your phone directory for a local district office of the association, or contact its Washington office at 1735 K Street NW, Washington, DC 20006, or call (202) 728-8221.

- The National Futures Association is a self-regulatory organization for all registered individuals or brokerage firms. Contact the association at 200 West Madison Street, Suite 1600, Chicago, Ill. 60606, or call (800) 621-3570. In Illinois call (800) 572-9400.

15

It's a Wonderful
(Retired) Life

The goal of this book has been to help you achieve an active retirement, whether your choice of action is to launch a new business, join the Peace Corps or sit on that porch rocker.

The over-fifty generation is the fastest growing segment of the population, therefore redefining what the word retirement means. Today, it means making new plans, starting anew. Today, you do not retire *from* something, but rather, *to* a new life.

You can retire to the activities you never got around to before: sports, creative arts, volunteerism. Above all, with sound financial planning, your options are open.

Nonetheless, retirement, as with any new phase of life, can be an alarming proposition. You have no idea what the next decades will bring, or how you will adapt to them.

Marvin, sixty-seven, was a senior partner in a well-known management consulting firm. Five years before he retired, he had led a team which reorganized a large insurance company. The chairman of that company called Marvin out of retirement to undertake additional studies on the company's direction, putting Marvin on a full-time retainer. He now hangs out his shingle as a consultant.

Consulting is a popular route for those who take an early retirement as a result of their company downsizing, particularly if you can consult for your former company.

Harry P. was a thread man—a merchant who sold thread to manufacturers, the classic American salesman. As a retiree Harry played golf, played cards, hung out with his buddies and enjoyed the extra time with his wife. But something was missing. Harry didn't think he "had the hang of retirement." Then he met another retiree who worked as a hospital volunteer.

Also the classic high-powered type A personality, Harry's buddy warned him emptying bed pans wasn't as glamorous as making a sale. But Harry didn't want glamor, he wanted, like many older Americans, to go on feeling useful.

With a lot of doubt, Harry signed up as a hospital volunteer. This community interest led, a few years later, to his being elected to the board of county commissioners.

Joseph U. took over his father's thriving company in the late 1940s and when he retired at the end of the 1980s it had grown even more successful in the directory printing field. In fact his only reason for retiring at close to age 70, was to give his son breathing space without the old man around. However, Joseph U. had no plans for quiet retirement. He had already signed on with the International Executive Service Corps, an organization based in Stamford, Connecticut, that arranges for retired executives to take their expertise to third world and developing countries.

Both he and his wife, after a few months reorganizing their lifestyle, were off to spend three months in Zimbabwe, at that government's invitation, to set up a company able to print telephone directories, catalogs, organization and government directories and the like. While both found the culture totally different from that of New York City, they also both found many similarities, particularly, Joseph remarked, in the young men and women eager to get their country's economy on a sound footing.

While Mrs. U. was not officially a member of the team (wives are invited by the government as a matter of course, however), she found she had a full calendar of events; and, as she pointed out, Zimbabwe is a country where age and the knowledge and maturity it brings are very, very respected. "It was wonderful, talking to those young working mothers, and the young women at the universities about what the working, homemaking life has been like the past forty years."

John J., a retired contractor, began devoting two afternoons a week to organizing games at a youth center. The obvious bonus to this was being around teenagers with all their energy and angst. The less than obvious bonus was that John J., with his administrative and organizational talents, was able to put a much needed but financially strapped club into the black simply by offering his years of know-how to the people running the club. As John comments, "I had all the fun, was able to offer input, but didn't have any of the headaches."

What you've learned all those working years, you may not even realize.

Mary K. had been a club woman for most of her married life. She knew how to organize, and when she realized that her country club pals were getting cranky from too much retirement, she organized a series of guest lecturers to come over and talk about volunteering in the community. Mary invited the heads of community organizations to her home or to the club to discuss their needs, first hand. She even went door to door with flyers soliciting volunteers. Largely through her efforts, volunteerism became a potent force in the community, not just an occasional whim or feeling of the need to do good. Prodded by Mary, many in her community took fresh interest in helping the less fortunate through their churches and synagogues. She inspired others to become active on behalf of causes they considered important to their quality of life and that of their grandchildren. Harry, mentioned earlier in these pages, benefited directly from these activists because it was their votes that boosted him onto the community board.

Admittedly, volunteerism isn't everyone's cup of tea. Some people become too frustrated watching administrators or managers badly doing a job they know they could do better. But you might find a cause that suits you. And, some people, who've worked for every dollar earned just couldn't, philosophically, work for nothing. Nothing to it.

While you are unlikely to find yourself making a larger salary than your "pre-retirement," or even the same, there is plenty of work out there. Our society is perilously short of support service personnel. In some metropolitan areas, finding a workforce that can type, answer the telephone and compose a letter is becoming impossible. The one time "steno-typist" job, so long a ghetto for women, has disappeared as ambitious young women move on to administrative positions and beyond. However, somebody still has to answer the phone, type the letters and open the mail. And these jobs, while not particularly high paying, and not necessarily available on a full-time basis, can be very satisfying, giving a retiree a place to be a few days a week. Many metropolitan local governments have senior job placement offices and this is a good place to start.

Wilma F. had been in banking her entire life. She took time out for marriage and children, and returned to work for twenty years before retiring. Unhappily, before she and her husband could enjoy their planned retirement together, he died, and Wilma wasn't up to moving off to Arizona by herself; or, for that matter, sitting at home all day with the occasional time out for grandmothering and her volunteer work with the local literacy program. Then again, she wasn't about to plunge back into full-time work, having felt that between her homemaking and banking lives, she had worked hard long enough. But someone did suggest that she look into the senior job placement agency in her city, and who should be hungering for part-time, though permanent, clericals but her old bank. While Wilma was somewhat amused by this, and wished them well, she didn't fancy returning to her old environs in a somewhat reduced capacity; it had taken her too many years to work up to vice-president, anyway. However, it did give her an interesting lead to a television network that was also looking for part-time people, though on a permanent basis. Wilma signed on as a "floater," which meant she roamed from programming to accounting to personnel to the nightly news, basically typing and answering the telephone, three days a week. While the money is negligible, and plays havoc with her Social Security payments, Wilma more than makes up for this with her tales of life behind the big-time scenes, and the general glamour associated with television.

You can, of course, take off entirely, as did BettyAnn and Jack L., who, after several years delightful retirement in Florida decided to move to Portugal. Why? Because Army man Jack was based on the Algarve many years before and of the many, many countries he had served in this was the one he liked the best.

BettyAnn admitted that leaving friends and children so far behind was a bit wrenching, and they both, as of this writing, have given up trying to become fluent in the language, hoping to at least learn enough Portuguese to "be polite and buy groceries."

Jim D. is a case in point. A career Navy man, he has retired at what a lot of us might consider "a young age" in that he is in his mid-forties. And, in our puritan work ethic society we might be expecting him to pick up career no. 2. Not Jim. Much as he's loved life at sea he is determined to settle into his new Kansas City condominium (yes, as far away from the sea as he could make it), he's allowing only one clock on his premises, and that hidden away, and has already tossed his watches overboard. He does have a list of things he "might do," which includes learning pottery, perhaps doing more of his painting, and mastering a language. The only thing he's sure of doing is reading. "Lots and lots of it. All the books I've loved all these years, and one I've missed." Well, all right, I suppose most of us give him six months of this sybaritic life. But it's his six months and he'll enjoy it for the rest of his life.

The point of all this is, relax and enjoy. We know you've worked hard, for yourself and for others. You've planned as carefully as you could, with a few diversions along the way. Life, after all, isn't perfect, but now you can step away from the mainstream and take a breath. You're back to being as free as you were as a kid, this time with the money and certainly more brains. Remember what it was like to be eight years old, with a whole dollar in your pocket and the entire day to play? This is what we should make of our retirement: playtime, whether for the good of the community, for a few extra dollars, for mental health, companionship or the plain heck of it.

Index